André Gide

THE THEISM
OF AN ATHEIST

André Gide

THE THEISM
OF AN ATHEIST

H. J. Nersoyan

SYRACUSE UNIVERSITY PRESS

Copyright © 1969 by Syracuse University Press
Syracuse, New York
ALL RIGHTS RESERVED

FIRST EDITION

Library of Congress Catalog Card No.: 69-17717

Manufactured in the United States of America

to

M.

About the Author

H. J. Nersoyan holds the Baccalauréat from
the Collège Champagnat des Frères Maristes,
Aleppo, Syria; he received the S.T.B. degree
from the Berkeley Divinity School, New Haven,
Connecticut, and the Ph.D. from Columbia University and Union Theological Seminary. He is
the author of *The Faith of the Armenian
Church* and *A History of the Armenian Church,*
and has contributed articles to journals such as
Ararat and *Religion in Life.* He is now assistant
professor of philosophy at the University of
Dayton, Dayton, Ohio.

Preface

Fifty years or two generations must pass, Gide surmised, before the full value and relevance of his books would be recognized. In these fifty years the idea has been gaining momentum that atheism must not be taken at face value, that it may indeed be a manifestation of the religious drive to reach God beyond the god of theism. Men who stand on the borderline of orthodoxy are now hailed as the announcers of a regenerated religious consciousness. Increasing interchurch and interfaith dialogues and ecclesiastical mergers coincide with, or closely follow, the emergence of such theories of knowledge as logical empiricism, and point to the fact that the established dogmatic formulations no longer command the intellectual subservience they once did. While the beginnings of Christianity are remembered with nostalgia, efforts to make faith conform to static, logical categories are looked upon with increasing disfavor. Well-publicized voices do not speak of the reform of the Church. They reject the Church altogether. Concurrently, there is a tendency to regard as myths pivotal scriptural reports that both Judaism and Christianity have been using as grounds for the validity of their central claims. A new morality emphasizes the notion that morality is, in the final analysis, a thing of individual responsibility; it is to be exercised in particular circumstances on the foundation of a courageous concern for the rest of the world. While the enjoyment of the here and now is itself advocated roughly within the context of that morality, Marxism and the Theology of Hope overcome a present disheartening situation by looking at it from a point of total fulfillment in the future. Marxism is certainly responsible for, and the Theology of Hope is not unrelated to, contemporary religious activism, whose purpose is to promote in the name of God the happiness of the greatest number in this life. God is the "problem" he perhaps never was before.

Between the ideas that stirred Gide and such developments as the above, the relationship may be viewed as one of seed or sapling to tree. These developments constitute at any rate the proper background against which to examine the religious and moral significance of Gide's creative output and of his entries in his *Journal*.

It is difficult if not impossible to write extensively on any aspect of Gide's work without being forced to deal with his religious stance to some extent. As a consequence many writers have had to comment on it. Several studies are devoted exclusively to the evolution of his religious thought. These are chronological reports which also offer valuable comments on such Gidian statements as contain conventionally religious terms.

Yet some of the conclusions arrived at on the premise the Gide's religious convictions changed radically at a certain point in his life stand in need of reconsideration. This becomes apparent when we desist from restricting the expression of religious concerns to "religious" terms. The present study will consider Gide's basic affirmations in this area as they appear and reappear in a succession of varying symbolisms.

One cannot complete a study of this nature without a feeling of gratitude toward all those who have engaged in studies of the same and related areas. Their insights have elicited some of the views expressed here while helping to eliminate other views which would have been held mistakenly.

For more direct suggestions and assistance throughout the work sincere acknowledgments are due to Professor Horace L. Friess of Columbia University. I am also grateful to Professor Justin O'Brien who first suggested that I write on this subject. His encouragement was particularly valuable in view of his internationally known erudition in the area of modern French literature.

My thanks are extended to Emily Schroeder and Evelyn Shaw for preparing large parts of the manuscript. There is an indeterminate number of people, some of whom are known to me only by sight, whom I also wish to thank. I refer to the staffs of the several institutions which had the books, journals, magazines, and pamphlets I did not own. I must thank notably the staff of that most remarkable establishment which must have won the gratitude of many an inquirer: the New York Public Library. To my wife my indebtedness is beyond words.

September, 1968   H. J. N.

Contents

The literature of the modern period is particularly exposed, I would say, to inner antagonisms and contradictions. Critics who are perturbed by these contradictions, preferring the writers they deal with to be of one mind, are prone to expend much ingenious cerebration in inventing unified creative personalities where none perhaps exists. They would do better to try getting at a writer's truth by fathoming the depth and intensity of the contradiction of which he is the carrier and which more often than not proves to be the wayward secret of his power over us.

Philip Rahv

The way of growth lies through a gradual increase in impersonality by an ever deeper and more intense unifying of the self with a greater than itself. In this process prayer, worship, meditation, philosophy, art, and literature all play their part since all help in purifying the inner being and disposing it more and more for contact with the divine.

Radhakrishnan

What we call Christianity has always been a pattern—perhaps a true pattern—of religion.

Dietrich Bonhoeffer

Introduction

There is a passionate—as distinguished from cool—sort of atheism which does not merely argue against the reasonableness of God's existence. The passionate atheist attacks God. He engages in mortal combat with God and announces his own victory. He has now reduced the enemy to everlasting silence. The shadow of the enemy will linger on, no doubt, but the slayer hero has saved the people. They will no longer have to feed to the monster their finest potentialities.

When God dies in this way, is man killing him, or is God killing a false image of himself through man? And is there a way of answering the question? Whatever the case, had Nietzsche's madman announced the death of *a* god, common sense would require us to assume that he was reporting a fact. Gods die in the course of history, and there is no apparent reason why "the God of theism" or "the God of Christendom" should be an exception. But the report that *God* died cannot be a factual account. Some have claimed that it is, but no attentive reader of their works will find that the claim is successfully maintained. On what logical or empirical bases can such a report be said to be factual? Death is the name of an event either between existence and nonexistence or between one mode of existence and another. In this second meaning it cannot without qualification be said of God or of anyone else that he is dead. If death is the name of an event between existence and nonexistence it does not apply to God. God either is, or is not, and not even Antony Flew's simple central questions are of much help in deciding between the alternatives. "What would have to occur or to have occurred to constitute for you a disproof of the love of, or of the existence of God?" The answer is, "we" would have to cease existing. But then, we would not be around to say or think that we were deluded.

Passionate atheism is rather an ethical than a theological statement.

1

It is rooted in the passionate atheist's active interest in human creativity and welfare. The god whom he kills is really the notion that there is a limit to human possibilities, as well as a fixed pattern of behavior, and that life cannot but be lived on this side of the limit and must remain within that pattern. But ever since the end of the Middle Ages the conviction has been gaining momentum that the future of man is entirely open and that people must revise their moral principles accordingly. This notion appears to entail not so much atheism as a religious conceptual adjustment. God did not have to vanish, but he had to change the place he occupied on the farther side of a void. The term "ground" came into use as relatively more appropriate to describe his relation to the world. He is still "the beyond," but "the beyond in our midst." Concomitantly we hear the phrase "God is Jesus" with renewed appreciation.

The modern need to bring God where the action is is certainly a consequence not only of the priority that movement, development, and energy came to have over rest, class, and matter, but also of new possibilities in interpersonal relationship. The more sensitive among men insist on treating as neighbors the strangers that technology brings into the family's living room. Yet a man's obligation to love his neighbor as himself does not follow from the neighbor's physical presence somewhere near him. No two friends are friends directly. Some third element is always the ground of friendship. Perhaps both friends like to read poetry; they happen to find the same objective overriding; or they can trace their origin to the same ethnic entity or country or father.

This age of mechanical cohesion but of personal estrangement, shot through as it is with dark Freudian suspicions, threatens to put an end to the attractiveness of the father-son image. On the other hand, the notion of substance, something that's all there independently of the individual self, is out of fashion. In these circumstances something dynamic, fluid, not so sharply distinguishable from the talking self, yet something that can be responded to, points to God or perhaps even designates him. This leads to the rediscovery of God's being love, along with the rejection of the view, once held by Feuerbach, that therefore love is God.

But even "love is God" is not sheer secularism. It is not equivalent to "love is love." It recognizes clandestinely that the limits of rationally graspable phenomena do not announce the limits of reality. It also recognizes that the worries with which we bother our heads every day do not constitute our real concern.

Existentialism analyzed this fundamental concern. It is born, to put it simply, from the expectation of death. A man knows that he lives in time. While time holds his life, it also kills him bit by bit. When he worries therefore, or when he fears things, he is under the immediate impression that he is fearing various objects for various reasons. In fact the one thing feared is diminution of life or loss of the "abundance" of life. Man's fundamental concern is to overcome this fear, an achievement which requires victory over time itself. Daily worries point to that fundamental concern—which they hide, as phenomena point to a secret reality. Our language is modeled on phenomena and therefore we really have no word for the reality hidden by phenomena, while we may not assume that anything we cannot name does not exist. On the contrary, it is possible to compose phrases or series of phrases which give us a feeling of that reality because phenomena, together, also reveal the reality they hide. The individual can test this truth by interrogating himself about himself. He will never see his own limits as one can see the floor of a pool, but each sounding will lead to a new fathom. Self-knowledge is never complete. The meaning of a phrase like "I am Adam" is not known exhaustively and without remainder. It is possible to say that to the extent to which self-knowledge is impossible, or the word *I* meaningless, the phrase "I build a house" is itself "meaningless." Our ignorance of other persons extends the limits of discourse that is meaningless in this sense.

The meaninglessness of sentences that have "God" as subject or predicate may be of the same sort. The theory that such sentences are meaningless may be related to the perennial theology that only negative statements may be made about God. Nevertheless, the theory does indicate a serious, relatively new crisis. Spatial transcendence and a specific code of morality came to be associated with the name *God,* and this gave rise to a host of theoretical and practical difficulties. From "God is dead" to "the *word* 'God' is dead" the process is one extended recognition of that mistake. The more recent theological concentration on the resurrection of Christ, and views of God under the aspect of future fulfillment, constitute a more positive handling of that mistake. It is one more mandate to make a distinction between the God of Christendom out there and the Living God in the center of things. It is also an invitation to face the post-"religious" era with enthusiasm.

Gide, who combined French and German characteristics, was attracted by the God-man relationship theme in Russian novels, and versed in what Charles de Gaulle would refer to as Anglo-Saxon literature, *lived* the utter defeat of God and his victory. To say that he was an atheist or a humanist at any period of his life is not only an injustice (for he did not want to be pigeonholed above all) but also nearsightedness. He simply mirrored the theological revolution taking place around him, and his use of several names in reference to the "more hidden" or "secret" reality—such as "virtue," "Future," and, most significantly, "Em."—reflects the confusion that is bound to reign wherever and whenever ideas are being remodeled and reshuffled to be rearranged in a way as to express new tastes and moods.

From the perspective of religious sensitivity Gide was probably the greatest creative writer of his generation, at least in his own country. He was drawn to religionless Christianity under the more delicate phrase, "unity of spirits without arbitrary unification." The irony is that he should find himself in opposition to that formidably orthodox Roman Catholic, Paul Claudel. The Church Claudel tried so stiffly to defend and to draw Gide into is now moving in a direction that Gide would welcome.

Gide used every means at his disposal—from insult to sarcasm to persuasion—to do away with Protestant puritanical and Catholic dogmatic rigidity. The Church's exclusive claim to given-once-and-for-all truths and her alliance with the secular powers were his constant targets. Both puritanism and dogmatism kept the individual in a straitjacket and hampered free development. This was a travesty of Christ's teaching, and bred hypocrisy and falsehood. But unlike so many others Gide did not, in the process of his denunciation of the churches' manipulation of men, introduce a basically non-Christian view of man. Man was not to him merely a material organism put together to function according to certain physical laws.

Gide recognizes that man is an isolated being, aware of his isolation, and unable, left to himself, to overcome this predicament. He can be saved or know himself, that is, recognize his own position in a spiritual community, after a struggle, one may even say after a process of self-emptying or *kenosis*. This process of reconciliation is through the artist who has himself a privileged position vis-à-vis "the ideal world." Reason does not reconcile a man to the foundation of his being because any reality beheld by reason is an *object*. Reason disjoins us from that with which it puts us into contact. Reconciliation is not through belief either, if *belief* means assent to the proposition that someone up or out there made me, watches over me, requires obedience to propositions he vouchsafes to men of his choice, and controls my destiny. When a god is defined in this way (or, to say the same thing in different words, when a god is set up over the whole world, in heaven) he becomes an answerer of metaphysical questions who allows no dissent, and a legislator. He robs individual man of his freedom, a development which means, in less image-ridden language, that men would rather escape their freedom than assume the responsibility of its exercise.

Gide took upon himself the task of telling men not to be afraid of their freedom, to be themselves, a precept which was always accompanied by the warning that the end of individualism is not an assemblage of disparate individuals. Rather, there is a plateau of fellowship where all individuals will stand in communion, equal to each other, but that fellowship is to be attained only through the realization of one's own potentialities. Self-realization is a means to an end, and the method to be used toward self-realization is receptivity, openness to the reality that both continues and envelops one. The method is to make of oneself, to use St. Paul's phrase, an earthen vessel. Gide was ostensibly opposed to Paul and there is no reference in his writings to the fourth chapter of the Apostle's second letter to the Corinthians. But he must have surely read it more than once, and must have liked *earthen,* not only because of its association with the earth, but also because *earthen* must have agreed with his ideal of renunciation. The word *ideal* is used here advisedly. Gide was born to wealth and is not known for his generosity. But the ideal of renunciation remained with him. It echoes Marx's warning against things whose private accumulation makes a thing out of the owner himself.

Gide may appear to advocate limitless receptivity and the other side of the coin, namely uninhibited self-expression. *Any* experience is welcome if you happen to be there to experience it. Do anything you feel like doing. Such suggestions are less startling and appear less callow when placed within the whole context of Gide's opus. They are, on the one hand, the exaggerated statements of his principles of receptivity and sincerity; on the other hand they may be meant to drive home the Dostoevskian conjecture that when God is dead everything is possible—or permissible. Yet Gide, though he remained the champion of zestful living, advocated neither anarchy nor irresponsible self-abandonment to sensuality.

A Gidian opinion that could be used against this last observation is the separation of love and sexual desire. Gide maintained that they do not involve each other. This is the curious consequence of a belief that he ostensibly rejects repeatedly: the separation of soul and body. He was brought up to believe that a good Christian must chastise the body in favor of the soul. His manner of opposing the theory that the body is evil was precisely to advocate the desire-love dichotomy in the sense that they both must and can be accepted, even when they happen not to be directed to the same object. Gide's point, in effect, is this: do not deny yourself a physical satisfaction if the only obstacle in your mind thereto is someone's commandment against it. Such a commandment may not be valid because the body must be welcomed and pleasure is not bad.

Gide frequently invites his listeners to give in to temptation. Close scrutiny of his text reveals that this is not an invitation to lasciviousness. After allowance is made for the show of daring that a champion of dissent must make, the reader realizes that Gide himself gives in to temptations involving pleasure in pursuit of a sort of unblocking of the self by way of entering into fuller communion with the surrounding reality. Here again morality to Gide turns out to be a means to a religious end. If we compare the end pursued to health, his position may be illustrated as follows: if a drug will make you healthy, do not refuse to take it just because it happens to be sweet. A health-giving drug *need* not be bitter. Painful repression and chastisement of the body do not guarantee spiritual freedom, or salvation.

Gide's general criteria for the goodness of an act are drawn with sufficient clarity, though they get less attention: an act in order to be good must be based on a principle that does not involve a denial of nature; it must contribute to the esthetic improvement of the world, and it must be useful to society, "society" including of course the doer of the act. These criteria do not add up to hedonism, let alone sensualism. Authenticity and constant determination to surpass oneself are dominant keynotes in a dynamic morality based on these principles. The advice that keeps surfacing is, "detect in yourself such traits as will make you surpass in excellence the generality of men, and do not shrink from the privations and effort required to develop them." It may be argued that the majority of men do not have such seeds of greatness in them, and many of those who do, do not have the leisure to pursue their preferences. The Gidian morality is for an élite. And it is largely for those who have their lives ahead of them. Its danger is that its emphasis on individual preferences may be adopted by men who are not already sensitivized by moral training or education or art, that is, by those who act impulsively as detached individuals and not as responsible members of society.

A circumstance Gide did not consider with enough care is that commands such as "do not destroy," "do not steal," "do not lie," "do not snoop," are not so much prohibitions, ways of leveling down individuality, as attempts at developing in the individual a sense of social responsibility. They are attempts at instilling respect for human life and for the rights of others. While it is obvious that there is no salvation or advance without the insubmissive, it is equally obvious that without the submissive—that is, without those who keep the law—there would be no society to save, no society worth carrying to a higher degree of perfection. And even this manner of viewing the scene is wrong. There are not some men who are submissive and others who are not; rather, all men are insubmissive in some respects and submissive in others. Submission and insubmissiveness are dialectically balanced at every level of their occurrence.

But it is somewhat futile to insist on these and other possible shortcomings in Gide's ethics. He did not have a detailed blueprint for the ideal society. He sought first the kingdom of God and had the carefree assurance that the rest would be given. Moreover, it is a mistake to think of him as a teacher. Gide is not a teacher. Gide is rather an example, or rather a case. The question is: How did *he* live? He knew his vocation, sought constantly to perfect his craft, questioned agonizingly the moral implications of his "inclination," and followed it only after he had honestly satisfied himself that it was according to the inevitable order of things, according—in another *façon de parler*—to a superior Will. He *accepted* what had to be. And even within its limits sought to improve the world. Moreover, indulgence in this inclination had salubrious effects on him, or so he thought, and did not damage anyone else.

Gide found the solution to his predicament as "this" man at the projected juncture of the vertical and horizontal dimensions of life. He foresaw a state of affairs where the vertical *Why* would no longer be a question different in nature from the horizontal *How,* a sort of paradise where the Dionysian and Apollonian, or such perennial kin-yet-opposites as love and justice, would no longer be in conflict. He overcame in joy his own inner conflicts. In joy too he overcame the tedium of life. He overcame that tedium in transtemporal joy and in the good *use* of time, which is work.

Gide, who refused to make moral decisions for anyone else—in the form of a moral code or otherwise—did not set himself up as a model of true living. Indeed he was acutely aware of his failures, and the observer who fails to find him admirable may have his good reasons. But then, how many sainted persons would we admire if we knew their lives in as much detail as we know Gide's? Moreover, his own suffering over the pain he caused other people—notably Madeleine—alleviates the impression that he cared more for himself than for anyone else. It is almost with fanaticism, but not always with ease or a sense of justification, that he appears to have insisted on being the man he thought he was destined to be, or to have done the work he knew he was destined to do. And the fervor which informs his writings, along with the example of his life, led many a beholder into paths which seem startling, but only at first sight.

Had Gide written in the forgotten language of Christianity, few people would have listened to him, and he would have been even less instrumental as he in fact was in leading many to the Christian faith. As he used symbolisms of his own without departing from the view that the center of history is outside history, Gide may be said to have strengthened Tertullian's famous claim that the soul is Christian by nature! He remained a Christian in yet another sense. Christianity is revolutionary not only because, as Gide said, it places the Kingdom of Heaven within man, but also because of a theme that permeates the Gospels: the last shall be first, and the first last. Thus Christianity is revolutionary not for any one of its teachings, but because it is the storehouse of a power of constant change. It seeks the demolition of *any* established order, regardless of its name and claims—including the Church—as soon as it becomes a den of thieves, that is, a locus and a vocabulary where one hides oneself not only from others, but also from oneself while pursuing selfish ends. Gide did not see this point about the revolutionary aspect of Christianity quite so clearly, but it was built into his mind, and it may account for his lasting appeal to youth. Nor is the Christian revolution an immature, headlong rush, heedless of damage and blood, toward some utopia. It contains within itself its own principle of criticism, inasmuch as its source is love.

Gide's use of secular terms to put forth an essentially religious attitude is, looking at it from the other side, the crystallization of religious—he would surely authorize us to say Christian—feeling on symbols that are not publicly acknowledged to stand for the sacred. This raises some problems. Does the substitution of secular for forgotten religious symbols mean that man's awareness of God's presence is inescapable, and that when one set of symbols become inoperative another set will necessarily replace them? Or does the rejection or replacement of the conventionally sacred symbols usher in the age of total secularity?

In Gide's case, the former of these alternatives appears to be true. The reality which he felt he must manifest without deflecting it in himself, which he nevertheless longed "to touch," is not limited to man, and Gide is not a humanist—or if the claim must be made that he is, then the already unmanageably large meaning of humanism must be extended further still. To Unamuno's question, Is man alone in the universe? Gide's unmistakable answer is No. He was a contemplative with a clear sense of ontological contingency. Reality to him was sacred, or had a sacred dimension, as we can gauge from the holiness that Em. (whom Gide loved) acquired in his mind in the course of his life. He hoped for an eschatological consummation without *relying* on a supernatural intervention which would set things right. He realized, in other words, that if there are no logical grounds to declare the world meaningful, there are no logical grounds to declare it absurd either. He opted for meaningfulness with what can only be described as an act of faith.

Gide was of course no theologian. The systematic investigation of the concept of God and of the nature of belief was not his responsibility. It is the critic's job to show how the experience of the creative writer blossoms forth—or does it die out?—in the theories of the systematic thinker. Gide's symbols were private or personal, and this guaranteed in a way his own and everyone else's religious freedom. This is in line with the view that authenticity consists in living out one's freedom, revealing oneself to oneself, in the process, as rooted in the larger reality. The fulcrum of human fellowship must not be external, Gide constantly insisted, because then it turns into an idol, which, itself being a mortal thing, is no bulwark against the fear of death. Nor should men belong to circles where loyalty is restricted to entities less than the universal.

There are two Gidian attitudes which in the minds of the unwary pass for atheism: anti-idolatry and mysticism. Anti-idolatry which may well subsume nearly everything said so far was the stated mission of his life. This is an indication of his ineradicable Protestantism. The Protestant principle, Tillich has written, is to protest against any absolute claim made for a relative reality. The God of Christendom, as a relative reality, was to Gide just another idol. He could not through this old idol overcome his alienation.

Gide's mysticism is manifest in *Les Nourritures Terrestres* (*The Fruits of the Earth*). This book seems to be a radical departure from his first published work, *Les Cahiers d'André Walter* (*The Notebooks of André Walter*), but the difference is largely one of literary maturity and language. In the new world of symbols adopted for *Les Nourritures Terrestres* Gide states the same fundamental concern and the same sort of answer to that concern: he wonders whether he is nothing but a "gathering together of sensations," and the answer is: "my life is always THAT, plus myself." The reader must reflect that "THAT" is potentially dissolvable in reality without a residue; but then there is "myself." Later in life, the hope of a "prodigious" relationship with the reality wherein he would both keep and not keep his selfhood was entertained by Gide under the category of love. The opposite of love—disruption—he saw as the work of the Devil.

To Gide, the isolated individual, no permanently held conviction brought solace. He overcame that isolation, a symptom of his solitariness, only in occasional heightened experiences. In these experiences he transcended time and space. As he remembered subsequently, at such moments his dichotomies, his sense of isolation were conquered. They remained the yearned for, focal points of his existence. This is the mystical way, a conclusion which is reinforced by his declaration made as late as 1942 that "solitude is bearable only with God." In this way the very difficulty connected with being, and yet not being, conscious of oneself in the Whole, vanishes.

The meaning of the word *theism* is undergoing radical changes at the hands of contemporary theologians. We must likewise modify our understanding of *atheism*. An atheist can no longer be described as a man who refuses to believe in the existence of a disembodied Spirit beyond the firmament. A cool atheist is someone who considers the following questions trivial: Why is there anything? What is the sacred? Also, perhaps, Why should I love my neighbor? These questions are trivial to the cool atheist in the sense that they are not genuine questions. They seem to promise to take the questioner beyond (or below or above) himself to the source of his being, but this promise is illusory. Actually, the cool atheist says, there is no source to be taken to and no point in asking these questions at all.

These questions were constantly present in Gide's mind, and he sought the answers by way of satisfying deeply existential needs. The charge of atheism leveled against him is therefore inaccurate, even if understandable. Atheism—in the old sense—and mysticism have often been not-so-strange bedfellows.

1

Gide's Method and Problem

André Gide, a French, or rather a European, classical writer, was born in 1869. Toward the end of his long literary career he was recognized as one of the most important writers of France, who had changed men's ideas and image of the modern world, while the Nobel Prize for Literature which he won in 1947 acknowledged in effect his importance as an artist who mirrored the characteristic emotions and philosophical preferences of an era.

The family to which Gide was born combined northern and southern French habits of mind and was the theater of clashes between sharply divergent moral and religious tendencies. His father was a rather liberal, scholarly man who enjoyed an occasional walk in the countryside with joyful companions, careless of the hour. He died when André was a boy of eleven, in 1880. André's mother, an earnest, stringent Puritan, survived her husband by fifteen years. Quite free of financial worries, she made her only, rather unconventional child the principal concern of her existence.

Gide was still an infant, of course, when the Parisian insurrection of the Commune broke out. He lived most of his life at the time of the Third Republic, nicknamed "La Gueuse," whose instability may be gauged from the less than twenty-four-hour duration of Ribot's government in May, 1914. He died in 1951, during the Fourth Republic which was an interpolation between de Gaulle's Provisional Government and his Fifth Republic. Thus the political situation in France was almost continuously chaotic from the day of Gide's birth to the day of his death.

The celebrated roaring gaiety that swept the capitals of the Western world before and after the First World War appears in retrospect to have been a deceptive veneer. Gide, who did not share in that gaiety, was encouraged in his introspection not only by the political confusion but also by the unprecedented pace of technological progress: at Gide's birth the machine gun was not yet in use; toward the end of his life he had occasion to write to a Japanese scholar victimized by the atomic bomb dropped on Nagasaki.

In a world which exhibited no external uniformity and where the accepted standards of conduct had broken down, the individual was driven to reappraise his own potentialities against society and its idols, to seek a basis of moral behavior within himself. Gide elicits the interest of the moralist and the student of religion in his capacity both as a learned and sensitive individual reacting to the forces defining a fascinating period of Western civilization and as a man in whom the dominant claims of that period are put to the test.

Contradiction, Free Association, Visibility

As a creative writer Gide does not present his philosophical views systematically. These views are to be found scattered throughout his *Journal* and his work, which Denis de Rougemont aptly describes as simply different manners of making the same revelation. The author's real portrait, de Rougemont goes on to say, is not in his creative work nor in his diary, but in their "mutual refraction."[1]

Yet it is not so much the disarrangement of Gide's thoughts as his contradictions that baffle his critics. Indeed so pronounced is his indifference to logical consistency that Thomas Mann summarizes the moral of his work in the aphorism, "Every principle is nothing but the corrective of its opposite."[2] Gide refers both to himself and to Edouard, the protagonist of his major novel *Les Faux-Monnayeurs* (*The Counterfeiters*), as Proteus. He noted in 1929 that he changed his opinions with a facility that even he found disconcerting, and stated two years later that he could not undertake anything consecutive. He spoke of his equal aptitude for contraries, among many other pronouncements to the same effect. In *Les Faux-Monnayeurs* two of his characters display the same attitude: Boris, a boy of thirteen, is madly in love with Bronja, the daughter of the psychologist who is in charge of him. Bronja, who is about two years older than Boris, invites him to go with her for a walk. His answer is: "Yes, I will. No, I won't." Bernard in the same novel keeps a notebook in the manner of Edouard—or of Gide himself, though

Edouard is not to be confused with Gide in every instance. "I write down an opinion on the right hand page," says Bernard, "whenever I can write the opposite opinion, facing it, on the left hand page."

It is evident that far from objectionable, contradiction is for Gide an effective means of getting at truth. Though he is too French to contradict himself without twinges of conscience, he would no doubt sympathize entirely in this matter with Walt Whitman's asseveration in "Song of Myself": "Do I contradict myself?/Very well then I contradict myself. (I am large, I contain multitudes.)" Gide wrote on one occasion that when he reasoned he did so "willy-nilly," and on another that "if I feel like contradicting myself, I will contradict myself without scruple: I will not seek 'coherence.' But I will not put on airs of incoherence either."[3] Hence criticisms leveled against him largely by Roman Catholic writers to the effect that he fails to respect the law of contradiction are pointless. Gide simply ignores that law; he chooses not to concern himself with it. Nor can one observe only incidentally that Gide contradicts himself, and proceed to select for presentation those of his statements which support the critic's own preferred view of the writer.

The ways in which Gide expresses himself—either by inclination or by deliberate choice—are far from irrelevant to the study of his religious and moral convictions. These convictions and the manner of their expression are interdependent and mutually illuminating, as are a philosopher's theory of knowledge and his philosophy. Examples of contradiction, free association, and what we may call the visibility of Gide's thought will be given and their implications from a religious and moral perspective pointed out.

Though Gide is committed to the proposition that system-building is not a fruitful procedure in the pursuit of truth, the occurrence of contradictions in his writings is much less common than one is led to believe by the writer himself or by many of his critics. Many of his propositions are contradictory in appearance only. When I say "I believe in X" and then "I do not believe in X," the second proposition is not opposed to the first if I change the referent of "X" from one proposition to the other. Gide's propositions are often contradictory in this sense. In the case of the term "God" in particular, two complementary circumstances may account for the impression that the statements where it occurs are contradictory: First, Gide is often groping for a solution to his religious problem, and this is reflected in the uncertainty, under his pen, of that term. Secondly, he sometimes uses "God" in the sense given to it by conventionally religious people, while at other times he does so to refer to his own indefinable feeling or vision of the ultimate, as shown in Chapters 5 and 6.

As revelatory as Gide's contradictions—whether apparent or real—is his attitude toward contradiction itself. It is possible to argue that two really contradictory propositions add up to nothing. They may be compared to sallies in two different directions only to return to the place of origin. But a reader familiar with Gide can almost hear him replying to such an argument—Ah! but the silence to which contradiction leads is precisely the one where one has a glimpse of the truth; if contradictory language leads the hearer to a source of meaning which is itself beyond linguistic expression, then contradiction must not be frowned upon. No doubt the ultimate in contradiction is to make contradictory statements about the advisability of contradiction. Gide advocated contradiction, but he also condemned it. Thus he recognized "that without Descartes's rigorous reasoning nothing solid or lasting could have been established."[4] He also declared, on the basis of his imperious "habit of logic," that "errors in logic always seem" to him "the most serious."[5]

Gide's lifelong contradictory attitude toward contradiction itself leads to the inevitable conclusion that he did not trust reason, even if he was not always indifferent to formal logic. Unfaithful even to itself, reason was, to use Luther's famous word, a whore. By the same token philosophy was an intolerable "arrogance," for it depended on reason, oblivious of a central paradox: reason could be trusted only on the assumption that it was given by God—but then it was reason itself that denied God. "Even if we pretend that [reason] is born only through a slow transformation, a successive adaptation to phenomena, it will very well be able to discuss phenomena, but beyond?"[6] Gide wrote this in his earliest published book. He did not thereafter modify his attitude toward reason, and he did not abandon his concern with the beyond which "reason cannot reach." Also lifelong was the substance of his conviction that "we can only opine" and that "affirmation is guilty."[7]

It is clear that Gide's low regard for reason is not due to his own lack of logical competence. Remy de Gourmont considers him "a very logical mind."[8] Francis Jammes speaks of his natural tendency to reason and even of his "exaggerated need for dialectics."[9] Yet another critic, Ramon Fernandez, describes him as "a very stubborn and very subtle logician."[10]

While these writers may not be known as judges of logical acumen, their testimony is sufficient evidence that Gide's theory of knowledge, indicating as it does an Augustinian-Lutheran frame of mind, was a consciously preferred alternative. His unsystematic statements amount in effect to the following estimate by Paul Tillich, who belongs in the same tradition. "Reason as the structure of mind and reality is actual in the processes of being, existence, and life. Being is finite, existence is self-contradictory, and life is ambiguous. Actual reason participates in these characteristics of reality."[11]

Gide's approval of contradiction is precisely his recognition that existence itself is self-contradictory. The word *therefore,* which is symbolic of a state of affairs where all things fit together without friction, must not be used by the poet, Gide said. The poet must not "know" that word. Self-contradictory existence cannot be overcome by *thinking* it harmonious. Philosophy which is the expression of consciousness for itself (*pour soi*) may seek to force the facts of existence into a pattern whose elements are logically concordant, but creative literature is the expression of consciousness in itself (*en soi*).[12] Its refusal to use "therefore" is the very mark of its genuineness. Gide does not wish to have his existence within the artificial self-consistency of intellectual elaboration. The "antagonistic proposals" of his nature, or what he called "the dialogue" in himself must not be "suppressed" for that would amount to "stopping the development of life."[13]

The dialogue of which contradiction is no more than the linguistic manifestation may turn on occasion into fierce and persistent discord, but then the ensuing reconciliation will be that much broader, Gide says, and he concludes that "everything leads to harmony."[14] This is so because contradiction is rooted in sincerity. "To contradict oneself," Gide wrote, "is to be sincere twice."[15] In other words, a proposition does not owe its validity to another proposition that precedes or follows it, but to the reality of which it is the expression. Each of two contradictory propositions may very well express two different items of the same reality without hanging logically together.

Contradictory statements may be compared to the spokes of a wheel, which are related to each other through the hub. Logical consistency on the other hand is like the outer rim of the wheel, which may constitute a flawless circle, but will not lead to the center. Gide's own simile to explain his approval of contradiction, or his existentialistic rejection of conformism to the dictates of any systematic philosophy is as follows: ". . . the spark of life can flash only between two contrary poles, and . . . it is larger and more beautiful the greater the distance between them and the richer the opposition with which each pole is charged."[16]

By way of saying the same thing somewhat more literally, he jots down a thought of Octave Mirbeau: "Only those never contradict themselves who are dead, or almost."[17] Evidently each pole in his own more vivid statement receives its initial charge from the depths of human existence—as each spoke is rooted in the hub. By the same token Gide maintained, on one hand, that a "more hidden continuity" lies behind the "apparent" inconsistency or fragmentariness (*inconséquence*) of the world[18] and, on the other, that reason is not autonomous and that it is merely an instrument of deep-seated drives.[19]

The broadly Platonic-Augustinian bent of Gide's mind is further seen in his theory of influence. As if following the theory that knowledge is not acquired but breaks into consciousness when the unknowing holder of hidden knowledge is properly stimulated, Gide claims that what we call influence is only the awakening of dormant preferences.[20] Again, repeatedly in his fiction a person is recognized by someone else not primarily on account of his characteristics, but because he is *waited for or sought after*,[21] a procedure which suggests Gide's inclination to believe that truth is subjectivity. He clearly states that knowledge is illumination.[22]

Gide's thought, unconstrained by the fear of contradicting itself, is guided by free associations of ideas. Consider the following:

Henceforth, acting in any way whatever and not giving myself time to reflect, my least acts seemed to me more significant since they were no longer reasoned out. At the same time I delivered myself from anxiety, perplexity, and remorse. And perhaps that intimate gymnastic to which I had first submitted had not been altogether useless and helped me to achieve that state of joy which made me recognize my act to be good solely from the pleasure I took in doing it.

The Greeks, who, not only in the multitude of their statues but also in themselves, left us such a beautiful image of humanity, recognized as many gods as there are instincts, and the problem for them was to keep the inner Olympus in equilibrium, not to subjugate and subdue any of the gods.

It is not so much by his acts that a lover of humanity makes himself useful as by his example. I mean: by his very figure, by the image he offers and leaves behind, and by the happiness and serenity it radiates.[23]

Many a scholar would disagree with Gide about his sweeping remarks regarding the Greeks and their gods, but that is not our concern. We are concerned with the order in which his thoughts are set forth in the passage quoted. This order is determined largely by subjective factors: the link that associates Gide's thoughts is his deep-set conviction that Christianity is the domestication of instincts, as we shall see in Chapter 2. Thus the "Christianity" practiced early in his life brings forth, by contrast, the alternative according to which he would have liked to have lived, namely "the Greeks." Then the phrase "beautiful image of humanity" gives rise to the last paragraph just quoted where the word *image* occurs again and which is otherwise unrelated to anything said before.

Gide, contradicting himself and associating freely, is nevertheless held in control when an *image* guides him. His thought is often "visible" and held in check by the image. Contrariwise, whenever an image is not there to guide his mind at work, he becomes impatient. This is certainly a factor contributing to his famous—and rather vague—contention that "the esthetic point of view" is the only sound one to take in discussing his work.[24] Gide does not engage in a sustained rational disquisition and analysis. When he catches himself doing so he simply abandons the issue, cutting it short with an ellipsis or an etcetera. The following paragraph, which deals with a subject of considerable importance to him, is one example:

Let us beware, Nathanaël, of all the instruments of happiness. And above all let us not choose them. To begin with, you cannot choose, but it is dangerous even to think you are choosing, since in order to choose you must judge, and judging always presupposes . . . ; besides, etc. etc.[25]

Mme Vedel of *Les Faux-Monnayeurs*—whom Gide likens to Lamartine's Elvire—has this same habit of leaving sentences unfinished. Gide interprets it in a religious sense: "[It] gives her reflections a kind of poetic vagueness. She reaches the infinite by way of the indeterminate and the indefinite."[26]

Such a disposition in Gide himself may account partially at least for the fact that not logic but visibility was a requirement of the thought of Gide the artist, in the sense, first, that he could not think without the aid of visible things. All of nature was to him a book of moral or even political reflection, and, his notions to the contrary notwithstanding, almost never a field of scientific investigation. When he points out that such animals that do not perspire are poisonous, he is not making a disinterested scientific observation. His aim is to drive home the point that repressed emotions fester in man and eventually result in harmful action. When seven bees wear themselves out at the closed window of his room while a slight detour would give them their freedom through another, open, window, he reflects that the bees would think themselves lost if they left the light for an instant. "It is," he says, "the story of the fish in the net." The fish, in turn, divert his thought to "the French in the Ruhr."[27] The theme of *Saül,* where a man is dispossessed of himself by his demons, was suggested to him, Gide said in a letter to Christian Beck, by a chrysalid of bombyx entirely occupied by small chrysalids of ichneumon flies.[28] Nor are his lessons learned from animals or from natural phenomena only. Not even a mechanical problem is a matter of mere mechanics. He writes in 1947, at the age of seventy-eight:

Individualism:
Mme Theo's clock, stopped for three months now, suddenly began again this morning by itself, *sponte sua* and without anyone's having touched it: we hear it strike eight o'clock; it is noon.[29]

On the other hand, when Gide wishes to express a moral or religious notion with any degree of finality, an image, often magnificently built in its minutest detail, is his instrument of communication. This gives all his creative writing its bidimensional character: nearly all the objects in Gide's fiction, whether persons or things or relations, are themselves, and ideas or principles beyond themselves. The effectiveness of Gide's bidimensional style is due in part to its total transparency. His images are there, and then they mysteriously vanish from between the reader and the idea they incarnate. One may pick at random the physical description of Armand's bedroom in *Les Faux-Monnayeurs,* which is also the analysis of the young man's psyche.

Gide analyzes the condition to which Armand is reduced. Armand's father, a pastor, confuses the mouthing of noble-sounding phrases with genuine charity. The father's contact with the son is formal. There is no genuine communication between them: ". . . he has never been inside the place. . . . It's magnificent to hear him," Armand confides to Olivier. "A pity he never has any time for a little chat." The bedroom in which he receives his friend

was a small, narrow room, reached by the backstairs. Its window looked on to an inner courtyard, on to which the water-closets and kitchens of the next-door house opened also. The light came from a corrugated zinc reflector, which caught it from above and cast it down, pallid, leaden and dreary. The room was badly ventilated; an unpleasant odour pervaded it.[30]

The other dimension of this beautiful example of Gidian writing is easily detected by one familiar with the writer's religious views. No detail is there for its own sake alone. The "backstairs" suggest that Armand is a difficult man to reach except in a roundabout way. As if in response to the water-closets that limit his horizon, the young man has written, we subsequently learn, a poem entitled the *Nocturnal Vase*. He is the sort of adolescent who will satisfy his covert incestuous drives by locking up a friend in a room with his sister. On another occasion, on the point of leaving Olivier's room, he pushes up the *portière* placing his walking stick in its hole. The precise account of this gesture seems irrelevant until the reader realizes its sexual and sadistic implications. "I respect her because she is virtuous," says Armand of his sister Rachel in the very next paragraph. "And I always behave in such a way as to offend her virtue."[31]

To be contrasted with Armand's room is Edouard's studio. It is on the top floor of an apartment house. Here, behind a wide open window, Edouard brings Olivier back to life. Gide is clearly intimating that his mission as a writer is to expose young men to light, namely to truth, directly. Armand, a pastor's son, receives *his* light as deflected on a zinc surface, that is, through a lusterless and even poisonous body of moral and religious formulae.

Gide was bound to prefer images to logically conditioned statements inasmuch as an image allows greater freedom: an image has the curious virtue of conveying the artist's idea without necessarily carrying the suggestion that the reader must accept or reject it as meant by the author. This is in keeping with the well-known advice that the reader of *Les Nourritures Terrestres* receives from its young author (Gide was twenty-eight at the time of its publication): "Leave me . . . when have I said that I wanted you similar to myself?"[32] The advice has become a Gidian hallmark, though it has been given by many a teacher before Gide.

I insist on giving to those who read me power, joy, courage, defiance, perspicacity—but I am careful above all not to give them directions, inasmuch as they can and must find these only by themselves—I was about to say in themselves. To develop at once the critical spirit and energy, those two contraries.[33]

Yet an image has requirements of its own and may falsify an observation when the user of the image does not abandon it at the proper moment. Gide's presentation of his doctrine of *déracinement* is a case in point. Since the very word *déracinement* evokes in the mind the forcible extraction of an actual tree from the ground, there came the time in his long debate with his opponents on this subject when the moral problem was lost to view altogether and it took the form of discussions in arboriculture.

That culture is sometimes defined in terms of deracination is a matter of common knowledge. Gide himself looked upon instruction as *an uprooting through the head*.[34] But his concern in this debate with Maurice Barrès over *déracinement* was rather psychological in nature. The ever new surroundings where one ought, according to this doctrine, thrust oneself, may be conducive to self-examination; such self-thrust may cause one to reappraise the convictions that have come to be held by the generality of men, for the simple reason that one does not take for granted things that are new or unfamiliar. Gide proved to be a better artist, more perceptive than his opponent. He saw that it was necessary for the individual to have the fortitude to stand on his own moral ground in a world where the certainties of a bygone generation were crumbling. Yet the image, as used by Gide, stood in the way of a sustained, accurate observation. He writes:

... I wrote a whole book, of a deeply reasoned madness, to exalt the beauties of travel, striving, perhaps through a mania for proselytizing, to teach the joy there would be in feeling free of ties, or "roots" if you prefer ...

And by way of elucidation:

... But might it not also please us to see a man demand of himself the greatest possible merit? In comfort every virtue is vitiated; new, arduous paths necessitate virtue. I like (forgive me) everything that calls on man to perish or become great. The historical events that have forced men out of their element are assuredly those that have made the most victims; they have also excited and enlightened the greatest number of heroes. It is a process of sifting; in the calm of habit, wings unextended, with no need of being widespread, forget how to be so; the higher the wind rises from abroad the more a powerful wingspan is necessary.

Yes, but the weak will perish in it.

Need we console ourselves by saying that they were weaklings? Let us say rather: true education is for the strong alone. Taking root is for the weak, sinking into the hereditary habit that will keep them from cold.[35]

Gide speaks here with the passion of a revivalist, and makes as much sense. It goes without saying that the word *great* is meaningful only in relation to *small,* as *strong* is meaningful only in relation to *weak.* Hence the injunctions "be great!" "be strong!" have no definable positive content. In the passage quoted, *strong* seems to mean "adventurous, dissatisfied with the customary and the familiar." Getting out of one's element (*dépaysement*) is presented as the greatest virtue, as an end in itself, justifying all the means, including large numbers of killings. Gide's enthusiasm would probably have been dampened if he had known clearly, as he wrote these lines, whether he was enjoining a course of action or describing a historical process, or both. Columbus, for example, would qualify as a "strong" man. Since he left behind the customary and familiar shore of the Mediterranean several centuries before Gide wrote against Barrès, one may say that the tendency to go beyond the known limits of one's experience is part of human nature. Gide wished to encourage this innate tendency, and fell into an error of exaggeration, misled as he was by the pictorially suggestive word *dépaysement.* The fact is that seldom if ever do people abandon the familiar for the purely negative reason of getting *out.* Rather, they seek familiarity with a larger world which is but dimly perceived prior to the voyage out. Thus getting "out" is an attempt at getting "in." To be sure there is a measure of strength involved in leaving the familiar, but that strength does not necessarily deserve praise if it is exercised for a decidedly harmful purpose. Gide himself did not praise strength uniformly: he admired the exceptionally beautiful flowers of sick plants, condemned the Spartans for failing to realize the value of delicacy,[36] and berated "The Brotherhood of Strong Men" for bringing about the destruction of Boris in *Les Faux-Monnayeurs.* Nor does he define here such words as *valeur, vertu,* and *héros,* all of which, while invariably eliciting praise, may apply to a variety of conducts. The passage is therefore quite obscure in spite of its apparent lucidity. In similar instances Gide confuses thinking with the drawing of pictures in his mind; he confuses the examination of religious and moral issues with the observation of natural phenomena. The clear outlines of a visible object become for him a proof of the validity of the idea. As an artist he was more sensitive than many a thinker to the contemporary condition of man. And the very condition of his artistry —his sensitivity to images—caused him at times to go off on a tangent.

"Solitariness"

The dominant manners in which Gide expresses himself—contradiction, free association, and image-building—already reveal his fundamental concerns. In all three the thing refused is the use of reason, for reason to him, as to Dostoevsky, is an instrumentality of isolation. This may account for the curious fact that the words *logical, philosophy, reason* itself, have in Gide's writings unexpectedly moral connotations. He will use the word *illogical* synonymously with *unjust,* while *logical* on another occasion will practically mean *monstrous*.[37] Reason keeps one, he clearly intimates, from communion with reality. He admits the presence in man of a region where reason becomes useless, of a spiritual depth that reasoning does not reach. By the same token, all knowledge that is *distinct* from one, that is, held by reason, will so remain until the consummation of time.[38] Reason does not overcome, but deepens the human predicament of alienation. From the time of *Les Cahiers d'André Walter,* his earliest work, to the last years of his writing career Gide kept casting that problem into a soul-and-body or heart-and-mind terminology, rarely using other variants.

One of the factors that complicate the soul-and-body problem is that "soul" and "body" are taken to be the names of two substantially different things. They may in fact refer to two dimensions of the same human existence, or even to two perspectives from which to view and evaluate that existence. Gide argues in *Les Cahiers* that the body is inferior to and possessed by the spirit because it dies, an argument which puts to mind the old Pindaric view that "each man's body follows the call of overmastering death; yet still there is left alive an image of life, for this alone is from the gods." According to the same Pindaric view, the soul "sleeps while the limbs are active; but while the man sleeps it often shows in dreams a decision of joy or adversity to come."[39] The occurrence of dreams is construed here as empirical evidence that the soul is an entity independent of the body and imprisoned by it. Gide must have meant less literally his statement that at night, when the body abandons itself, the soul escapes, and that in the morning the body recovers possession of the soul which is caught in a cage once more. Thus the body, or that which dies, is also the instrument of individuation. It is, moreover, that which is impure; it pulls down.

The body is that which gives the individual, to use F. H. Bradley's term, an adjectival status.[40] It keeps man from reaching the substance of things. It keeps him away from the Whole. Gide was driven by this notion until the time when he discovered that the body which is an instrument of isolation is also an instrument of communion. This new perspective in turn gave way to enthusiasms of a socio-political nature. Thus, though *Les Nourritures Terrestres, Numquid et tu . . . ?,* and *Les Nouvelles Nourritures* (*The New Fruits*) appear to be widely different in outlook and content, Gide's concern remains identical to itself in all three. The books differ as symbolic expressions of that concern. They coexisted in him as he himself was very much aware. *Les Nourritures Terrestres* is "the physical accompaniment" of *Numquid et tu . . . ?,* as the phrase is used in the following passage: ". . . in the theatre the mere name of Agamemnon is enough: I weep torrents. From this physical accompaniment my emotion derives the guarantee of its authenticity." *Les Nourritures Terrestres* is the "physical accompaniment" of *Numquid et tu . . . ?* as *Les Nouvelles Nourritures* is its "social" accompaniment. Gide himself has said in effect that what he sought in communism was "communion," and that he had *always* been a Communist.[41]

Nevertheless Gide never solved intellectually the old body-soul problem, and his repeated use of the imagery where the truth about a person (his secret, his name, his diary) is discovered in a tightly closed receptacle[42] is strongly reminiscent of Plato's doctrine, put forth in *Phaedrus,* that we are imprisoned in the body, like an oyster in his shell. Even when Gide tells himself that in the name of wisdom he must not separate body and soul, the notion of their separateness underlies his thought. As a child, he informs us, he had an exquisite dream of better things as his soul freed itself from his body:

Then I separated them so much that now I am no longer their master; they go, each its own way—body and soul; the soul dreams of caresses ever warmer, the body abandons itself and goes adrift.

Wisdom would require that they be put together, that their pursuit be made to converge, and that the soul seek not loves too distant in which the body may not share.[43]

Gide elsewhere expressed the belief that body and soul are one and the same thing. He has said that he has found "calm" in their "identification."[44] He has spoken in the selfsame paragraphs of the "interdependence" of body and soul and of their "harmony," making of these passages a series of perfectly bewildering statements. He does not reflect, though there are signs in his writings of familiarity with Eastern religious thought, that the user of the possessive adjective *my* in the phrases "my soul" and "my body" is an entity other than the soul *and* the body, and that dissatisfaction with the soul-body dichotomy is perhaps a covert yearning for the non-dual, the Advaita.

Either the conscious self or the sensible elements in a man's makeup, that is, either the soul or the body, could be, to Gide, instrumentalities of isolation and of death, witness the change in his symbolisms from *Les Cahiers d'André Walter* to *Les Nourritures Terrestres* to *Numquid et tu . . . ?* This anxiety informs his other works, and to the extent to which A. N. Whitehead is correct in defining religion as "what the individual does with his own solitariness," Gide's fundamental problem appears to be a religious problem. This conclusion is strengthened by the great emphasis he places on sincerity coincidentally with Whitehead's observation that "the primary religious virtue is sincerity, a penetrating sincerity."[45] In his autobiography, published in his late fifties, Gide recalls the following incident from his childhood:

> . . . it was a few years later, a little after my father's death; that is to say, I must have been about eleven. The scene again took place at table, but this time my mother and I were alone. I had been at school that morning. What had happened? Possibly nothing. . . . Then why did I suddenly break down? Why did I again feel, as I fell convulsively sobbing into mamma's arms, that indefinable anguish, the very same exactly that I had felt at my little cousin's death? It was as though the special sluice-gate of some unknown, unbounded, mystic sea had suddenly been opened and an overwhelming flood poured into my heart. I was not so much unhappy as terrified; but how was I to explain it to my mother? All she could distinguish through my sobs were, repeated again and again, these blind despairing words: "I'm not like other people . . . not like other people!"[46]

In this context of terror and despair Gide is not reiterating his feeling of being "one of the elect,"[47] as some commentators have suggested. He is describing as a childhood memory the anxiety of separateness. He felt it throughout his life. "One is alone" is practically the key sentence of *Les Cahiers d'André Walter*. In his last work, *Thésée*, the Greek king goes forward "alone," beyond the level of "constancy in friendship." Between these two tales nearly all of Gide's works are studies of man's solitariness and of his reactions to it. The characters of his only "novel," *Les Faux-Monnayeurs*, are solitary individuals, rarely related at any appreciable depth. The one scriptural quotation that governed Gide's religious philosophy, and which remained uppermost in his mind during most of his literary career is: "Except a grain of wheat fall into the earth and die, it abideth by itself *alone*," a verse which incidentally governed the thoughts of such diverse contemporaries of Gide as Berdyaev, Thomas Mann, Van Gogh, and Jacques Rivière. One may attribute Gide's own solitariness to his wealth, to the untimely death of his father, to his childhood under the protective wings of his mother and to his—perhaps consequent—homosexuality. Yet these are the peculiar circumstances which made him acutely aware of the human predicament of alienation. A remark of Simone de Beauvoir applies to him: "If any individual—a Pepys or a Rousseau, an exceptional or a run-of-the-mill character—reveals himself honestly, everyone, more or less, becomes involved."[48]

Gide belongs to a generation of intellectuals including Bergson whose importance Georges Sorel has described as transitional.[49] He was himself quite conscious of living in a period of transition. While he saw "our old world crumbling . . . around us," he waited and hoped for, observed with all his attention, "something unknown" being formulated and slowly taking shape.[50] Gide represents a transition between the enthusiasms of the nineteenth century and the sober reappraisals of the human situation in the twentieth. He is a transition between Symbolism on one hand and Existentialism on the other, many of the fundamental elements of the latter's elaborate theoretical structure being found in one or the other of his symbolisms, such as holding one's own lamp in total darkness, and of peregrinations, whether on land or on sea, without any guideposts, without any known or projected destination.[51]

This transitional character of Gide's importance becomes an element of more than casual interest as we recall that the phrase "failure of nerve" originally applied by Gilbert Murray to the Hellenistic period has been used to characterize our own times also.[52] If it is true, moreover, that there is a correlation between the theological systems of the thirteenth century and the consecutive emergence of Eckhart, Ruysbroeck, and others; or between the Renaissance and such mystics as Teresa of Avila and John of the Cross, then Evelyn Underhill is probably correct in her observation that from a cultural point of view a phenomenon of transition is mysticism,[53] mystics being torch-bearers who overcome the tergiversations and anxieties that mark the periods between established certainties.

In Gide's time a new foundation of meaning was being sought: "everything must be questioned, doubted again."[54] Mysticism was the subject of renewed interest not only in France with the publication of Henri Brémond's *Prayer and Poetry,* for example,[55] but also in England and the United States with Inge, Underhill, and William James. The central dilemma with which Gide was always faced is itself the basic concern which informs all mysticism. He had hardly passed his twentieth year when he wrote: "Communion will never be perfect; or, if perfect, it will not be felt,"[56] a statement which amounts to the repudiation of all rationally controlled solutions to the problem of alienation, and claims in effect that alienation is built into the fact of being an individual. Another variant of the same problem is Gide's constant reiteration that humility—a virtue whereby an individual may overcome his alienation —is in fact pride. This is certainly not true in every instance of humility, and Gide would have been less dogmatic about the impossibleness of that virtue had he not been conditioned to think as a Calvinist that man is hopelessly depraved. Though he denies man's moral helplessness vigorously and often, that conviction keeps finding less direct ways of insinuating itself into his writings.

Alienation and the search for a ground either to integrate the individual into the Whole or to make him autonomous was of course the problem of Gide's era, as it was the problem of German Idealism between the Enlightenment and Romanticism, when it received a different solution. The affinities between Gide and such contemporaries as Nietzsche, Dostoevsky, and Sartre have been studied extensively, though two of his significant differences from Nietzsche have not been dwelt upon,[57] namely Gide's refusal to think that the individual should "regard *himself* as an aim," and his implicit rejection of the doctrine of eternal return, a doctrine which insists on keeping man within the realm of time.

The religious kinship between Gide and Simone Weil has received only one fleeting notice, when the similarity of views between the two authors is in fact remarkable.[58] Weil has repeatedly propounded in her major works the necessity of living fully the present moment, the virtues of sincerity, *déracinement,* total detachment, "obedience" (akin to Gide's determination to follow nature), the investigation of reality by means of pairs of contraries, and the necessity to follow one's "inclination"—to mention only some of her views which agree with Gide's.

Gide's desire to touch God, expressed in *Les Cahiers,* as well as in many a paragraph of *Les Nourritures Terrestres,* was condemned by Marcel Schwob, a Jewish convert to Catholicism, as "a sinister and desperate parody of the need for the Host," yet that desire could be sympathetically viewed by a man of Teilhard de Chardin's religious sensitivity, for example.[59] Of interest too by way of understanding the religious nature of certain characteristic Gidian stances is an aphorism by Simone Weil, who said that carnal love is a search for the Incarnation. There are elements of modern Protestant theology that have been fore-shadowed in Gide's work. Bonhoeffer's famous statement that "God is teaching us that we must live as men who can get along very well without him," could easily be read as a quotation from Gide's diary.[60] Another remark, equally important for the critic who wishes to see his way clear through the complexity of Gide's contradictions, free associations, and images is made by Paul Tillich:

The name of this infinite and inexhaustible depth and ground of all being is *God.* That depth is what the word *God* means. And if that word has not much meaning for you, translate it, and speak of the depths of your life, of the source of your being, of your ultimate concern, of what you take seriously without any reservations. Perhaps, in order to do so, you must forget everything traditional that you have learned about *God,* perhaps even the word itself. For if you know that God means depth, you know much about Him. You cannot then call yourself an atheist or unbeliever.[61]

Such an affirmation, occupying as it does an important place in contemporary religious thought, proves useful as a perspective from which to examine Gide's statements. Only then will these be seen in their depth and relevancy.

2

Criticism of the "Christian" Answer

St. Paul

In the disagreement between St. Paul and St. Peter, as related by the former in his Letter to the Galatians, Gide would certainly have sided with the Apostle for the uncircumcision. The apostle contributed to Gide's turn of mind both as a direct influence, and because of his pervasive presence in the religious atmosphere of both home and school where the future writer received his training.

Gide's determinism and his cardinal conviction that true individualism is selflessness, as well as his antinomianism (including the "flesh-" or "letter-spirit" opposition), antinationalism, and antirationalism, are decidedly Pauline. A major Gidian moral and religious requirement is sincerity. Paul himself had laid emphasis on sincerity both in the ordinary sense of practicing what one preaches—"thou that abhorrest idols, dost thou rob temples?"[1]—and in the more profound sense of making of oneself an open channel for the flow of truth, which is the obligation, to use Gide's word, "to manifest": "for with the heart man believeth unto righteousness; and with the mouth confession is made unto salvation."[2] Few people in history had more fervor than Paul. He taught it to the Romans: "never flag in zeal, be aglow with the Spirit."[3] Gide taught it to Nathanaël, the disciple in *Les Nourritures Terrestres*. Gide bade Nathanaël make of himself the most irreplaceable of beings. The bidding is satisfactory only—for Rasputin and Hitler were quite irreplaceable—if it implies obligation to excel in one's own way along a morally praiseworthy path.[4] Some such notion must have been present in Paul's own mind when he observed that ". . . each of us shall give account of himself [not to men but] to God" and advised each Corinthian to "lead the life which the Lord has assigned to him."[5]

31

Paul was as "available" (*disponible*) as Gide, for he was all things to all men. Neither minded contradicting himself; they did the things they did not wish to do, believed in the educative value of the law, expressed antifeminist sentiments, and deprecated family life. Gide spoke in effect of what Paul called the "body of death"; both yearned after transparency, after a world, that is, where no truth is hidden from view and where a given object does not cause the beholder to stop short of the infinite, a world where things are not isolated. Both Paul and Gide had an equal need to love and be loved. "For God is my witness, how I yearn for you all with the affection of Christ Jesus," Paul wrote to the Philippians.[6] Both longed for serenity. Paul wrote both to the Colossians and Ephesians to make the very most of the time. Gide exalted effort.[7] Both preached *dénûment*, the virtue of stripping oneself of things material. The list of views common to both could be extended.

Gide's disagreements with Paul are less significant though he pointed them out with considerable vigor.[8] In certain instances of his opposition to Paul, Gide was simply confused. Echoing in 1928 the body-soul conflict which he had maintained in *Les Cahiers d'André Walter,* he wrote: "Nothing is heavier, more important than this: necessity of option between the temporal and the spiritual. The possession of the other world is based on the renunciation of this world."

His own assent to this "either/or" did not prevent Gide from blaming Paul for the same dualism. Again he claimed erroneously that Paul had focused the world's attention exclusively on Christ crucified. He himself preferred Christ in his condition "before the torment."[9]

We may infer that Gide was interested not so much in understanding Paul as in shaking off the Apostle's hold on him. He wished to exercise his freedom to interpret the gospel according to his own light.[10] The Apostle's conceivable confusion of himself with Christ, and his enervatingly repeated invitation tendered to his correspondents to imitate himself, must have caught Gide's attention. He could not have seen in him an example of humility, or of tolerance. He resented above all Paul's authority. He wrote at the age of sixty-four, referring to the "Communist religion": "Whether the text invoked be by Marx or Lenin, I cannot abide by it unless my heart and my reason approve it. I did not escape from the authority of Aristotle or St. Paul to fall under theirs."[11]

The reference to Aristotle is altogether startling; Gide does not seem to have been subject to Aristotle's authority for any appreciable length of time, even if agreement with some Aristotelian advice can be detected in his work—such as exertion of effort and preference for a short intense life over a long, humdrum existence. Besides, the Greek philosopher could easily be cited in support of the spirit of inquiry which he advocates elsewhere.[12] We may suspect on the other hand that the phrase "unless my heart *and my reason* approve it" is used as a broadly accepted formula. Seldom if ever did Gide require the assent of his reason as such in the acceptance or refusal of a proposition. What he means to say in the quotation above is that a given proposition loses its attractiveness to him as soon as it is mandatory, even if it is acceptable otherwise.

The flesh-spirit dualism had been Paul's way of deploring the human predicament of alienation, for while the spirit is the instrument of limitless communion or "peace with God,"[13] the flesh, this tangible principle of individuation, is an instrument of isolation. It has its existence outside the Whole and therefore dies. Paul, who inevitably borrowed his imagery from his own milieu, based the solution of that predicament on the transformation of the body in a future life into something spiritual. His assurance that this would come to pass was based on the resurrection of Christ in the glorified body. As to the earthly approximation of the heavenly community, it was to be an enlargement of the one Community which received the Spirit in the Upper Room. This vision is identical to Dostoevsky's dream as defined and heartily subscribed to by Gide: "unity of minds without arbitrary unification."[14] Yet Gide could not accept it in Paul's name, or within the context of the Apostle's premises: his hopes for his self-conscious existence almost never went beyond the grave; Christ was not for him the exalted Messiah whose coming had completed the process of divine self-revelation, though this statement—like most others about his beliefs—cannot be made categorically. "I come back to you, Lord Christ," he wrote in his sixties, "as to God Whose living form you are. I am tired of lying to my heart. It is you I find again everywhere, while I thought I was fleeing from you, divine friend of my childhood."[15] His predominant attachment to the "Greek legend" notwithstanding, he found Christ's teachings of an infinitely superior kind, even perfect. He rediscovered Christ in the renunciation of all things.

As to Gide's firmly held notion that Christ's and Paul's teachings are opposed, it is not of course new. There were those in Corinth who said: "I belong to Paul" and those who said: "I belong to Christ."[16] But then the root of his resentment of the Apostle must be sought ironically enough in his mystical leanings. He accused Paul, "the man behind the priest,"[17] namely the originator of Christian legal requirements, of plunging us "back into time," of moving away from "the permanent and eternal character"[18] of Christ's words. This is the principal reason for his opposition to Paul, though the Apostle's doctrine of the New Adam and his overt opposition to homosexuality must have influenced Gide's attitude considerably.[19]

Protestantism

A sustained criticism of Protestantism in general occurs in Gide's tale, *La Symphonie pastorale*. This is the story of a pastor who is divided between his wife and Gertrude. Gertrude is the name of a nondescript object which grows up to be a girl. The pastor falls in love with her in the process of caring for her. When first discovered near a mysterious lake in a dark hut she was a crouched, uncertain being, her face almost entirely covered with hair. She had been nourished, but never spoken to. Gide's description of her suggests a baby about to be born. Throughout the story and in the course of her growth, the girl, like so many of Gide's characters, is herself and something other than herself. She is a force coming from the murky depths of the pastor's subconscious to the surface of his consciousness. As if to lead the reader to this interpretation, the author informs us that Gertrude slept at the pastor's house above a staircase leading down to the cellar.

To care for potentialities buried out of sight is a duty: did not Jesus go after the lost sheep, forsaking the ninety-nine tame ones? "I bring back the lost sheep" the pastor announces to his family as he brings Gertrude home. As the story unfolds it becomes progressively clearer that she represents the instincts which, in Gide's opinion, must not be "domesticated" by Amélie's brand of Christianity. Amélie, the pastor's wife, does no more and no less than her duty. Her Christianity is unmistakably that of Gide's mother. Those of the pastor's family who are formed by the mother are cold. They are indifferent to the fact that something new, something living, is emerging from the pastor's carriage.

One of the torments of Gide's life was that while he craved for his wife's approval, he was not willing or, as he thought, capable of fulfilling the conditions which she required for the granting of that approval. He gratified his unorthodox desires secretly so as to spare her the grief of knowing. Nor was he certain, until his wife burned his letters addressed to her, that she knew of his escapades. He never knew—nor does anyone else—whether Madeleine had obtained precise information about, or correctly surmised, the fact that Gide had a daughter, Catherine, born out of wedlock.[20] This pattern of life is portrayed faithfully in *La Symphonie pastorale*. The pastor cannot admit to himself his love for the blind Gertrude because he finds it against the rules. He is constantly reminded of these rules by the presence of his wife. Indeed the tension wherein the pastor lives with Gertrude on one side and Amélie on the other is the tension between spontaneity, which has its source within man, and discipline, which is imposed from the outside. Gide described himself as a child-pastor combination.[21] He probably did so in a Bergsonian sense, the child standing for *élan vital,* the Protestant pastor representing the recall to restraint and established duty.

It is against the background of the discovery and presence of this natural, vivacious, metamorphic force, Gertrude, that the pastor proceeds to a reappraisal of certain Protestant tenets. His heated conversations with his son Jacques represent Gide's own debate with himself on the merits (or lack of them) of Protestant fundamentalism. Inevitably the question of justification is brought up. Luther had said that the believer who has faith cannot be restrained. Neighbor-directed life and effort are necessary to help the neighbor attain grace, and as a test of Christian discipleship. "Christ never gave any other commandment than that of love," Luther specifies, "because He intended that commandment to be the test of His disciples and of true believers."[22]

This conviction informs the pastor's thinking in *La Symphonie pastorale* in a context meant, oddly enough, to be directed against St. Paul. The pastor observes that submission is the effect of love, but that love does not come by way of submission. Happiness is not to be obtained through prescribed conduct. When a course of action is the effect of happiness, it is good. People lie, for example, when they are not happy. This is, in secular dress, the Lutheran doctrine of the relationship of faith to works, itself inspired by St. Paul. The pastor, a spokesman for Gide in this passage, has come to these conclusions through the ordeal of his peculiar relationship with his wife. He reevaluates the gospel as a method whereby one achieves the blessed life, *blessed* being associated with, or meaning, *joyful.*

Joy is ordinarily the name given to a certain inner state of being which depends partly at least on external circumstances. It is an emotion due to some sort of a contact, and it wanes to the extent to which such contact is abolished. To Gide it is a capacity which one can use at will, apparently without the employment or aid of anything external. Each being, the pastor assumes, is more or less capable of joy, and his duty consists in tending towards it. To present the same idea in different terms, there is such a thing as joy tucked away, in different quantities, in the soul of each individual, and each individual's duty is to clear the way for it to come to the surface. The name of that which stands in the way of joy is *sin*. Sin is what darkens the soul. It is what is opposed to joy. It is, moreover, the work of the Evil One, for the realm of the Evil One is where love is lacking. An unusual saying of Christ, the restorer of the sight of blind men, is quoted by Gide: "If you were blind, you would have no guilt," precisely because in Gide's mind blindness is a condition where one does not need the external world in one's quest for joy.[23]

The pastor declares that conduct must be the spontaneous expression of love. He observes on the other hand that men have "made the world ugly." Neither ecclesiastical legislation nor the hope of a compensatory bliss in a supernatural realm will fill the gap between ugliness and love. The happiness anticipated by the puritan Amélie as she awaits Gertrude's return to her home results in frustration. Gertrude's recovery of her sight and her fall into freezing water, followed by her association with Jacques (that is, the seeping into her soul of such convictions as Gide himself held as a youth), mark her conversion to Christianity, the domestication of instincts. Her emergence from the water is not unto "newness of life"—as Paul claims the emergence of people from the font of baptism is[24]—but unto death.

Justin O'Brien observes that Gide's "most revealing comment [on *La Symphonie pastorale*] is found in a note on the Pastor inserted into a letter to an American scholar":

Through him, rather than trying to express my own thought, I have depicted the pitfall to which my own doctrine might lead, when that ethic is not rigorously checked by a critical spirit constantly on the alert and little inclined to self-indulgence.[25]

It is because the pastor lacks "the indispensable critical spirit" that he is unaware of his genuine motivation in being so very solicitous of Gertrude. He was constantly under the impression that he was carrying out a biblical injunction, when the plain fact was that he was enamoured of her and jealous of his son. This was "a form of lying to oneself" which Gide, as he said, criticized in the book.[26] In a letter to Victor Poucel he observed that La Symphonie pastorale was also a criticism of the principle of everyone's being his own uncensored interpreter of the Bible, uncensored, one may assume, even by "the light of the Spirit" which Calvin said ought to preside over such interpretation.[27]

La Symphonie pastorale argues indirectly that that principle is dangerous, for it may be used to justify self-centered deeds, words, or thoughts. Should this be the case, the Bible turns out to reinforce individual or collective selfishness, while its user goes about thinking that he is being an earnest servant of the Lord. Protestant Gide was accused by Roman Catholic François Mauriac of doing precisely this in writing Numquid et tu . . . ? Yet neither the pitfalls of everyone's being his own interpreter of the Bible nor Catholic criticism could turn Gide to the Catholic view of biblical interpretation. According to this view the Bible is to be interpreted by the Church. The written word must, in other words, pass through the sieve of the collective experience of the properly structured community of orthodox believers. Only then does it become an objective frame of reference.

Gide remained thankful to his own Protestant tradition to the point of indulging in some quaint exaggerations as when he said that renunciation is a purely evangelical doctrine, or that love of mountains was a Protestant invention—in which case Petrarch ought to be counted a Protestant.[28] His criticisms of Protestantism are themselves made from a Protestant vantage point in the manner of his passionate rejection of Paul while following the major lines of the Apostle's outlook. Thus in order to mark his disappointment with both Protestant orthodoxy and Catholicism he decides to go, in good Protestant fashion, "to the very source." "And this I began to do passionately. That is to say, I began to read the Bible."[29] The writings of Virgil replaced in time the Holy Book, both as sustenance and as counsel. The authorization which Gide implicitly obtained from that author—who was something of a prophet in the eyes of medieval Christianity—cannot be discounted in a consideration of his defense of homosexuality. His habit of reading the Bible as an adolescent changed in old age into reading Virgil's works with almost the same assiduity and devotion.[30]

Gide had left his Bible behind when, both as a result and as an affirmation of his emancipation, he left Europe for Africa. The context in which the account of that resolution occurs sheds further light on the religious and moral attitudes that he favored. The following oft-quoted statement stands out in the first pages of Part II of *Si le grain ne meurt (If It Die)*, marking as this Second Part does, in contradistinction to Part I, a sort of conversion:

In the name of what God or what ideal, do you forbid me to live according to my nature? And where would my nature lead me if I simply followed it? Up to the present, I had accepted Christ's code of morals, or at any rate, a kind of Puritanism which I had been taught to consider as Christ's code of morals. By forcing myself to submit to it I had merely caused a profound disturbance in my whole being. I would not consent to live lawlessly, and I required my mind's assent to the demands of my body. . . . Then I saw at once that . . . harmony must be my supreme object, and the endeavour to acquire it the express reason of my life. When in October '93 I embarked for Algiers, it was not so much towards a new land that my impulse sped me, as towards *that*—towards that Golden Fleece.

That Golden Fleece designates the Greek "ideal of equilibrium, plenitude and health" that Gide could not find in the Christianity of his youth. Goethe had helped him widen the distance between the two ideals. He writes:

It was, I believe, indeed, my first aspiration toward what is now known as "classicism"; how contrary this was to the Christian ideal I began life with, it is impossible to say; and I realized this so thoroughly that I determined not to take my Bible away with me. This, which may perhaps seem a trifle, was of the highest importance; up till that time not a day had gone by without my going to the Holy Book for both sustenance and counsel. But it was just because this sustenance seemed to have become indispensable, that I felt I must do without it. I did not bid farewell to Christ without a wrench at my heart, so that I ask myself now whether I ever really left him.[31]

Whether his determination to leave his Bible behind was or was not a trifle, an evangelical pattern of life, part of which he eventually filled with secular symbols, was irrevocably built into Gide's outlook. Nor did the Greeks or Virgil succeed in gaining Gide's allegiance exclusively. He found Catholicism "inadmissible" and Protestantism "intolerable," but he *felt* himself profoundly Christian.[32]

"The Christ of the Gospels," Etienne Gilson has said, "belongs to everyone; he belongs even to the philosophers, if they want him, outside of all religion."[33] This is precisely the Christ Gide wants. At one time he toyed with the idea of writing a book which was to be entitled *Christianity against Christ*.[34] He was under the impression that the "saints" too are "against the church,"[35] the church being an instrumentality that imprisoned or crippled Christ by assimilating Him to itself, instead of itself to Him. From this perspective "Christ" represents the ideals of emancipation, freedom, abnegation, and joy.[36]

The Catholics

When Gide uses the word *Christianity* as opposed to Christ, he means generally the Roman Catholic Church. While the Church functions in the name of Christ, Christ would not recognize himself in it today. We must therefore combat the Church, and this must be done in the name of Christ Himself. If religion has turned into something hateful, it is the priest, not Christ, who is to blame.[37]

There are personal reasons that disposed Gide against the Catholics. His mother's passionate dislike of them, his childhood experiences with Catholic ruffians, Madeleine's being wooed away from him by Catholic proselytists must have been particularly influential in the atmosphere of anticlericalism which was rampant in France throughout the nineteenth century and during most of his life.[38] And then there was always the issue of homosexuality: "How could complete frankness with you [meaning largely the Catholics] have been possible," he asks, "since it implied the confession of what I knew you to consider abominable, and I not, since you considered abominable a part of me that I neither could nor would sacrifice."[39]

Gide was given at times to worthless outbursts of anger in which he called the Catholics "gassed" men,[40] said that they "do not like truth"[41] and that they permit and encourage idolatry. The Catholics, he wrote, "are more abject and miserable than pagan idolaters because their religion is more distorted and debased in them and because they make it fall from a greater height; and also because superstition is closer to magic than to faith."[42] He went so far as to compare a conversion to Catholicism to a first visit to a brothel.[43] He denounced Catholicism as something of a gangrene,[44] and declared that the Catholics are indifferent to human happiness: "They prefer humanity unhappy to seeing it happy without God, without their God."[45]

There is, or rather was, relatively more objectivity in Gide's accusations of staticism and dogmatism directed at the Catholics. The pictorial presentation of this reaction is his *Isabelle* (1911), with the suggestion that a post-Christian era is at hand. In an earlier story entitled *La Porte étroite (Strait Is The Gate)* (1909), the Church was already placed on the sunset side of the house.

The castle described in *Isabelle* is decrepit. In it live some remnants of aristocracy, a priest, and a theologian. As if to insure the reader's understanding that the crumbling castle is an image of the benighted Church, Gide compares it to a ship, the Church's traditional symbol of itself. Lacase from the Sorbonne moves into this unhealthy atmosphere to study not the contents, but the chronology of the works of Bossuet—the symbol, for Gide, of Catholic theology which is now, therefore, of mere historical interest. The stove in Lacase's room is extinguished, and, as his coachman warns him, in the country one has to be satisfied with what one finds. He opens the window of his room. The moon is about to vanish, the trees are weeping, the air is damp. Then it seems to him that the house is weighing anchor for the night crossing. The doctrinal rigidity of the Church is seen in the person of M. Floche, Lacase's teacher. He lives in the past, and he is physically stiff, unable to turn his head at all. When Lacase proposes to dedicate his study to him, Floche answers: "when one is so close to leaving the earth, one smiles willingly at anything which gives promise of a measure of survival."

Isabelle is also Gide's announcement of his own role in the advent of a post-Christian culture. Casimir, born deformed on account of his mother's prudish fears, helps in the end to destroy the old estate. His parents are cousins, as Gide and Madeleine were. Lacase and the Abbé had collided over the education of the boy who obviously stands for the coming generation. As the story ends we see that the Abbé has lost the boy altogether.

In line with his conventional atheism, Gide regarded the Roman Catholic Church as a purely secular organization whose human failings were magnified in his eyes—and sometimes shown as in *Les Caves du Vatican (Lafcadio's Adventures)* to be grotesque and ridiculous—because of the Church's claim that it was *not* merely human. As to the position of the Catholic Church on any one issue, he learned it from Bossuet and the

stray pronouncements of his Catholic friends. He had generally inter-
rogated life more than books, as he put it,[46] and had no patience with
learned treatises and laboriously advanced proofs, as is evident from this
entry in his *Journal* of June 4, 1930 (in view of Gide's Platonic leanings
his preference for St. Bonaventure is a matter of course) :

I have been told that X. was not completely satisfied with his new state of
grace, that he remained unhappy, restless, that St. Thomas had disappointed
him, that he found merely categories, a mystic card-file and abstractions, where
he had hoped to find contact, and that today he inclined rather toward St.
Bonaventure. It must be added that he came to conversion (so it is said)
through a great desire and need to approach the beyond, the suprasensible,
and to communicate with the realm of souls, particularly with his dead parents.
For a long time he apparently indulged in spiritualism, knocking on tables
and questioning spirits. Maritain, aware of the situation and always lying in
wait, wanted to tackle him. In short, X. became a Thomist. But I believe he
got the wrong Thomas. The one he should have had was the other, the
Thomas who, before believing, first had to touch.[47]

One of the disputes that repeatedly flared up between Gide and his
neo-Thomist and Thomist friends, notably with the formidable Paul
Claudel, concerned the relation between virtue and reward. It was far
from uncommon in France. Bossuet himself, who represents historical
Catholicism in *Isabelle,* had argued in his *Avertissements aux Protestants*
against those who mystically claimed that perfection consists in a habitual
state of pure love. The thesis of retributive justice in heaven which
Bossuet defends was taken up once more by Claudel against Gide.

Though Gide has often been subjected to unduly severe, altogether
uncharitable, Catholic criticism and his works have been placed on the
Index,[48] his own reaction to the Church was not uniformly inimical. His
angry and vilifying comments on Catholicism notwithstanding, he declared on one occasion that "as for them he cannot hate them; on the
contrary"; and on another, that Catholicism would have been for him a
salubrious environment to grow in.[49] In his late sixties he was almost
reconciled with the Church. Having listed the League of Nations, the
League of Rights of Man, the Russian Revolution, and communism as
bankruptcies or profound discomfitures which "we have impotently wit-
nessed," he asked himself whether the Church, meaning the Roman
Catholic Church, at least had been faithful and solid, and the answer is

on the affirmative side. While Gide gives us to believe that he is somewhat satisfied with his own role in the new situation, he attributes it largely to historical circumstances. The Catholic Church, he says, faced with danger and attacks, has caught hold of herself, and many complaints that had angered Gide against the Church have disappeared. While Hitler presented a menace to her sovereign mission, the breakdown of communism restored to Christianity its revolutionary implication, a set of circumstances from which Gide draws the lesson that "Catholicism betrays as soon as it becomes conservative," conservative, that is, of title, of fortunes, of privileges. "It is the spirit that is important to hand on, not the 'letter that kills.' That some Catholics felt this, I have never doubted. But it seems to me, today, that the Church even understands it; . . ."[50]

Gide was sensitive to the conflicts between the liberal and conservative elements within the Catholic Church, which broke out into the open during the pontificate of John XXIII. On the specific issue raised by him in the above quotation there is of course no disagreement. No one would deny that it is the spirit that must be handed on. The problem is to find a way of realizing that aim without the letter that kills. Gide uses the very words of Paul—his declared foe!—to condemn tradition, because he was conditioned to believe in the depravity of man. Protestant fundamentalism relies on the written word which may be preserved intact, while tradition may reflect, not prevent, the corruption of the spirit in the course of history.

One source of friction that never ran dry between Gide and his Catholic friends was the latter's claim to exclusive possession of certain supernatural truths. Gide would rather follow Nietzsche and ripen for death in combat than bask in the security of such knowledge.[51] He had other reasons for opposing the Catholic teaching in this respect. In *La Symphonie pastorale* he had concerned himself with this problem and had pointed out the danger present in reliance on scriptural authority in deciding upon the course of one's life. In his attempt to free people from the authority of the Church, he sought to invalidate that authority. The Church, he persistently maintained, does not hold a set of truths entrusted to her and to her alone by a supernatural being. He did not believe in revealed truths.

A young Moslem whom he met in 1933 told him "with tears and sobs in his voice" that no religion held the promise of peace among men and nations outside of Islam. Gide remarks that Berdyaev thinks the same of Greek Orthodoxy, that a Roman Catholic and a Jew will each make the same claim on behalf of *his* faith. Since every religion presents itself as the sole depository and the true interpreter of revealed truth, the men professing it will fight in the name of God, and this is a matter not of ethics, but of *revelation*: "Thus it is that religions divide men, though each one claims to unite them. Each one claims to be the sole possessor of *Truth*. Reason is common to all men and is opposed to religion, to religions."[52]

Contrary to what Gide suggests, the problem raised here is not of course a religious problem, for the attitude which consists in saying "my way is the only way" is not a specifically religious attitude. Moreover, *my* way may very well *be* the true way. There is a failing when the assertion takes the form: "my way is the best way *because* it is mine." Berdyaev has nowhere claimed that the Greek Orthodox description of the human condition is accurate *because* it is expounded by the Greeks or the Russians. No respectable expounder of any doctrine has ever claimed that his truth is the truth because it is his. Indeed the fact that a truth is said to be *revealed* implies the exact opposite. As to the last sentence of the above quotation, it is not a dominant Gidian opinion. Gide generally agrees with Protestantism that reason is broken and unreliable. Nor would history bear out his contention that reason is a legislative, unifying power. That it is "opposed" to religion, to religions, is, to say the least, open to debate.

A clue to Gide's real reasons for opposing revelation as conventionally understood is given in *El Hadj*, published in 1899. *El Hadj* is subtitled "treatise of the false prophet," and the prophet's falseness consists in his pretensions of speaking on behalf of a prince who is, in fact, dead. *El Hadj* is a short treatise on the existence of God and of a supernatural order with the sustained argument that no man can be transmitting to us messages from another world for the simple reason that such a world is an illusion. Yet the illusion may have a practical usefulness to those who care to entertain it. The following passage assigns to hope—in line with recent theological emphases—a central position in man's moral and religious quest, and is in accord with the fictionalism of Hans Vaihinger, who speaks in his *Philosophy of the "As If"* (1911) of the irresistible power of the ideal, even though the ideal is the work of the creative activity of the mind, in contradiction with itself and in contradiction with reality. (The word *miragineuse* is probably coined by Gide himself):

Thus from virtue to virtue we shall walk, El Hadj, till death, in hope; and we shall maintain ourselves till the end by the miraginous vision of some unknown bliss—as the man who would assiduously prepare a dream to his irrevocable sleep, in order to sleep therein.

El Hadj, the prophet, alone has access to the tent where the prince had his being. He could and can speak on behalf of the inhabitant of the tent because that inhabitant was silent before and now he is dead. There is no doubt that the tent stands for the Temple, namely the house of the prophet's God. Gide suggests this with extreme subtlety. The lines "Be lifted up doors of cloth/And let my desire come in" are strongly reminiscent of Psalm 24:9: "Lift up your heads, O gates!/and be lifted up, O ancient doors!/that the King of glory may come in!"

The temple is empty, Gide implies, and man's vitality must occupy the premises heretofore reserved to God. He further argues that falseness is built into the nature of prophecy. Indeed he seems to be turning the tables against those who would claim that prophetic utterances prove God's existence. If there were a God he would speak for himself to each man; prophets prophesy *because* there is no God: "For if He did not keep silent, what good then would our words do?" It is the death of the prince that gives the prophet the gift of prophecy: "Prince! I knew how to speak to your people from the moment you yourself could no longer say anything."[53]

There were contemporaries of Gide, including Lévy-Bruhl, Durkheim, Bergson, Brunschvicg, and notably Julian Huxley, who advocated a religion without revelation. Behind the more or less theoretical arguments against revelation his own more serious reasons for opposing it are moral. In a pathetic scene in the Third Act of *Saül*—written four years after *El Hadj*—the king, who has ordered the execution of all the sorcerers in Israel, wishes there had been an oversight. He has lost his bearings, is in urgent need of advice. "What's to be done? Nothing! Nothing! The least soothsayer would know better than I. (Running suddenly to the door) Ah! High Priest! (Re-enter the latter) Your God? Is He still silent?" Saul's high priest is no help, though he does answer the king. He proceeds sheepishly and irrelevantly to recite the first commandment, and on Saul's own suggestion asks him in biblical terms whether he has broken that commandment. Saul shrugs his shoulders with impatience, then, upon hearing the words, "for I am the Lord thy God," he yawns. Saul had told the priest to hurry, for he was expecting the barber. As the latter appears, the king says to the priest with a sigh of relief: "You will go on with that another time."

This parody points to the irrelevance to man's disorientation and anguish of the theistic stance as formulated in the language of a bygone era.

Moreover, a truth that is allegedly received from God may turn into an instrument of domination in the hands of a priestly caste. Belief in revealed truths is thus downright dangerous. In *Saül* the high priest is an accomplice of the queen, herself the real ruler behind the king, for as long as she lives. After her death we see the high priest cut the ridiculous figure just observed, and then he vanishes from sight. Creon in *Oedipus* makes this ominous statement: "We who rule should use [the oracles] to reinforce our authority, and interpret them as suits us best." This Machiavellian advice given by Creon to Oedipus reflects a conviction which Gide held even before his sentimental adherence to communism.

Two years later he saw clearly that capitalism and Catholicism have a common interest in a religion that teaches men whom society strikes on the right cheek to hold out the left. The teaching will benumb the oppressed and soothe them with hopes of an afterlife: "How could the man who knows that Christ said: 'happy those that weep' fail to take advantage of Catholicism, and how could 'those that weep' not accept submission if they know that 'the last shall be first'?"[54]

This same argument is presented elsewhere in Gide's *Journal*.[55] It is readily traceable to the famous aphorism that religion is the opiate of the people, but while valid interpretations of this estimate of religion are possible within the context of Marxist existentialism, Gide's simple argument remains invalid. Indeed the Russian masses of 1917 were certainly among "those that weep," they were taught that "the last shall be first," yet they did respond to the call of rebellion and to the promises of a better life in the world. Nor is there any empirical evidence that belief in life eternal reduces the desire for comfort. The typical Buddhist who does not believe in life eternal will care less for the things of this world than a Christian who does, and it is quite conceivable that of two Christians, believers in life eternal, one will and the other will not seek to accumulate riches. The pomp and wealth of both the Omayyad and Abbasid Moslem dynasties were proverbial. They believed in life eternal. Against the background of these considerations a Christian's claim that far from debilitating, belief in life eternal may prove to be an invigorating force, remains a live option.[56] It is fair to conclude, on the other hand, that if Christian hierarchies supported the oppressors of men they did so not because, but in violation, of their profession of faith. Nor did this observation escape Gide himself who writes: "The fact that capitalist society sought support in Christianity is a monstrosity for which Christ is not responsible, but rather the clergy."[57]

Strictly speaking the immortality of the soul is not a revealed truth. The Catholic Church considers it a philosophical certainty, though not an altogether desirable state of affairs without the assurance of the risen life. Gide, we have seen, had no patience with such fine distinctions. As far as he was concerned the doctrine of immortality was itself, in the hands of Catholic clergy, a means of self-perpetuation. Having stated that he always strives to set up a new hope in the place of one that he injures, he goes on to write:

I should like to be able to believe in eternal life, not for my own happiness, but for the consolations that it allows to give. But they [i.e., the Catholics] as soon as they possess that assurance, feel the need of casting a gloom over this life, in order to make necessary what will console us for it.[58]

The suggestion that pious lies are to be allowed as long as they console some poor souls cannot be taken seriously against the entirety of Gide's work. But the point, made without supporting evidence, that "they" cast "a gloom over this life *in order* to make necessary what will console us for it" was one of his more permanent beliefs. Tiresias representing in *Oedipus* the idea and the institution of priesthood expresses his concern over the fact that the mind of Oedipus is *too* peaceful. "His mind is already too much at rest," he tells Creon, "his soul is like some sealed vessel, to which fear can find no entrance. My authority is based on the fear of God, and there is blasphemy in Oedipus' untroubled happiness." Tiresias cannot rest as long as that happiness is not disturbed, or gloom is not cast over life, for it is "by means of that disquieting little crack that God will find a way into his heart." Priests and those driven by political and materialistic ambitions cooperate, as manufacturers of untested and harmful drugs cooperate with advertisers, in order to create a market for their wares. Only frightened men and women need a god who has a prescription of his own to reveal as the solution to a given misery. Consequently Tiresias must frighten the people in order to dominate them with his oracles. Gide thinks of Revelation as a series of dictated truths; and "everything that is dictated is constraint," he wrote in his *Retour du Tchad*. Shortly after the publication of *Oedipus* he was writing in his *Journal*:

Man can know the truth only through the revelation of which we are the guardians [say those pious souls]. Any felicity, any harmony achieved without the aid of God seems to them criminal; they refuse to consider it real; they deny it and with all their piety oppose it.[59]

The point of view which governs the problem of revealed moral principles in *Oedipus* coincides with that of *El Hadj*. The author puts all his contempt for revealed truth in this question, laden with irony, asked by Oedipus: "Has the oracle foretold what I must do next? Must I still consult it? And find out, O Tiresias, what the birds have to say?" Oedipus' own defiance of the oracles consists, first, in his acceptance of the human predicament: "I was caught" and "what I did I had to do." Then he transcends this predicament, without any supernatural help, in a supreme act of freedom. In his self-inflicted blindness he is on a par with Tiresias:

In your jealousy of my light, did you [i.e., Tiresias] seek to drag me into your darkness? I, too, gaze now upon the celestial dark. I have punished these eyes for their failure to guide me thither. No more can you overwhelm me with the superiority of the blind.

Ordinarily one does not associate revelation and priesthood. The opposition in the Old Testament between priests and prophets is evident enough, and since both prophets and priests believe in the Lord God, the evils of ecclesiastical bureaucracy and priestcraft are not directly traceable to belief in God. This is not the view that underlies *Oedipus,* or Gide's thinking on the whole. "I put myself in your hands," Jocasta says to Tiresias, "for it is through you that we learn the decisions of the Most High." Elsewhere in the same play Tiresias describes himself as "merely God's instrument." He is an instrument not of kindness but of cruelty: "since He is working through me, He will not now stay His hand." In an atmosphere dominated by him Jocasta hangs herself.

According to traditional Christian theology the self-revelation of God was completed in Christ. Oedipus is made by Gide into a Christlike figure, following the apotheosis of the original Greek model. He is in, but not of this world, for he has taken as guide Antigone—his sister? his daughter? Oedipus no longer cares. The words *sister* and *daughter* are meaningful in this world only. In heaven, where men and women "neither marry nor are given in marriage,"[60] those words are meaningless. Oedipus no longer feels guilty, for he has become, without any external assistance, a citizen of that realm. Antigone asks him where he wants to go. The answer is: "I don't know. Straight ahead. . . . Henceforward with no roof, no country for my own." The reader is reminded of Christ's words: "Foxes have holes, and birds of the air have nests; but the Son of man has nowhere to lay his head."[61] Oedipus is no longer a king. He renounces his possessions, his great name, himself, in that order. He no longer discriminates between Thebans and non-Thebans. "Whoever they may be, they are men. I shall be glad to bring them happiness at the price of my sufferings." The point seems to be that in this Christlike figure it is not God who has revealed himself, but man who has shown his ultimate potentiality, but then Gide may be pointing out that God's revelation of himself is not a series of propositions but a concrete universal event. Man's own realization of his ultimate potentiality is not in conflict with that event, while man is not God and God is not man. "In escaping from you, Tiresias, I shall remain faithful to God," Antigone tells the priest.[62] God is not opposed. A false conception of him is corrected.

The end pursued by Oedipus has never been happiness. Toward the conclusion of Act II there is this altercation between him and Tiresias:

Tiresias: That fortune-teller had also predicted to Laius that he would be killed by his own son. Oedipus, Oedipus, foundling and blasphemous ruler that you are! It is in ignorance of your past that you have become sure of yourself. Your happiness is blind. Open your eyes to your misery—God had withdrawn from you the right to be happy.

Oedipus: Get out! Get out! As if I had ever sought happiness! It was to escape from it that as a boy of twenty I ran away from Polybius on my toes, with fists clenched. None can say how beautiful was the dawn above Parnassus as I went forward in the dew to hear God's oracle. I had nothing but my own strength to help me, and I didn't yet know who I was, but with all the possibilities of my being I was rich enough.

"The past" of which Oedipus was "ignorant" and because of which, according to Tiresias, he was "sure of himself," is a thinly disguised reference to the Christian doctrine of original sin. Nor can one fail to detect in Oedipus' vehement, emotionally charged answer a reference to Gide's own escape to Africa. The more universal interest of the passage resides in the fact that Gide's alternative to happiness, as an end-in-view, is self-knowledge. This is to be contrasted with Tiresias' alternative to happi-

ness which is salvation, consisting partly in dogmatic (i.e., revealed)
utterances. Gide, who classified the dogmas among what he called "truths
of convention," was opposed to any formulation of man's ultimate concern which robbed him of the opportunity to listen to God "directly."[63]

We shall see when we come to Gide's "sincerity" that he was not opposed to a revelation stripped of all conventional religious terminology.
We may note before closing this chapter Gide's observation that Mallarmé or Einstein were "accessible to but a few rare people." This was
proof of their greatness, and not an excuse for the many to condemn
them.[64] It is doubtful whether he would allow a Catholic to use the
same, rather weak, argument to say that one does not discard, for example,
Athanasius, simply because one does not understand him. Nor does he
appear to have considered the difference between the revelations made to
the Old Testament prophets to whom God said things from above and
the completion of the revelation in Christ to whom—and this is of course
the most fundamental claim of the orthodox Church—God did not speak
as if he were someone wholly other. Christ the man hid God, and yet it
is in and through him that God is to be known and seen.

Gide stood in need of a revealer who would disclose the nature of the
real beneath appearances, inasmuch as his end-in-view was, as Harold
March puts it, "a firm contact between his lonely and rather frightened
self and a solid reality outside."[65] He would not dispute the theory that
the sources of such ideas as become thoughts or images in our minds are
hidden in regions not open to simple observation. But since the Church's
monopoly of revealed truth led to the evil of exploitation and the im-
position of dogmatic propositions on captive minds, the revealer must be
looked for outside the Church. It is because Gide is not opposed to
revelation *per se* that he can refer to Christ as the living form of God.
More generally, however, the revealer for him is the artist. This is already the theme of one of his earlier works, *Le Traité du Narcisse (The
Treatise of the Narcissus)*. As long as the voices of literary characters of
a universal appeal have not resounded either in books or on the stage,
he wrote later, "they languish or become impatient under the cover of
mores, waiting, waiting for their hour . . . these new forms of humanity
have no knowledge of themselves."[66] Art too fulfills its function in a
paradoxical manner: it simultaneously veils and reveals the truth:

Are so many words necessary? and the concentration of the mind, the effort
to construct a plot, in order to stretch before the reader that motley embroidery

which, for a time, shimmers before him and veils reality. On the other hand, it is to that reality that I want to recall him constantly, to reveal it to him in a better light, to present it to him as even more real than he has been able to see it hitherto.[67]

This is precisely the aim of every apologist: deliverance from ignorance, from self-limitation to that which is apprehended by the senses only. As Saint-Exupéry puts it in *Le Petit Prince,* " the essential is invisible to the eyes."

Eventually combining this view of the artist as the revealer with his division of the human cognitive activities into those of the "mind" and of the "heart," Gide spoke of two sorts of novels: "the first, exterior and commonly called objective, which begins by visualizing others' acts and events and then interprets them. The second, which begins by paying attention to emotions and thoughts and runs the risk of being powerless to depict anything that the author has not first felt himself." Gide recognized that these two "sorts of novels" may well be "two ways of looking at and depicting life." Whatever the case "everything derives from [the author]. He is the only one to vouch for the truth he reveals, and the only judge."[68]

Revelation and Sincerity

It is because art is the gateway to truth in a broadly religious sense, and the artist the revealer, that sincerity plays in Gide's writings a uniquely important role. Henri Peyre refers to him as a "martyr and hero of sincerity."[69] Gide often underlines the word *sincerity* as if conscious of giving it a load of meaning greater than its capacity, and he seldom uses it in its dictionary meaning of "the state or quality of being in reality as one is in appearance." It does not denote merely the Rousseau-istic disposition of telling the whole truth. *Sincerity* in Gide's special vocabulary is synonymous with *disponibilité,* but it applies almost uniquely to the artist. Gide would agree with T. S. Eliot concerning what the poet does: "The poet," Eliot said, "is occupied with frontiers of consciousness beyond which words fail, though meanings still exist."[70] The artist's special sensitivity that places him at these frontiers puts to mind the capacity certain men have of hearing the Lord God directly. Thus the second verse of Psalm LXXVIII as quoted by Matthew in his gospel[71] practically anticipates the Gidian conception of art: "I will open my mouth in parables, I will utter what has been hidden since the foundation of the world."

In view of this emphasis on sincerity a statement by Gide on a literary trend which he himself helped create comes as a surprise:

A singular misunderstanding today causes the virtue of *sincerity* in the work of art to be extolled above all. Everyone wants the artist to be, before everything else, *sincere.* . . . As to knowing just what they mean by that, no one quite dares say. . . . The task of the public is to constrain the artist to hypocrisy.[72]

Gide's somewhat obscure meaning appears to be that there must be familiar symbols for the artist to use, if he is to perform his function in society. For example, Catholic symbols were used by the Renaissance artists to "cover" their sensuality "so naturally pagan." There is therefore a sense in which their public constrained them to hypocrisy.[73]

A novelist is sincere according to Gide when he writes as a man dreams. In a dream, as in an artistically successful story, the subject or the writer gives expression to the truth in an entirely original or personal manner without tampering with the truth in the process of dreaming or writing. Gide, having declared that "the most important thing to do in art is to be sincere," asks the question: "What do you call sincerity?" The answer is: "Sincerity begins where imitation ceases."[74] Such comments must be read against the background of recommendations to the effect that the artist must not let the word precede the idea, and that there is a sincerity which consists "in striving to *see true*,"[75] this last observation coinciding with the correct reading of phenomena as advocated by Simone Weil.[76] A sincere artist is not concerned merely with the true expression of his experience; these experiences must themselves be true, a circumstance which points to the biblical source of Gide's emphasis on sincerity. The worst hypocrisy according to the New Testament, writes E. F. Scott, is that of *self*-deception: "If the light that is in you is darkness, how great is the darkness!" As against this darkness:

[The] exercise of a perfect sincerity is to be based on the knowledge that God is present everywhere. From Him nothing can be hidden, and men are to feel at all times that He is aware of their secret thoughts, and requires them to be in harmony with His will.[77]

It is difficult to think of any period in Gide's life—including the period when his eschatological enthusiasms took the form of *la question sociale*—when he himself would not have written in the same vein. It is not altogether inadvertently perhaps that on at least one occasion he gives the name "God" to the mysterious sources from which the artist will draw his truth: "God proposes," he writes, reversing the order in the adage, "man [i.e., the artist] disposes."[78]

Evidently, if the world of art is the incarnation of a hidden reality, it is not itself fictitious or unreal. It is a world in which a man can live and have his being. The world that is known as real by the generality of men fades into unreality, or into less reality, when confronted by the world of art: "The supreme art supplants the nonexistent reality," Gide writes. Indeed, art is the means of resurrection: "The imaginary Vera becomes more real than the real, dead Vera.—" The so-called real world is not, Gide repeats elsewhere, much more real than the world of *Les Faux-Monnayeurs* or *Les Thibault*.[79]

Nevertheless, after all the parallels between the world of art and the Kingdom of God are established, one difference remains: a man will not go on living in the former of these worlds after death. But then this difference may not be altogether radical from a broadly religious point of view. St. Paul's evidence that we shall rise from the dead was the resurrection of Jesus Christ, cautiously referred to nowadays as the Easter event. Is it anything more than a myth? "If the individual has infinite value and infinite depth he cannot surrender his meaning," Paul Tillich writes:

But he can surrender finite elements including the future existence for the sake of his infinite value. This implies, of course, the participation of the individual in Love itself, in the eternal ground of Being (but it does not imply the symbols of immortality and of a transcendent reward).[80]

Gide's endorsement of this view would have been enthusiastic:

I have never managed to take this life quite seriously; by no means because I have ever been able to believe (in so far as I remember) in eternal life (I mean in an after-life), but rather in another facet of this life which escapes our senses and of which we can have but a very imperfect knowledge.[81]

And as if to reinforce the claim that discourse about life after death is quite meaningful even if everlasting self-conscious existence is not literally expected, he wrote at a mature age: "I would like to return to God, no matter what happens to me, a grateful and enraptured soul."[82]

3

Salvation or Self-discovery

The Prodigal's Concern

Gide's views on salvation follow from his views on revelation. They are developed in *Le Retour de l'enfant prodigue*. The word *retour* is used by Gide in two other titles: *Le Retour du Tchad* and *Le Retour de L'U.R.S.S.* He does not write of his *impressions* of the USSR, but of his *return*. In all three titles *return* has the connotation of disillusionment, of reawakening to a greater intellectual or spiritual clarity. In *Les Faux-Monnayeurs,* too, Bernard leaves the paternal house, but then he returns to it because he can now look upon his father from a more mature, one might say more spiritual, perspective. This theme of departure from the paternal house and return to it is eminently biblical not merely because it is patterned after the story told in Luke's gospel, but also because the Bible is itself the story of man's departure from God and return to him.

There can be no doubt that *Le Retour de l'enfant prodigue* is a treatise on the ultimate destiny of man, and a critique of the conventional Christian, more specifically Roman Catholic, teachings on that subject. Gide's Catholic friends had repeatedly confronted him with the claim that the true church of Christ is the one in communion with Rome, and that there was no other avenue to salvation. In *Le Retour* the father says to the son: "It is he [i.e., the elder son] who summoned me to tell you: 'Outside the House, there is no salvation at all for you.'" Thus the word *Maison* (written with a capital M) has a bidimensional meaning: it stands for the Prodigal's home and for the Catholic Church. By the same token the elder son becomes a symbol of the Catholic hierarchy. Gide's contention is that the Catholic Church's claim that she is the sole agency of salvation has always been baseless. It may even be fraudulent: "The House is not You, father," the Prodigal says. "Though in Your name, the House has been built not by You, but by others."

53

The apparent root of Gide's objection is that the Catholic Church is not catholic. It is simply another man-made, shackling institution. The Prodigal leaves it because he wishes to confront the Infinite, and this is an adventure to embark upon by oneself alone. Is this pride? Perhaps one ought not to disregard or, riskier still, to challenge the wisdom that a structured society accumulates in the course of time. "Man needs a roof to rest his head under," the Prodigal's father informs him, echoing the elder son. "Man of pride! Do you think you can sleep in the open air with the wind blowing?"

The metaphor, notably the use of *wind,* is certainly not fortuitous. At Pentecost a sound came from heaven "like the rush of a mighty wind."[1] The Catholic Church captures and channels the wind—or the spirit. To break loose from that confinement is not an act of pride. Answering the "reprimand" of his father, the Prodigal argues that there are those who have nothing to be proud of—and cannot therefore be said to be proud—who nevertheless have left the Church.

The answer is not in fact convincing: one may have nothing to be proud of, and still be proud; or else the argument is a tautology in the sense that "I have nothing to be proud of" may simply mean "I am not proud," in which case *therefore,* used by the Prodigal, serves no purpose. Yet the argument advanced by the Prodigal is only incidental to Gide's purpose. A question of greater import is: can anything of value be said to be a man's own if he is not allowed to carry it where he pleases, or make use of it as he prefers? To quote the householder in the gospel according to Matthew: "Am I not allowed to do what I choose with what belongs to me?" Gide probably had this question in the back of his mind as he made the Prodigal proclaim: "I have changed your gold into pleasures, your precepts into whims, my chastity into poetry and my austerity into desires." The accumulated values of the past are given to a man so that he may transmute them into a new fervor. The Prodigal has done precisely that, and now he is left with the memory of his pleasures. Having spent the energies of whatever nature that were his own, he feels nearer to God. He does so, we may presume, inasmuch as bottled up energies intensify a man's awareness of himself and thus alienate him from the source of his being. The Prodigal's heart fills with love as it is emptied of all.[2] Not only, therefore, is there salvation outside the Church; salvation is outside the Church only, a finding which elicits the question: "Then what is it that made you come back? Speak!"

The imperative "Speak!" implies the Prodigal's silence as a result of reticence or uncertainty. The exact reason which impelled him to return cannot be formulated easily. When pressed, he will say: "I know not. Perhaps laziness." In the Church the answers are given. All one has to do is learn and follow directions. The Prodigal, in this story written by Gide seven years before the First World War, ventures forth into the signless world of the Existentialists.

The formal clarity of *Le Retour* is deceptive. With the Prodigal's mother an element of mystery is introduced into the problem of man's destiny. In Luke's story the son separates from the father only to arrive at the conclusion that self-fulfillment consists in serving the father. Gide's Prodigal does not return to the father. He returns home, to the mother: "Kiss me now on the forehead as when I was a little boy and you watched me fall asleep. I am sleepy." He yearns for the completely integrated life, a life of perfect communion with the environment, of which life in the womb is of course the perfect example: "How sweet it is, half lying at the feet of your mother, herself sitting, your forehead hidden between her knees, to feel her caressing hand bend the rebellious nape of your neck!" This is said by the mother. Later the son will reply: "Mother! I come back to you, very humble. Look how I place my forehead lower than your heart!"[3]

The father and the elder brother reprimand him. They both dwell on the period of his absence from the House. There is no exultant joy over his being alive and found now. The father merely tolerates his return: "I know what pushed you on to the roads: I was waiting for you at the end. You would have called me . . . I was there." One does not come to the Father, for the Father is to be found anywhere at all. However, if the Prodigal felt weak it is good for him to have returned. Pretense of strength is worse than frailty. For the elder brother anything is good as long as it brings a man back to the fold. In this case it was the Prodigal's tiredness: "Well then, blessed be your tiredness!"

No doubt Gide's conclusion is biased, or at least hasty. The Catholic Church has had too long a history, is much too complex and vast to be made the subject of any one satisfactory judgment of value. It certainly does include a number of men and women to whom the adjectives *weak* and *tired* do not apply. They are not there out of weakness. The Church includes notably those who helped shape its doctrine and did not, therefore, live on theological handouts. Perhaps Gide would be the first to admit that *Le Retour,* like his other works, is an exaggeration. He wrote it shortly after his thirty-fifth year, an age at which a man's problems are said to be essentially religious.[4] Forty-two years after the publication of the book he told Christian Beck that he had put into it his "whole heart" and his "whole reason."[5] He marshaled all his analytical powers in an effort to find an answer to the question, If salvation is not in or through the Church, how is it to be attained?

The Prodigal is asked insistently to formulate his motivation for his departure from the House; he cries when the question is put to him again by his mother. He then says: "I can hardly understand, near you, why I went from the House." He certainly did not do so in order to satisfy an intellectual curiosity. The adjective *emotional* on the other hand does not reach the depth of the problem. The phrase "ultimate concern" would describe the Prodigal's search, and account for his inability to define it. The Prodigal went away, casting off a set of acquired values because of this concern; his values had to be genuine, and the criterion of their genuineness was that they be experienced directly by himself. His existence had to be authentic. In Gide's secular frame of thought the ultimate concern, the quest for salvation, takes the form of a search for one's identity: "I was looking for . . . who I was." One must find, and then be, oneself.[6]

Salvation and Self-knowledge

Gide presents self-knowledge as an *alternative* to salvation. The fact of the matter is that "self-knowledge" and "salvation" describe differently the *same* state of affairs.

In his early twenties Gide inscribed in his diary the formula *"Dare to be yourself"* and added: "I must underline that in my head too."[7] The injunction never acquired clarity or a uniform meaning in his head. Jean Cocteau suggests the reason in an interview recorded in *Gide vivant*: "Dare to be what you are"—in order to carry out that program, Cocteau says, "one must know who one is and that is impossible in view of that part of the invisible of which we are the carriers and the servants."[8] This remark rests on the assumption that in order to know oneself one must engage in a mental activity which will eventually cause one to come face to face with an object—the self—and to have an immediate knowledge of its characteristics. Cocteau is saying that to pin hope on such a mental process is futile.

Cocteau was not the first to have made the observation that the self is, strictly speaking, unknowable. More competent thinkers have been baffled by the same problem. Socrates wonders in *Charmides* whether the knowing self can be the object of its own knowledge and concludes that he does not have the genius required to answer the question. Many prominent thinkers have argued likewise from various vantage points. Simone de Beauvoir, to cite a recent example, writes that "self-knowledge is impossible, and the best one can hope for is self-revelation."[9]

Gide did at times exhibit awareness of the impossibility of positive self-knowledge: "The sentence that begins with: 'I know myself . . .' always ends with a negative. 'I know myself: I . . . not . . .'"[10] He repeats on another occasion: ". . . the expression 'I know myself' is never used except in a restrictive sense ('I know myself: I do not . . .') and that in a broadening sense, on the contrary. 'I no longer recognized myself,' which is always followed by the assertion of something or other of which one would not have thought oneself capable."[11] He once declared that in a recognizable (physical) world he, to himself, is the only unknowable (*méconnaissable*) entity.[12]

He gives this view a practical twist when he writes that "if it is still fanciful at the age of sixty to think you know yourself thoroughly; it is dangerous at twenty to try to know yourself thoroughly."[13] Yet it would have been unlike Gide not to have made a number of other statements invalidating partly or completely what has just been quoted. He was once angry with a critic for attributing to him the statement "I am never what I think I am." He had said "I am never *but* what I think I am,"[14] thus implying that he was to himself an object of total knowledge. His fertile imagination presented him to himself as a thing of many layers. Much more important to note, however, is Gide's notion that beneath a heap of debris one could discover, if one looked assiduously enough, what he called "the unspoiled self." At the age of twenty-one he thought this was the condition for making "really sincere" entries in his notebook: "I shall have to undertake such a disentangling in my cluttered brain that, to stir up all that dust, I am waiting for a series of vast empty hours . . . ; during which my sole care will be to rediscover myself." "To rediscover, underneath the factitious creature, the unspoiled self was not, or so it seemed to me, so easy a task,"[15] he wrote over thirty years later. Both

Gide and Michel of *L'Immoraliste* were anxious to get back to the old Adam, "that authentic creature" and new self.[16]

The effort directed at the discovery of this unspoiled self is not, one gathers, to be confused with concern with self. Gide chided vehemently the young men of his age for nurturing precisely such preoccupations. He thought they were frightfully concerned with, and never knew how to get away from, themselves. He found Maurice Barrès, the advocate of devotion to one's land and ancestry, responsible for this trend. He attributed Barrès's political activity to despair and boredom and surmised that the self-centered young men were turning to Catholicism for the same reason.[17]

Gide himself had spent nearly every day of his life observing himself, trying to know himself. Nor does his behavior reveal a genuinely generous, outgoing, other-directed person. Nevertheless he wrote in *Les Nouvelles Nourritures*: "All through my life I have never sought to know myself; that is to say, I never sought myself." He adds: "rather poor and limited personalities succeeded in finding and understanding themselves."[18]

That is a revealing statement. It explains Gide's surprising, bitter opposition to the famous inscription in the temple at Delphi: Know thyself. He calls it a "pernicious" and "ugly" maxim.[19] We saw Gide advocate self-knowledge. Are we to conclude from his estimate of the Delphic inscription that he is contradicting himself, now advocating self-knowledge and now opposing it? The contradiction is, once more, apparent. It disappears as the attentive reader realizes that Gide's opposition to the Delphic maxim is occasioned by a limited understanding of it. This understanding is not what "self-knowledge" meant to him on other occasions, as noted above. It is not what the Greeks themselves understood by that maxim. Gide says in *Les Nouvelles Nourritures* that to observe oneself is to arrest one's development: "If the caterpillar tried to know itself, it would never become a butterfly."[20] That is to say, the caterpillar would say to itself "I am a caterpillar" and this very conviction would prevent it from developing into a butterfly. It is in this sense no doubt that "rather poor and limited personalities succeeded in finding and understanding themselves." The same idea is more explicitly expressed in terms of a personal dilemma and preference: "I still do not know, at thirty-six, whether I am greedy or over-generous, sober or gluttonous, . . . Why should I form, facetiously imitating myself, the factitious unity of my life? It is in movement that I can find my equilibrium."[21] In the case of the artist who has discovered himself seeks to be not sincere but consistent. "The genuine artist remains always half unconscious of himself."[22]

Whenever Gide condemned self-knowledge, the thing condemned was not genuine and successful self-scrutiny and its rationally beheld consequences but, rather, *self-labeling*. He had reasons for being emotionally involved in that condemnation for he "knew" himself as a pederast, for example. He looked for, and found evidence to prove to himself that he was a pederast and then remained one all his life. It is conceivable that if he had not labeled himself he would have overcome that inclination. Gide was opposed in principle to the application to oneself of certain epithets, for fear of acting accordingly. The application of epithets to oneself is self-definition. It is, by implication, refusal to let oneself be invaded by reality at each moment. A believer might describe that sort of self-labeling as "opposition to the will of God."

Gide condemned the inscription at Delphi because he thought it meant "label yourself!" The Greeks did not take "self-knowledge" to mean self-labeling. Nor can one attribute to them Gide's other meaning, namely discovery of an unspoiled self. What the Greeks did mean by "self-knowledge" was a condition where one is healthily related to one's environment. This was the meaning of the Delphic inscription; it is entertained also by St. Augustine, as paraphrased by Etienne Gilson. To the question, Why is the command "Know thyself (*Nosce te ipsum*)" issued, the answer is: "Only that the soul may know its true nature and live in accordance with it, that is to say, take its proper place, which is beneath Him to whom it should be subject and above that which it should rule—above the body and under God."[23] It appears that the known "true nature" of the soul is really the position of the soul between God and the body. The opinions referred to above to the effect that one cannot know oneself in the ordinary sense of the verb *to know*, also lead to the conclusion that the desire to know oneself is a quest which is satisfied not when something called self is made into an object of knowledge, but when estrangement is overcome.

Self-discovery and Relatedness

There are cases of self-discovery in literature where no "unspoiled self" is discovered. The seeker "finds himself" when he establishes satisfactory relatedness with the environment. The self-discovery of Peer Gynt is a good example. Gide has been compared to Ibsen, while Ibsen himself is recognized as having affinities with Kierkegaard. It was Marcel Schwob who introduced Gide to Ibsen's works,[24] all of which Gide had certainly read before he wrote *Le Retour de l'enfant prodigue*. Noteworthy is the fact that *Peer Gynt* was conceived and written at a time when Rimbaud in France was writing *A Season in Hell* with the basic theme of flight from a Dionysiac paradise. "Do I still know nature? Do I know myself?" Rimbaud asks, and in his expectation to worship—among the very first to do so—Noël on earth he bids the slaves of the world not to curse life.[25]

Peer Gynt, a prodigal of sorts, journeys through a hell of his own making of which the different stages are recapitulated in Act V, scene v. He is "on all-fours on the ground, grubbing up wild onions. 'Now, my dear Peer, I'm going to peel you, however little you may enjoy it,'" he says to one onion. Then, after a good many layers have been peeled off: "Are we never coming to the kernel? (*Pulls all that is left to pieces*). There isn't one! To the innermost bit it's nothing but layers, smaller and smaller. Nature's a joker! (*Throws the bits away from him.*) Deuce take all thinking!"

The point of the passage seems to be that the way to self-knowledge is paved when we desist from conceiving of "self" as of a thing or from taking *knowledge* to mean *knowledge of*. It is significant that both Peer Gynt and Gide's Prodigal—one willingly, the other not quite willingly, and still expressing the sort of yearning couched in Rimbaud's "O let me go to the sea!"—conclude their quest by returning to their "mother and wife."[26] Discovering oneself turns out to be finding one's place in the universe. To put it more modestly, to discover oneself is to establish a harmonious relationship with those who, or things which, surround one.

Some statements of Gide placed next to each other would substantiate that view. He said: "Some people work over themselves to obtain the unity of their person. I let myself go"; or, "the best means of learning to know oneself is seeking to understand others."[27] These "others" may be characters created by poets. Thus Bernard of *Les Faux-Monnayeurs* knows himself through Theseus and Hamlet.[28] Having observed that to follow a system of morals is neither wise nor possible as long as one does not know who and what one is, Gide stops looking for himself, and it is in love that he finds himself again.[29] It is as if he were advocating a second birth or salvation inasmuch as "God is love" and according to Christian doctrine salvation is, in the final analysis, to live in and with God.[30]

The story of the Prodigal Son as told in Luke's gospel is itself of course a lesson in the procedure and the conditions of salvation. According to this parable—and in the Christian epic—man realizes his destiny as he realizes his sonship through the Son of God. The "mythology"—as Gide might call it—of going to heaven is there, in the same Christian tradition, to convey the view that no unimpeded communication will be established among men in a material world. The only pure relationship is spiritual. By the same token with Solveig, for example, to whom Peer Gynt returns, one feels a holy feeling. Peer Gynt is at the end of his peregrinations on the face of the earth: "I will rock you to sleep and guard you!" Solveig tells him, "Sleep and dream my dearest boy!" The solace that Gide's Prodigal receives from *his* mother is similar but not identical: "Go, I will presently pray for you all."

"You all" includes the younger brother. It is he whom we find dreaming, but his dream is wakeful, restless: he too must leave the House—and he must be strong enough not to return. There is a book at the head of his bed. It is torn. There is an open pomegranate brought to him by a swineherd. He is said to have brought it to him after an absence of three days. These symbolisms are unmistakable: Scripture has lost its relevance to the younger brother, and when he leaves, he will be like one risen from the dead. To be sure, he will not find in the desert a fruit that will quench his thirst, but he will, in the long run, come to like the thirst itself. "Thirst itself," unlike any one specific fruit, has at least the connotation of limitlessness. Gide constantly tried to reach beyond the outer limits of his (i.e., of human) capacities and cannot be said to have been satisfied with mere humanism. What he consistently refused was to define the "beyond" as a space inhabited by disembodied spirits.

No reason is given in the story why the younger brother should succeed where the Prodigal did not. It is even possible that he too will return in the end, having known the desert merely as an episode in the process of his growth. Whatever the case, something of the theory that a man's salvation consists in the giving of his naked self to a reality that lovingly envelops the self persisted in Gide. Twenty-seven years after *Le Retour,* having heard a sermon on the theme *"Ein Gott, ein Volk, ein Land,"* he judged it "rather stirring" so long as its implications were not spelled out. "But hateful by reason of the exclusivity it involves. 'Kein Gott, kein Volk, kein Land' is the still Utopian program that tomorrow may save the world and to which I subscribe already."[31] This "Utopian program" is not to be taken to mean anarchy. It is again that dream of the unity of spirits without arbitrary unification that Gide had entertained during and after the writing of the Prodigal's story. In that unity, as in love, there is self-discovery.

The modern preoccupation with identity—of which *Le Retour de l'enfant prodigue* is a symptom—appears to be a quest for what is referred to in Christian doctrine as salvation, while both self-discovery and salvation refer to a state of affairs where the problem of the rift between a self and the Other is solved. The self finds its place in the Self of the Whole (as the branches are "in" the vine) and is neither lost nor forced into a mold at the cost of losing its own given shape. The question is, Who is Gide's "savior"? By what means does he hope to overcome the ambiguities of existence on earth? It is certainly not the Church.

Salvation and the Artist

In *Les Nourritures Terrestres* Gide compared himself—probably borrowing the image from Rimbaud—to a cork—"a poor cork on the waves."[32] He found this condition undesirable. In *La Porte étroite* Jerome dreams of feeling himself *"together and alone"* on the uncertain waves.[33] In *Thésée* the hero ventures forth alone to kill the Minotaur, but then he is holding a thread—which is substantially a way of feeling oneself "together and alone" with, in addition, an end in view.

These images are expressive of Gide's double-sided desire both to yield to the Whole and to resist disintegration. From this point of view there is a difference of degree but not of kind between *Si le grain ne meurt* and some of his other major works. *Si le grain ne meurt* is only the least disguised of his creative works. It is, as confession, a way of self-giving to the world, and as autobiography his self-safekeeping for presumably endless years to come. The protagonist of *Si le grain ne meurt* is to André Gide, the man, what a believer's risen self is to the believer. The metamorphosis of André Gide into the protagonist of that book is, as is evident from its title, the resurrection described by Saint Paul in his first epistle to the Corinthians, the obvious difference being that that through which the miracle occurs is not belief but art. This is the heart of the matter. On this basis the Church's claim becomes false in Gide's eyes. To him Christ is not the Savior, a conclusion he could arrive at by simple logic: Christ the Savior is said to lead to heaven; there is no heaven; therefore Christ is not savior.

Gide finds himself in, or is saved through, an artist such as Dostoevsky. He describes his relationship to him in religious terms: ". . . everything I find a means of saying through Dostoevsky and apropos of him is dear to me . . . It will be, just as much as a book of criticism, a book of confessions, to anyone who knows how to read; or rather: a profession of faith."[34] Self-discovery by this means is not peculiar to Gide. One can think of Nietzsche who knew what and where he was, through Schopenhauer. Through Schopenhauer Nietzsche "saw the land,"[35] but the attraction that the artist and his world exercised upon Gide is something more than intellectual enlightenment. The art world where form (time) and content (eternity) blend in the act of creation is his kingdom, the realm of his salvation. In two remarkable entries in his *Journal* made in January, 1892, Gide sets forth in clearcut terms his views concerning the role art plays in leading a man to the fulfillment of his existence: "A man's life is his image. At the hour of death we shall be reflected in the past, and, leaning over the mirror of our acts, our souls will recognize *what we are*."[36]

It is instructive to recall before quoting the sequel that many years later Gide looked upon the blank page, the void which he was to fill with his creative work, also as upon a mirror.[37] Pursuing his reflections of January, 1892, he had spoken of a "reverse sincerity" on the part of the artist, who, rather than recount his life as he lived it, must live it as he will recount it. In other words, the portrait of him formed by his life must identify itself with the ideal portrait he desires.

And, in still simpler terms, he must be as he wishes to be. It must be observed that *recounting* does not mean giving a factual report. It is an artistic function. It is art which will reveal what we are. Salvation is through art.

It is not surprising therefore that in an entry of the *Journal des Faux-Monnayeurs* Gide the artist should speak as if he were a priest. Speaking, for example, of two characters in *Les Faux-Monnayeurs,* he says that they remain nonexistent so long as they are not baptized. He likens the moment, just before the moment of composition, to that of the convert who is on the point of approaching the altar and who "feels his faith suddenly falter and takes fright in the emptiness and dryness of his heart."[38] *Les Faux-Monnayeurs* itself portrays a world of makers of false coins, of promoters of false values which prevent genuine interpersonal relationship. Edouard has a saving presence in this world. To see in the novel either the record of Gide's and Cocteau's fight over French youth, or an imaginative transcription of his subconscious drives,[39] is incomplete. *Les Faux-Monnayeurs* is to be viewed primarily as the story of a combat between the artist and the anti-artist, as between Christ and the Devil, the revealer and the deceiver.

The artist's role in *Les Faux-Monnayeurs* is not merely moral. It is to be compared to that of the Demiurge, a prototype of Christ, described in Plato's *Timaeus*.[40] The maker or craftsman—or the creator—builds the forms, or the form of the good into the world, though matter resists him to a certain extent. This describes fairly closely the function of the artist according to Gide: we see Edouard at work in *Les Faux-Monnayeurs* ordering his material into an artistic creation. Nothing is, properly speaking, "imagined" in *Les Faux-Monnayeurs*. Every character is someone Gide knows in real life from Passavant (Jean Cocteau) to Sophroniska (Mme Sokolnicka, a disciple of Freud, who popularized her teacher among the *Nouvelle Revue française* group shortly after 1918), to Paul-Ambroise to whom one or two very brief references are made and who, with his "habit of saying that he refuses to take count of anything that can't be put down in figures," is unmistakably Paul Valéry.[41]

The plot of the novel—or whatever there is of it—is itself the elaboration of an incident which Gide had seen reported in a newspaper. Several details within that framework are clearly autobiographical. Thus a multiplicity of related persons and incidents constitute the equivalent of formless matter given to the craftsman in Plato's cosmogony. The artist wishes to build his idea into them or them around his idea. "I should like a novel," Edouard says, "which should be at the same time as true and as far from reality, as particular and at the same time as general, as human and as fictitious as *Athalie,* or *Tartuffe* or *Cinna*." This novel will not have a subject, "stupid" as the notion may sound. If it were materially possible, the appointed task of the novelist would be to use all of the facts of the history of man to fashion with them the artistic cosmos. The artist's function is therefore to return the fragmented world to an original—or rather final—coherence. Edouard is critical of the "slice of life" novel of the Naturalist school, which cuts its slice in time, arbitrarily. As for himself, he says, he should not like to cut at all. He wants to put everything in his novel, because any cut of the scissors would limit its substance arbitrarily. "For more than a year now that I have been working at it, nothing happens to me that I don't put into it—everything that I see, everything I know, everything that other people's lives and my own teach me . . ."[42] The craftsman meets with resistance in his project to bend the formless into the forms. The novelist who has the same problem must "represent reality on the one hand, and on the other [the] effort to stylize it into art . . ."[43]

Had Gide lived in the age of St. Bonaventure he would probably have adopted the prevalent beliefs of thirteenth-century Europe, suppressed his excessive sensuality—of which he was ashamed and was led to absolve himself by attributing it to heredity[44]—and written mystical verse, oblivious of goings-on here below. Living as he did in an age where facts acquired importance as facts, where process and dynamism were dominant concepts, he could not be satisfied with any static world view. For this reason his artist differs from Plato's craftsman, if it is true that the craftsman orders *his* universe according to preexisting ideas. Edouard rejects that procedure. His book does not have a plan, that is, a scheme in the artist's mind, to which the novel will seek to conform. If anything were settled beforehand, everything would be falsified. "I wait for reality to dictate to me," he says. Though his novelist wants to abandon reality, he shall continually bring him back to it. Edouard's mention of "my novelist" presumably indicates a conflict or a dialogue within himself. Then the subject of the book is put in a nutshell: "the struggle between the facts presented by reality and the ideal reality."[45]

One would expect "ideal" reality to do the dictating in question. Edouard waits for the non-ideal reality to dictate to him. At the same time he is critical of the Naturalist school. The ideal reality of which Edouard speaks has a certain objectivity and concreteness about it, since he insists that the artist is the expositor of a struggle; evidently "the facts presented by reality" cannot engage in a struggle with nothing—or pure fantasy. This struggle and, by inference, the ideal reality are not things of the imagination. "Don't think," Bernard tells Edouard, "that I didn't understand what you said about your book and about the conflict you imagine between brute reality and . . ." Edouard's answer is: "I don't imagine it, it exists."[46]

The ellipsis with which Bernard's remark peters out is significant in that the world which stands over against brute reality is beyond definition. But this does not mean that the world is now entirely given in the manner of the realm where Plato's ideas are often said to have their ever-lasting, immutable being. Edouard acknowledges the reality not of the ideal world itself, but of the struggle with it. The point seems to be, from a broadly philosophical perspective, that we must not entertain an arbitrary scheme of perfection in our heads and then try to force history to conform to it. Rather, mankind must have the consciousness of moving toward a fulfillment as a concrete possibility. That fulfillment is there, though it cannot and ought not to be visualized in detail ahead of time. If, moreover, there is a fulfillment, then history is more than the sum of phenomena. That which propels the phenomena toward the fulfillment is not to be identified with them.[47]

This being the case, the function of the artist is not to present an unchanging ideal. It is to witness and communicate to the less sensitive an unfolding, while the artist himself experiences in his person the birth pangs of the ever new. This experience is that of a struggle, for it involves a consciously adopted, profoundly hopeful stance against natural evil, Edouard's "brute reality." In this manner will art take up brute reality into an ideal reality, which is another way of saying that the function of art is essentially to save. It is because Gide looked upon art as salvation that he disregarded good sentiments as material for good literature. It is bad sentiments that *can* be saved. Those features of our workaday world are saved which have been re-formed and re-presented in an artistic masterpiece. In a more conventionally orthodox frame of mind Gide speaks of the idea becoming—in the manner of the Word—flesh. And the idea that becomes flesh is a living thing: "it palpitates, it lives, you caress it; you adopt it intimately; you know its contours, its limits; its deficiencies, its relief, its recesses; at once its genealogy and its descendants."[48]

From Gide's most comprehensive exposition of his theory of art we further learn that his conflict is fundamentally the conflict between the vertical and horizontal dimensions of existence. This conflict, which is therefore universally significant, is solved in the work of art in the manner in which divinity and humanity meet in Christ: "Of love and thought, here is the subtle confluence . . . the white page gleams before me . . . As God becomes man, so my idea clothes itself, submissive to the laws of rhythm."[49] As such art is the link between heaven and earth, a rainbow, which is interpreted in Christian circles as a prefiguration of the Prince of Peace. It also stands above brute reality, in the sense that it judges it.

Edouard, the Artist, lives in Gide as he in Edouard. They are not identical, yet not different. The paradox of the eternal Christ's living in Paul who nevertheless was a man of his times and place is reflected in Gide's mutually exclusive claims that the poet must have no personality of his own, but must have his own philosophy and ethical outlook.[50] Moreover, the world of art is the locus of Gide's enthusiasms, its discovery the moment of his salvation. Thus he is born to life with the discovery of a poet, namely Heine.[51] He uses the soldier's or the explorer's or the mystic's terminology to describe his reading of a book with a comrade: "We both went directly to the thick of the work, to the heart of the burning bush, to Faust, and not to the first Faust. Daringly we threw ourselves into the second."[52] This terminology of adventure befits the discovery of a new world. Coming out of a bourgeois environment as he did, Gide speaks in the manner of Columbus who was under the impression, upon landing in the Windward Islands, that "here are truly the Islands of the Blessed in the region of the Setting Sun where reigns perpetual spring, and where the nightingale sings from the boughs."[53] Here is his impression of his first visit to the studio of Jean-Paul Laurens, a painter:

. . . everything was as cordial and simple as could be; it was nevertheless with a beating heart that I first entered a world so different from any I had ever known. . . . All around was harmony, severe, purple, dusky, filling me at first with an almost religious awe; here, everything I saw seemed soothing to the eyes and mind, and conducive to some delicious kind of studious contemplation. That day, my eyes were suddenly opened, and I then and there realized the ugliness of my mother's rooms; . . .[54]

Full of "shame and shyness," he felt at Laurens' studio as if some of the ugliness of hs mother's rooms must be clinging about him. He was, under a new guise, the sinful penitent overwhelmed by the spectacle of religious purity. He was a new being. So pervasive was his desire to escape from the bourgeois, false, illusory respectability and its symbols, that he took physical delight in the world where his readings carried him. In the manner of mystics who use concrete, sexual symbolism to describe their spiritual experiences, he speaks of the "healthy appetite" and "gluttony" with which he reads, and recalls the marvelous sensation accompanying certain readings in his childhood, "so voluptuously penetrating that I felt the sentence almost physically enter my heart."[55]

In his youth Gide read "with" Em. even in her absence. On one such occasion Balzac's *Le Cousin Pons* caused him to experience an unusual *ravissement,* an ecstasy. "Real life holds no such transports," André Walter says to Emmanuele. Gide sobs reading *Athalie* at the age of sixty-nine.[56] We saw him weep torrents at the mere mention of Agamemnon. At a time when he has had his "fill of poetry," he observed that everything was getting confused in his "heart and head." He no longer knew where he stood. "From the practical point of view, this can become most embarrassing;" he said, "as, for instance, to confuse the characters of a play or a film or of life and to mistake one for another."[57] Gide regards this confusion of art and life as a deficiency, for he had said earlier that "if social questions occupy my thought . . . this is partly because the creative demon is withdrawing from it. Such questions do not take over the field until the other has already surrendered it."[58] In this cleavage between the worlds of art and of daily existence, the former is clearly preferred.

An indication that Gide lives his authentic life in the world of art is his constant appraisal of himself and of this world in terms of that world. The social questions themselves which he opposes to "the other world" where "the creative demon" is at work, interest him in the manner of a "Balzac novel."[59] In the very first entry in his *Journal* he looks upon Paris as a Balzac character would. He is enchanted at being known as "the idiot" by village urchins because it is enough like Dostoevsky.[60] He notes in 1932, probably having Kierkegaard in mind, that he "used to compare himself to Icarus, lost in the Labyrinth from which so many mystics think they are able to free themselves only by a leap toward heaven,"[61] a passage which, incidentally, is the key to the understanding of his *Thésée.* Eventually his accumulated esthetic experience turns into a pair of lenses which he simply cannot remove: "I see Rome through Stendhal despite myself," he writes in his *Feuilles de Route,*[62] and Bernard says to Laura in *Les Faux-Monnayeurs:* "Oh, if you only knew how maddening it is to have in one's head quantities of phrases from great authors, which come irresistibly to one's lips when one wants to express a sincere feeling."[63]

An ordinary tourist would see upon arriving at the port of Tunis in the nineties of the last century a swarm of Arab paupers in tattered clothes. This crowd is to Gide, "straight out of the Arabian Nights."[64] The people are no longer themselves, in their abject misery. They are

details in a wonderful world. When Meriem, an Algerian prostitute, fails
to come at the expected time Gide is disappointed even though there was
no real desire behind his resolution to sleep with her. He is "as Cain
when he saw the smoke of his offering beaten back to earth: the holo-
caust was not accepted."[65] Then the girl is compared to a "bacchante—
the one on the Gaeta vase, for instance—because of her tinkling bracelets
too, which she was continually shaking."[66] In *L'Immoraliste* a Sicilian
boy is said to have been "as beautiful as a line of Theocritus,"[67] certain
African women are "very Maillol"[68] and the Tunisian coast, on one occasion "very Delacroix."[69]

The reference to the world of art is not limited to esthetic experiences
only. The declarations of the nationalists will make him think of the
protestation of Lear's daughters, and he will conclude that "the deepest
love does not leap so easily to the lips." He holds, he says, "for the silence
of Cordelia."[70] On the other hand, he quotes from Molière's *Don Juan*—
Act III, scene iii, as he carefully notes—when he feels during his honey-
moon with communism that to be silent about certain abuses is to become
an accomplice.[71]

Gide writes at the age of eighty, and eleven years after the death of his
wife: "I can see her again on her deathbed. With no more of that smiling amenity left which always tempered her gravity, she seemed like a
Jansenist painting by Philippe de Champaigne."[72] Given to this esthetic
other-worldliness, he will note, confounded by the complexities of life during the Second World War, that it is all "very Kafka."[73] Such associations where the reality at hand is transposed into, and valued in terms of,
a higher level of reality could be multiplied.

Reference has already been made to the healing power of art. Where
there is youth and happiness and a strong sense of belonging, the intima-
tion is, the work of art is not only uncalled for, but also impossible,[74] a
consideration which leads him to the eschatological pronouncement that
the time will come when—as if following the same destiny as that of the
church militant—there will be no need of art.[75] The artist, the mediator
between the actual and ideal, will have accomplished his mission at the
end of time. Life will apparently have completed its imitation of art, and
the perfect wedding of content and form or soul and body will have
come about, for the "world of art" in the final analysis is the ideal realm
where Dionysus and Apollo live together in peace. It is a condition where
the conflict between "madness" and "reason" are reconciled.[76] In the

meantime we all share to some extent in a dialogue of sorts, *dialogue* being a euphemism for the disruption that Gide himself experienced in his person. He did not always regret that dialogue, for it brought into operation all the potentialities of his being. This disruption leads to art or, to consider the process from the other side, art is the means to achieve the highest good: "That *state of dialogue* which, for so many others, is almost intolerable became necessary to me. . . . , far from leading to sterility, it invited me to the work of art and immediately preceded creation, led to equilibrium and harmony."[77]

The "equilibrium and harmony" is to be compared to the peace that believers find in Christ, and the comparison is not fortuitous. Gide thinks of the calm provided by the work of art within a context of religious preoccupations. He wrote in 1893: "We shall not lose any of our anxieties. Their cause is within us, not outside us. Our mind is so constructed that everything unsettles it, and only in solitude does it find a bit of tranquility. Then the thought of God troubles it." He added immediately: "What I like in the work of art is that it is calm; . . . no one more than I has longed for rest, nor has loved unrest more."[78] Thirty-five years later he wrote of this same rest-unrest alternation, and presented the calm provided by art as an alternative to the serenity that the Catholics find in religion. Art leads to a harbor, a traditional metaphor signifying rest following fatigue, security after insecurity, stability after flux.[79]

That art leads from unrest to serenity was a favorite Gidian theme.[80] From this perspective there is a striking similarity between the life patterns of Gide's Prodigal and of Bernard of *Les Faux-Monnayeurs* on one hand, and, on the other, a fundamental difference. Both the Prodigal and Bernard wander away from home and come back. The Prodigal encourages his younger brother to look for kingdoms, kingless lands which he did not have the endurance to discover, but which the latter "knows," "feels" do exist. We do not see Bernard urging his younger brother Caloub to leave the house, but we know, as the book comes to an end, that Caloub will come into direct contact with Edouard. The turning point, the salvation of Bernard had begun when, holding in his hand the piece of paper that would give him access to Edouard's journal, he transcended the conventional notions of good and evil. He was not in a position to know Edouard intimately. That journal was in a suitcase, the key to which Edouard did not have. At this stage of the novel Edouard is known to the reader as one who never feels himself living so intensely as when he escapes himself "to become no matter who." It was therefore almost intentionally that he had lost the key to his suitcase containing his journal. Yet he knew as he checked it at the railroad station that the checkroom attendants were too busy to look into it. *He* will find Edouard who seeks him. Bernard was in a despairing mood, traversing a dark night of the soul, just before he saw the crumpled piece of paper that was to determine the direction of his life: "his gallant courage of the morning had left him. He felt abominably lonely and his heart was swelling with something brackish and bitter which he would not call unhappiness, but which brought the tears to his eyes." Evidently, he would not call his disposition unhappiness, for *happiness* would not describe the object of his quest. As he decides not to act in the manner of a "normal fathead" he recites to himself the first lines of Hamlet's soliloquy on suicide. In the terminology of Tillich, anxiety informs his existence. He is existentially aware of the threat of nonbeing. Or, to use Kierkegaard's phrase, he is "sick unto death." The Prodigal was himself in a similar mood at the end of his wanderings in the desert: "Nothing is more tiring," he says to his mother, "than the realization of one's dissemblance. This journey tired me in the end." Yet he is not certain that he did the right thing by coming home. Though he feels that he could not have done otherwise, his nostalgia for the desert is still acute. Bernard's return to the house of the man now referred to as his father—presumably because the relationship now between them is spiritual and not based on genetic ties—is, "indeed, . . . the best thing he could do." The decisive difference between the Prodigal and Bernard is that the Prodigal met no one in the desert. Bernard met the artist, a meeting which is not unlike, to use Martin Luther's words, taking hold of Christ by faith. The New Testament insistently teaches that interpersonal relationship must transcend physicalness. Bernard, following the insights he gained through Edouard and on the basis of his pure love of Laura, overlooks the fact that Monsieur Profitendieu is not his legitimate father. His return indicates that an order of relationship of greater validity has been attained.

Gide delivered his Dostoevsky lectures while writing *Les Faux-Monnayeurs*. A certain parallelism can be seen between his own self-discovery through Dostoevsky and Bernard's self-discovery through Edouard. The artist-savior functional identification in Gide's mind has more explicit expressions. He will say on one occasion that imagination, the *sine qua non* of art, opens "the gardens of heaven."[81] Ultimately art liberates man from the fear of death. It protests against it. Its very *raison d'être* is to overcome the anxiety of death inasmuch as without this anxiety there would be no art.[82] Gide went so far as to say, in 1922, that he writes in order "to have something secure against death."[83] To borrow Tillich's terminology again, through art as through religion, one defeats anxiety. The threat of nonbeing is ovecome. Nonbeing is taken up into being. In view of the similarity of the concept of nonbeing and darkness, it is significant that Edouard enters the world of *Les Faux-Monnayeurs* simultaneously with the rising sun.

In the Gidian world the artist has a privileged position as the revealer and as one who saves the generality of men from alienation, from the contradictions and limitations of finite existence. Nor is the relationship between the artist (novelist) and his characters unlike that of the relationship between Christ and the members of the Church in Paul's view. The novelist *is* in a sense his characters,[84] and their joys and sufferings are his: "all the heaven and hell of his characters is in him."[85] These characters are moreover "models furnished by society" and it is as a novelist[86] that Edouard is, as he says, tormented by the need of intervening, of effecting their destiny.

4

God

Gide asked the Catholics on one occasion whether they needed "the paternal clout" to force them to do their homework right.[1] The suggestion is of course that if they have come of age then they should not need God. He probes more deeply into this problem in *La Porte étroite*. Though *La Porte étroite* was meant to be a critique of Protestantism in the Kantian sense of *critique*[2] we learn in the story itself that the protagonist, Jerome, intended to write a book on the philosophy of religion.[3] Since Gide's protagonists usually write the book *he* is writing, we may safely assume that *La Porte étroite* is, before being a critique of Protestantism, a critique of religion. More specifically, it is an examination of the concept of God. This is dealt with so subtly that it may be asked whether Gide himself was entirely aware of his position. Yet *La Porte étroite* is a classical work, and we may recall that "our classical authors have a right to all the interpretations they allow of."[4]

The woman loved by Jerome is Alissa, his cousin. The principal point *La Porte étroite* makes is that Alissa's God failed to save her. He was of no help to her in her effort to overcome isolation and loneliness. In her last entry in her Journal she records how she saw the atrocious bareness of the walls of her room as if for the first time, and was seized with fear. It is a sudden and disenchanting illumination:

Even now I am writing to reassure myself, to calm myself. Oh Lord! may I reach the end without blasphemy!

I was able to get up again. I went down on my knees like a child. . . .

I should like to die now, quickly, before again realizing that I am alone.[5]

To the extent to which Gide could exclaim "Alissa c'est moi!"[6] we are entitled to see in this entry a poignant confession of the author's own solitariness.

The question arises, how does Alissa conceive of God? If there is a conception of God, other than Alissa's, which is valid, then Gide's condemnation of Alissa's religious behavior will turn out to be a condemnation not of belief in God, but of belief in *her* God, just as the condemnation of Amélie's Christianity in *La Symphonie pastorale* is in fact the condemnation of the domestication of healthful vitality. Alissa's relationship with her father provides a clue. The place that he occupies in her life in the novel is clearly suggested to Gide by his wife's reaction to *her* father in real life.[7]

There are a number of entries in the diary that Mme André Gide kept before her marriage that are particularly significant from this perspective. In her twenties, after the death of her father and the remarriage, soon thereafter, of her mother, Madeleine writes: "O grief and shame of having to think about it! How sweet it must be to have a mother! But we have had you, O Father all loved, and our heart has missed nothing."[8] Madeleine, who capitalizes *father,* could get by without a mother. The father's presence on the other hand is her fortitude and protection, he being the epitome of righteousness and honesty.[9] She has feelings of guilt that attend the very thought of her marrying Gide, such feelings being related no doubt to the place her father—or his memory—occupies in her life. They are thinly veiled as in this entry on the occasion of Gide's birthday: "Really! So you are twenty years old! I have wondered if that should give me pleasure or displeasure. The balance tipped towards displeasure."[10] She writes of him after some years: "But his life is absolutely separated from mine!"[11] She decides not to write to him, but then she changes her mind: "I am answering with a feeling where there is a singular mixture of black and of white—of severe blame for myself—of righteous anger against you . . ."[12] At the height of an intellectual and esthetic experience she yearns for his companionship, but this awareness unsettles her: "I was in a rage at reading this article without you—so much so that I called everyone André all day long. Which annoyed me beyond measure."[13] She lives in 1891 a whole succession of bad days, of silence, of annoyance, of revolt, of guilty thoughts. "I am a slave to myself when I could and should be a master."[14] In the following passage where she "repents of her weakness" as of a sin, the words *obsession* and *guilty* are particularly revelatory. The passage must be read in connection with such entries as: "O Father, where are you . . . do you still love me. Am I still your daughter, your older daughter? O Father come back—

or let me go toward you!" or "Papa, my father so, so much loved—when shall we all be reunited? We still had so much need of you . . ." It is in this attitude of yearning after the father that Madeleine at the age of twenty-four reads Gide's first book. She confides the following to her diary ten days later:

And during these ten days I lived in a *constant obsession* of the past—and also a *guilty* imagination of a chimerical future.
I awake and repent of my weakness.
My God, my God, deliver me.[15]

The future contemplated by Madeleine is chimerical to her in all proba-bility because it includes the impossible reconciliation of two courses of action: to be and not to be André's wife. Gide's *Les Cahiers d'André Walter* was intended as an invitation extended to her to marry him. One month after reading that book she congratulates herself for the success with which she put him out of her mind: "Thank you, my God! Make the separation complete, the distance gained impossible to cross!" This was in February, 1891. In October of the same year she discerns some-thing of a fiction in all proposition of marriage, which is fun and pleasant.

It's a bit, I think, the feeling that the Russians call *otchaiane,* which makes you lean over a project of marriage as over an abyss—to have a strong feeling of dizziness—and the mad desire to bind oneself—to say yes—in order to see what would happen.[16]

On December 29, 1894, her comment after a short visit in Paris with André is: "What a sad reunion!" She is determined not to see him again. Yet the death, six months later, of Mme Gide creates the ideal situation for the solution of Madeleine's psychological dilemma. She will not be betraying her father upon filling Mme Gide's shoes, under the pretext of becoming André's wife. She sees André again on the occasion of his mother's death and returns to Rouen to announce her engagement. Nev-ertheless the idea of marriage is still as fearful as ever. Five days later she writes to André: "I have no fear of death, but I fear marriage."[17]

Gide must have somehow detected the incestuous character of Made-leine's feelings for her father. He must also have known that that was the reason for her reticences, and he suggests it in *La Porte étroite* with uncommon artistic finesse. In one of the better-known scenes of that novel where Gide recreates a real experience of his own with Madeleine, Jerome describes the manner in which he surprised his Aunt, Alissa's mother, entertaining a lover in the presence of her other two children. Alissa in another room on the upper floor knows of this infidelity and is distressed. Jerome finds her "on her knees by the bedside" at a time when "through the window behind her came the last glimmer of expiring daylight." In view of Alissa's puritanism the reason for her affliction should be clear enough to one who has just seen her mother with a "strange young man in a lieutenant's uniform." Yet Jerome "doubtless . . . understood very imperfectly the cause of Alissa's wretchedness, but felt intensely that it was far too strong for her little quivering soul, for her fragile body, shaken with sobs." He is "drunk with love, with pity, with an indistinguishable mixture of enthusiasm, self-sacrifice, and virtue." In an attitude of complete religious commitment he resolves to shelter his helpless and innocent friend from fear, evil, and life.

I knelt down at last, my whole being full of prayer. I gathered her to me; vaguely I heard her say: "Jerome! They didn't see you, did they? Oh! go away quickly. They mustn't see you." Then, lower still: "Jerome, don't tell anyone. Poor papa doesn't know it."

That in her profound distress Alissa's principal concern should be to keep Jerome's visit a secret comes as something of a surprise. The reason why *they* must not see *him* is not evident. One can only conjecture that "they mustn't see you" really means "you should not have seen my mother in these circumstances." The subject of Alissa's concern is her father, and the last sentence gives it all away. Her reaction is not one of compassion for her mother. Nor is there any evidence of her being disturbed over the consequences of her mother's breaking a divine commandment, grave as these consequences—here and hereafter—doubtless were to her fundamentalist mind. It is her father whom she wishes to protect not only against the embarrassing discomfort of knowing of his wife's infidelity, but also against the aggravating circumstance that others, including Jerome, know it too.

The following incident recorded by Alissa in her journal may never have occurred in real life; the style of the narrative gives it the semblance of a dream. It may be Gide's analysis of the nature of Madeleine's painful hesitation to marry him. The passage must be quoted at length, for the least detail, masterfully used by Gide, contributes to the conclusion that repressed emotions, incestuous in character, inform the daughter-father relationship:

Yesterday evening, Jerome had just gone up to his room; Papa, who was sitting up with me for a little, left me alone for a few minutes. I was sitting on the sofa, or rather—a thing I hardly ever do—I was lying down, I don't know why. The lampshade was shading my eyes and the upper part of my body from the light; I was mechanically looking at my feet, which showed a little below my dress in the light thrown upon them by the lamp. When Papa came back, he stood for a few moments at the door, staring at me oddly, half smiling, half sad. I got up with a vague feeling of shyness; then he called me: "Come and sit beside me," said he; and, though it was already late, he began speaking to me about my mother, which he had never done since their separation. He told me how he had married her, how much he had loved her, and how much she had at first been to him.

"Papa," I said to him at last, "do, please, say why are you telling me this this evening—what makes you tell me this just this particular evening?"

"Because, just now, when I came into the drawing-room and saw you lying on the sofa, I thought for a moment it was your mother."

The reason I asked this so insistently was because that very evening, Jerome had been reading over my shoulder, standing leaning over me. I could not see him, but I felt his breath and, as it were, the warmth and pulsation of his body. I pretended to go on reading, but my mind had stopped working; I could not even distinguish the lines; so strange a perturbation took possession of me that I was obliged to get up from my chair quickly while I still could; I managed to leave the room for a few minutes, luckily without his noticing anything. But a little later, when I was alone in the drawing-room and lay down on the sofa, where Papa thought I looked like my mother, at that very moment I was thinking of her.

I slept very badly last night; I was disturbed, oppressed, miserable, haunted by the recollection of the past, which came over me like a wave of remorse.

Other passages in the book contain the same suggestion. Alissa writes in her diary some five months after her twenty-fifth birthday:

Though I am as tired as if I were very old, my soul keeps a strange childishness. I am still the little girl, who could not go to sleep before everything in her room was tidy and the clothes she had taken off were neatly folded beside her bed. . . . That is how I should like to get ready to die.

The entry prepares the reader for the last lines of Alissa's Journal, where she goes down on her knees like a child and wishes to die so as to be taken to the heavenly father before realizing her loneliness once more. The care with which she folds her clothes is certainly a symbolic gesture. Tidiness was certainly not a virtue that would appeal to her dissolute mother.

Between the lines of *La Porte étroite* one can easily read all the reasons which ought to oppose Jerome, in Alissa's mind, to her father. There is, instead, an overt opposition between Jerome and God. In one of her letters to Jerome the vacuum left by him is filled by God. It is a matter of either/or: "Good-bye, my friend. _Hic incipit amor Dei._"

Alissa is not clear about the reasons which prompt her to avoid Jerome; "The reasons that make me fly from him? I no longer believe in them. . . . And yet I fly from him, sadly and without understanding why I fly." She will, on occasion, ask God to authorize her to love him: "My God, Thou knowest I have need of him to love Thee. . . . give him to me so that I may give thee my heart." But such authorization is not forthcoming. She simply cannot love them simultaneously. Sometimes they are separated because she stands between them—"Alas! I understand now only too well: between God and him there is no other obstacle but myself;"—another variant of the same disposition being her belief that, accompanied by Jerome, she is not acceptable to God. She considers the possibility of their walking together, like two pilgrims, toward God, along the way of life. Neither she nor he will be overcome by weariness, for it will be enough for them to feel near each other. "But no! The way Thou teachest, Lord, is a strait way—so strait that two cannot walk in it abreast."

The same either/or (God/Jerome) is present in a question she asks Jerome, her "friend" and her "brother": "Do you think we are ever nearer to each other than when each of us forgets the other as we pray to God?" Or in an entry in her Journal: "Why, then, between Thee and me, dost Thou everywhere set his image?" This question is put to a God who is recognized as "jealous."

"God" in _La Porte étroite_ is an alternative to Jerome, as was Alissa's father. In her religion her father and God are fused into the same entity, who is thus a limited being, an idol. In keeping with his avowed mission to destroy idolatry, Gide berates that god and declares him incapable of overcoming human estrangement. We can begin to see what he meant when he said that he was an "unbeliever," but not "ungodly."[18]

Atheism or Anti-idolatry

Gide's atheism, his refusal to recognize God in any man-made object, coincides with Paul's attitude as set forth at the council of the Areopagus.

The god whom he rejected is "someone up there." He is someone very much like Monsieur Keller, the founder and head of a pension where Gide studied for a time as a boy. The impression Keller had made on him was unforgettable as is evident from an arresting description given in *Si le grain ne meurt*. He appears again in *Les Faux-Monnayeurs* as Azaïs. A comparison of the two portraits—one remembered, the other an artistic recreation with symbolic overtones—provides a fairly accurate description of the god Gide rejects. It is this god he thought, not without reason, in whom the generality of Christians believe. This is Monsieur Keller:

Though [M. Jacob, Keller's son] himself was getting on in years, he subordinated his thoughts, his plans, his life to this Old Man, who was almost unknown to the pupils, for he only appeared on the most solemn occasions; his authority, however, weighed heavily on the whole household and M. Jacob returned clothed in it, when (like Moses coming down from the mountain with the Tables of the Law) he came down from the room on the second floor, where the Old Man lived in seclusion. Into this sacred abode I was only allowed to enter very rarely, and then accompanied by my mother—for I never should have dared to go alone—but I can answer for it that the *Aged* really did exist. You were shown into a small Evangelical-looking room, where the old man sat installed for the whole day in a large green rep armchair, beside a window overlooking the playground, so that he was able to keep his eye on the boys at their games. . . . In spite of his great height, the weight of years had bowed him over much. His glance was unswerving, his voice severe, and it was impossible not to understand, not to feel, that the orders transmitted by M. Jacob to the rest of the school, had been received by *him* straight from God.[19]

In *Les Faux-Monnayeurs* old Azaïs can look over the playground and keep an eye on the pupils' "goings and comings." He is entirely out of touch with the world in the sense that there is no genuine rapport between himself and actual occurrences. The atmosphere of his room with its mahogany, rep, and horsehair furniture is so austere that it seems "as if any flower must wither in it at once."[20] Edouard goes up to the second floor to see him. Having recorded in his Journal the illusions nursed by old Azaïs, he writes these lines hoping secretly that Bernard will be indiscreet enough to read them. Bernard will know what Edouard means if he frequents Azaïs a little longer.

In speaking so of Azaïs, it is I myself that I render odious. . . . I like the old fellow very much, and "moreover," as he says, I respect him; but when I am with him I have the greatest difficulty in containing myself; this doesn't tend to make me enjoy his society.[21]

Gide may be willing to be ridiculed by conventional believers for the sake of the younger generation to whom he is conveying the message of the death of God, but the reader may not assume that Azaïs does no more than represent the rejected god. It is undeniable, on the other hand, that whenever Gide fills *God* with a referent to be rejected, this referent holds in his world a position and plays a role similar to Keller's in the pension. This same sort of entity is made fun of as "Monsieur le Principal" in *Les Caves du Vatican*. Gide once accused Francis Jammes, a converted Catholic, of believing in a god with a beard like Jammes's own.[22]

It does not occur to Gide that if Catholic theology entertained belief in the god he rejected, the enormous place occupied in that theology by the mystery of the Holy Trinity would be quite unexplainable. Inasmuch as Christ, the Second Person of the Trinity, is both God and man, that mystery affirms and denies simultaneously the existence of a void between God and the world, or God's being another person. There is thus a certain inaccuracy in Gide's rejection of traditional orthodox theism. It reflects difficulties experienced with a wholly other God, difficulties which the dogma of the Trinity itself raises and claims to have overcome. His quarrel remains nevertheless with a theism which regards God simply as someone external to the world. Nor can one detect a radical change in his religious attitude—as distinguished from the verbal expressions of it—during and after the publication of *Les Cahiers d'André Walter*. The "liberating crisis" in terms of which some of his critics[23] describe his putative conversion to atheism is merely another expression of his anti-idolatry.

As soon as the images Gide used to describe that conversion are discarded in favor of the thing described, the conclusion can be reached that from the dangers of idolatry inherent in the symbolic expressions of his earlier youth Gide is turning in the direction of less common expressions of anti-idolatrous religious attitudes with *Les Nourritures Terrestres*. Here, as in Trinitarian orthodoxy, the distance between man and the reality where he has his being is not a vacuum.

There is no reason to think that at the time Gide was writing *Les Cahiers* he was less or more of a "believer" than at any other time in his life. It is in *Les Cahiers,* for example, that he declares the absence of any difference between possessing and *believing* that one possesses: both states of affairs are equally "sweet" and equally "chimerical."[24] He loves the Lord even if the Lord is not. The Lord exists, he says, in his thought. Evidently these are not the reflections of a "believer." One or two examples from the period immediately following *Les Cahiers,* when he presumably wavered between faith and unfaith, will further illustrate the underlying sameness of Gide's religious stance over the years. He writes in 1892, one year before his first journey to Africa—which is the external concomitant of his presumed movement away from the faith of his youth: "To know . . . to know what?"[25] and in April, 1893: "We shall no longer ask God to raise us up to happiness. Why, indeed! We know very well that *I* am weak. (Too many things in that sentence. Let's not deny anything. Let's go on)."[26] During the fifty-eight remaining years of his life Gide never wavered from this notion. "A clear understanding of God," he wrote in 1894, "makes one want to follow the direction of things, the direction of oneself."[27] *Les Faux-Monnayeurs,* published in 1926, develops that same theme among others.

Gide could at short or long intervals express the same basic idea with or without conventional religious terminology. There is no practical difference, for example, between the advocacy of the pursuit of truth, as distinguished from its possession, and the declaration that "to know God is to seek him." Both notions were entered by Gide in his *Journal* in October, 1894. He speaks in the same year of God as "the rewarder, the just supervisor."[28] Decades later, as he observes in Chad the payment of a homage to a tribal chief, he is led to wonder whether God will "likewise" take pleasure in hearing prayers and litanies.[29]

The expression at different times of identical concepts through changing symbols is not a process to which the name "evolution" properly applies. Beneath Gide's diverse imagery there is, first, the god that is held in the mind as if a specific, mentally encompassable object corresponded to it, and, secondly, God, the indeterminate reality that includes, envelops, and transcends one's own being, somewhat in the manner of Jaspers' *Umgreifende,* translated as the "Comprehensive" or the "Encompassing." In the former of these he never quite believed, while he always maintained his faith in the latter. A reality that included him should at least be personal, as Gide indicated in various ways.

Gide maintained both in his youth and later in life that it is impossible to "believe" and "know" simultaneously, inasmuch, he said, as these two concepts are mutually exclusive. He regretfully admitted in 1937 that he used to localize God in a certain suprasensual region,[30] which is another instance of one's knowing God in one's head, since the objects of rational knowledge are, by the fact of their being known, totally other than the subject who knows them. Gide gave expression to his own, antirationalistic theology in other ways:

> To try to prove that God exists is just as absurd as to assert that he does not exist.
> For our assertions and our proofs will not create him . . . or suppress him.[31]

The implication here that only that god can be proved which has been created by man is incidental to the basic declaration of lack of confidence in metaphysics. Gide intimates elsewhere that metaphysics is a form of poetry. He sings in *Les Nourritures Terrestres* the "roundelay of the beautiful proofs of the existence of God," of which there are "one thousand and one." He lists six of these. His treatment of them as poetry would have been akin to logical empiricism had he resisted the temptation of advancing, not without a measure of facetiousness, six counterproofs. In the one against the argument from motion he regrets the fact that "we" were not there to ascertain the claim.[32] Belonging as he does on Augustine's and Anselm's side of the fence of theology, he writes in the same vein in 1916: "No, I shall not help you to believe. You know well that on the contrary . . . so that there may be nothing but what is absurd and loving in your faith; and so that it may be withdrawn from the learned and permitted to the humble."[33]

The opposition of humility to learning is of course a piece of pious inanity. Gide is using *learned* here in the special sense of "proud of knowing and clever in discursive reasoning." He had written more positively in the same year: "I can believe in God, believe God, love God, and my whole heart inclines me to do so. I can make my heart dominate my mind. But, I beg you, don't look for proofs and reasons. That is where man's imperfection begins; and I felt myself to be perfect in love."[34]

God does not therefore name an entity that can be reached at the top rung of a rationally constructed ladder. Such an entity may be "your God," who must be dethroned in order to make room for God. Thus when Gide writes for example, announcing Bonhoeffer, that "the best means of keeping Him from failing us is to learn to get along without him," he is advocating not the absence of God but a certain attitude toward God whose reality is thereby affirmed.[35]

Five Reasons for Rejecting "Your God"

A first reason that leads Gide to reject "your God" is that there is discrepancy between the manner in which good and bad things are distributed among men, and "your" notion that God is a good and omnipotent person, with known moral preferences, who cares for each human being. Actually this distribution, unrelated as it is to any humanly discernible standard, makes belief in such a god unwarranted. These ideas can be gathered from Gide's *Prométhée mal enchaîné (Prometheus Illbound)*, the story of man's self-divinization by lifting *himself* up. Decades after *Le Prométhée* Gide admired Baron Munchausen for "tearing himself from the morass by pulling himself by the hair."[36] Prometheus is a product of our urban culture. His story begins "on the boulevard leading from the Madeleine to the Opéra." He is also a product of the Industrial Revolution. He is a manufacturer of matchsticks: he produces his own fire, does not steal it from heaven. He is neither bound nor unbound, but ill-bound: he is neither unfree nor free, but *can* free himself, provided he commands the means thereto, and, more importantly, provided he is willing to exert the required effort.

One may see in Gide's Prometheus and the latter's eagle a certain parallel with Christ and the Dove. The eagle comes from above, but unlike the Dove he is ugly, meagre, and famished. Prometheus chooses to feed him his liver, and accepts the necessary pain which is a way of taking up the challenge of man's expulsion from Paradise. Adam was driven out of Paradise as he proceeded to decide for himself what is good and what is bad. Gide's answer to the writer of Genesis is that man cannot but *be* the author of his own moral judgment and take upon himself the agonizing responsibility of perfecting his own conscience. It is neither healthy nor useful to entertain the regret of an original innocence, and expect a fictitious agency to help man regain it, or a heightened form of it.

The god who is criticized in *Le Prométhée mal enchaîné* appears under the guise of a banker of limitless means, his money being a most appropriate symbol of what Christians generally call "blessings." He—"the Miglionaire"—is no less a god than Zeus himself. The manner in which he hands out his blessings ushers in the central problem of the book which was also that of Job: not so much the existence as the senseless distribution, of good and evil. There is, Gide intimates, a wrong way that men can adopt in their effort to make sense out of this senseless-ness; it consists in looking for and eventually finding a supernatural dis-tributor of blessings. There are devotees of such a distributor who allege that one basis of his seemingly erratic behavior must be a judiciously held secret of his own. Damocles, one of the principal characters of *Le Prométhée,* accidentally receives from Zeus the sum of five hundred francs. He looks for someone who, responsible for the windfall, must have brought it to pass for a reason. This supposition fills him with anxiety and drives him to his own destruction.

Thus the problem of the absurdity of the world is posed, but the reader is not permitted to acquiesce in it. Gide, unwittingly perhaps, leads the reader's gaze beyond the limits of the world. Potentialities, we are told, are "lent" to people. It is the Miglionaire who purveys eagles, though he himself does not possess one. It is clear, at any rate, that the sort of humanism advocated in *Le Prométhée* does not entail atheism. The eagle represents man's *raison d'être,* and is a power that overcomes the dis-junction present in man's self-consciousness. On the other hand, the Miglionaire, who gives the eagle, lets people call him the good God—an indication that the generality of believers are mistaken not as to the existence of God, but as to his identity. The point of *Le Prométhée* is that there are those to whom Zeus the Banker, a caricature of God, *is* God. It is an indictment of the notion that belief in such a god is an effective or the proper cure against the anxiety induced by the world's absurdity.

Gide who was and remained a dualist constantly drawn toward monism, makes in *Le Prométhée* a sharp distinction between men as moral agents and men as products of nature. While this position follows the pattern of the soul-body dualism of his youth, he tells us in an essay written considerably after *Le Prométhée* that God is two very different things: he refers to them as the Zeus side and the Prometheus side. Zeus is reality minus everything that is personal and moral. It is things which do not change—"cosmos, the natural laws that regulate it, matter, forces, ener-gies." The Prometheus side could also be called the Christ side. It is the opening up of man in the manner of an opening flower as well as his progress in virtue. "*This* God" does not at all inhabit nature. He exists in and through man. He creates himself through man. Nor is there any point in trying to exteriorize him through prayer. The conflict between Zeus and Prometheus Gide finds irreconcilable. He finds Christ's words on the cross meaningless because Zeus is the Father and the Father had not really abandoned the Son (i.e., Prometheus or Christ); indeed he had not *adopted* him in the first place. Gide tells us towards the end of his little essay that he believes in and worships the Son of Man or Prometheus, or Christ, which is not the cosmos but an indwelling, personal power of cohesion and the promise of salvation.[37]

Not much can be retained from this phantasmagoria of a creed. How, for example, is it possible to make such a radical distinction between "nature" and "man"? However, if we do not try to understand the essay in detail—which would be a fruitless endeavor—but concentrate on its general suggestions it becomes evident that the God in whom Gide believes is all-inclusive, that He is man's hope of salvation, and that He is, in the final analysis, worthy of worship in His nonmaterial side. Elements of the Christian doctrines of the Incarnation and of the Trinity seep into this creed inasmuch as Prometheus or Christ, who is a side of God but also God, exists through man and creates himself.

A second reason for Gide's impatience with conventional theism is that it is an obstacle to human achievement. "Who dares say," he wrote in 1931, "that man without God is capable of less virtue, of less effort?"[38] This rhetorical question announces a conviction voiced more positively during his Socialistic enthusiasms of the mid-thirties, when he was under the impression that theism is in the way to the millenium.[39] Communism, he then thought, was devoid of mythology and paved its own scientific way toward the ideal society. His eventual disenchantment with that system did not prevent him from continuing to encourage the project of bringing about the ideal society without supernatural assistance. In 1915 he had already condemned "the confidence based on a faith in Providence" as a form of irresponsibility.[40] The initial urge to improve the world could come as a consequence of the conviction that the present state of things is *intolerable,* and only a few Christians were dissatisfied with the status quo to the point of being moved to correct it: "Why, how, do they happen to be the exception among Christians? It is, alas, only too easy to answer this question with another question: how can one consider intolerable what one believes to be willed by God?"[41]

Actually theism and zeal for social betterment are not mutually exclusive.[42] It is, moreover, Gide himself who often claimed that that which is is because it ought to have been—a philosophy hardly conducive to the expenditure of the planned effort required to improve the world. Nevertheless, his "comrades" were told in *Les Nouvelles Nourritures* that the new man will emerge out of man himself, man being, as Gide incongruously acknowledged in the very same breath, insane and ferocious. He then says unexpectedly "that all that can be will be, if man *helps.*" Who or what it is that will *receive* the help Gide does not care to specify[43] because he is not certain—as a general survey of his writings reveals—that the course of history is determined by man. But a man can discern the direction in which history is bound to move, and opt to behave accordingly; he can make of himself, reflectively, an instrument of historical realization, and thereby transcend time—to transcend time meaning to make of oneself an active witness of the obliteration of the distance between that which is possible and that which is. Another manner of summarizing Gide's approach to history is to say with St. Paul that those who have the first fruits of the Spirit wait for adoption as sons. The point is that the entity whom Gide conceives as an obstacle to human progress is not the God of concerned Christians. God is not "the gods" of the following entry made in 1940.

When a certain stage of history is reached, everything appears in the guise of a problem. And man's responsibility increases as that of the gods decreases.

It devolves upon man alone, in the final reckoning, to solve all these problems which he alone has *presumably* raised.[44]

One of these problems concerns the very fate of mankind: "The gods have decidedly failed," he writes some ten years later in *Ainsi soit-il (So Be It)*, "and man himself must check humanity's collapse."[45] Gide's sitting in judgment of "the gods"—who have failed to pass the test of their divinity required by men—makes the gods inferior to men and temporal entities. Perhaps the clearest exposition of this second reason for Gide's opposition to "your God" is an entry of August 2, 1931: "Struggle against what? . . . As soon as one considers man and not God as responsible, one can no longer resign oneself to anything." Atheism is therefore the condition of the removal of evil. But to understand properly this thought, announcing as it does the beginnings of Gide's more or less formal adherence to communism, one must read it in connection with the following, written six years earlier:

In this world: real sufferings; imaginary sufferings. The first can be attenuated; the second almost suppressed. They most often result from a belief in *idols*— or in bogeymen. The former are constructions that are venerated and do not deserve to be. The latter are phantoms that are feared and do not deserve to be.[46]

A third reason for Gide's refusal to believe in "your God" is that such belief curtails human freedom and does not permit one to act in the direction of one's value, for the alternative to acting in this direction is self-suppression: "If I do not act in the direction of my value, it is as if I were suppressing myself."[47] Gide was aware as most other people that there is a logical conflict between "God's prescience" and "man's freedom" which is the moral counterpart of the impossibility of God's being all if man is something in his own right. "Adoration kills the individual,"[48] he said very early in his writing career. He wrote again much later: "Amazing intellectual acrobatics in order to get to the point of believing that only one's own weakness keeps one from reconciling God's prescience with man's freedom, the X with the M, etc."[49]

He is probably referring here to an article he had read. His own undeclared position in this matter is that as the existence of "your God," of "the fierce Jehovah" is admitted, the necessity arises of finding a *modus vivendi* with him, which may end in the practical clash of two wills. In such a situation only one of the two wills must and can prevail. Gide subjected himself for a time to the other will, to a puritanical code which had been taught to him as the rule of Christ, but he never did so without difficulty, without misgivings. Contrary to what some of his entries may suggest, he always asked himself whether God really exacts such constraints, though it was some time before he analyzed these constraints as continual rebellion, a stance against God. "I gradually came to wonder ... whether, in the struggle that divided me, it was reasonable to consider the opponent always in the wrong. It dawned upon me at last that this discordant duality might possibly be resolved into harmony."[50]

Several strands of thought run into each other in this outcry, and the whole passage becomes confusing. A question immediately precedes the passage just quoted: "In the name of what God or what ideal, do you forbid me to live according to my nature?" One ought therefore to be allowed to live according to one's nature, an injunction which does not exclude the principle that one must do what one feels like doing. But no sooner is this suggestion made than it is virtually retracted. The advisability of a course of action should be based rather on a consideration of its consequences: Where would that nature lead me if I simply followed it? There arises in the third place the necessity of avoiding impiety by living according to, and not ignoring, the will of God.

The outcry is Protestant in the sense that it is a secular echo of Luther's reputed "here I stand I can do no other." It has its earlier, more subdued variants. Gide was writing in 1894 that temptations or desires do not come from God and that they turn us away from his contemplation. They were not, however, all capable of being suppressed. In fact, a too-long resistance to desires might excite them and cause the soul to be unbalanced. He wanted to honor God with the totality of his being, and seek him everywhere, "suppress nothing with a view to a partial exaltation." He spoke of admiration where others felt gratitude. He wanted to know God only in the study of all things. "And that admiration . . . gave me the love of duty. The laws of nature are those of God: happy is he who can know them and follow them; what has he to do with commandments?"[51]

The position of the young writer is clear, a position which does not change, but gains precision and strength with the years: a detailed code of morality coming from Someone Else cannot be binding if it does not take into account the—largely psychological—well-being of the individual. Moral prescriptions must be flexible enough to allow freedom of self-expression to individual idiosyncrasies. Belief in an individual god stands in the way of this principle.

In connection with Gide's opposition to conventional theism, one may observe in the fourth place that God did not have to be Someone Else in order to be an agency curtailing man's freedom. He could do so as an *idea*. Gide was familiar with the work of Alfred Fouillée and welcomed his philosophy that certain ideas hold their own power within them. The theory of the *idées-forces* was a way of placing within man his motor principles, a manner of thinking which was bound to please Gide. "An idea continues to be a living force so long as all the nourishment in it has not been used up in phenomena," he writes in the same vein.[52] Occasionally God *is* the idea of God: "It is a disturbing thought," he was already saying in 1896, at the age of twenty-seven, "that man needs a tradition, a history, to understand an eternal God. The history of God can only be the history of what men have thought him to be."[53] He wrote again thirty-one years later, while proclaiming his stance against absolute nihilism and his determination to rebuild *beyond* that negative philosophy, after having passed through it: "It strikes me as monstrous that man should need the idea of God in order to feel steady on earth; that he should be forced by him to accept absurdities in order to construct something solid; . . . so that he lets himself go to nothing as soon as his heaven is empty."[54]

Some years before his death he tried to clarify to himself the nature of

his atheism and his motivations behind it: "Get along without God. . . .
I mean: get along without the idea of God, without a belief in an attentive, tutelary, and retributive Providence . . . not everyone can achieve
this."[55] Gide had long ago learned ostensibly from Leibniz to distinguish
between "truth" and "idea." "Truth," he writes, "belongs to God; the
idea belongs to man."[56] An idea is, at best, a piece of truth. It is broken.
Thus when God is thought of as an object, reducible to one idea among
many, the thinker is already in error. Gide is subject to the temptation
of "drawing" God mentally, while he reacts to the limitations inherent
in that habit. This leads to the fifth and possibly the major reason for
his opposition to "your God."

Gide the artist was tempted to ascribe existence only to those objects
which are artistically expressible, a circumstance which is the esthetic
equivalent of the identity of the rational and the real. In the following
observation made in 1931 he appears to be aware of the difficulties involved in religious symbolism, while he exhibits his abiding preference
for things new and untried. He quotes from a letter written by a soldier
to the soldier's mother: "What does it avail me to be spared by bullets
and shells if I lose my soul? *This is the way people would have expressed
themselves in the past.*" The emphasis is added by Gide, who goes on to
comment: "What no longer has a name for him [i.e., for Franz Blumen-
feldt, the soldier] is nevertheless what it is important for him to preserve.
Is there really any need to have recourse to idolatry?"[57]

One has recourse to idolatry, in other words, when one names the un-
nameable or draws that which cannot be drawn with words, lines, or
otherwise. We have seen Gide build images in order to lead the reader
beyond them. He was impatient with those who were not so led.[58] He
himself read the story of Christianity as he wished others to read his
own stories. His understanding if it is not always in purely moral terms;
indeed this understanding displays at times a poignant orthodoxy. Consider this passage written in reference to his concerns of a social nature.

I turn my mind away from such questions and refuse to grant them that
importance which they had, only recently, in my eyes. . . . It is *in order
to be crucified* that Christ comes on earth, and to save us by this indispensable
sacrifice toward which his whole life led him. Any effort to detach Christ
from that necessary cross thenceforth becomes outrageous, for it would reduce
his mission to nothing. In order to see merely an accident in the crucifixion,
as I tried to do, one must first take away Christ's divinity.[59]

Precisely because he was and remained a religious person, Gide was unusually sensitive to the now patent fact that "the category 'God' " had lost significance, and was engaged, in his own way, in doing what a New Testament scholar said must be done: "If the category 'God' as a propositional reality has lost significance along with the whole structure of thought to which it belongs, it is urgent that his reality be recovered in another context."[60]

Prayer and Faith

At a time when he was in the habit of using more conventional religious language Gide defined prayer as "praise of God" or, in a more striking phrase, as the "oratorical form of the soul."[61] He also defined it as "a reflection of You returning to You when You look upon me," which may be used as a definition of the "orison" of the mystics.[62] He will on occasion think of prayer as dialogue with oneself, a view which agrees with the theory, itself held on occasion, that God is a projection.[63] By the same token when he rejects prayer as a "telephone call"[64] he is rejecting the one who is supposed to be the receiver of the call. Both Anthime of *Les Caves du Vatican* and Michel of *L'Immoraliste* refuse to pray because that act would be a betrayal of their confidence in themselves.

A prayer of petition is an invitation extended to "your God," to induce him to change his mind or intervene in the affairs of the world. It is an admission of impotence, a sign of distortion: "I call a 'warped mind' the one that believes a God can come and keep his eye on, or poke his finger or his nose into, the tasks of this earth."[65]

Gide dealt with the question of faith largely in *Les Cahiers d'André Walter.* In that book three views are put forth with regard to faith. He expressed these same views more sharply later, without reconciling them. Faith was, in the first place, a manner of deluding oneself in order to make life more bearable. In the following passage the term "Providence" is used almost synonymously with "God," and meaning not, for example, "inner directedness," but supervision from the outside:

Providence: all their life is based on one hypothesis; . . . But . . . they will never know whether they were wrong in believing. If there is nothing, they will not be aware of anything.—In the meantime, they believe; they are happy, or console themselves with hopes.[66]

Uncritical consent to propositions stating, for example, the self-conscious survival of individual souls is the sort of faith Gide derides as unverifiable, opposed to reason, and blind. The idea is adumbrated in *Les Cahiers* and entertained throughout his life: "as long as reason has not spoken, no struggles are required in order to believe."[67] Besides the diagnosis of faith as illusion, and his consideration of it as opposed to reason, Gide viewed it more favorably, in the third place, as "confidence" in God, abandon of self. He went so far as to see within the situation of faith a transfiguration of reason. The "sacrifice" of reason was still required, but then it would be rediscovered a hundredfold. The meaning of the rediscovery of reason a hundredfold is not clear. Reason must mean to Gide in this as in certain other instances something other than reasoning reason,[68] perhaps a general term covering the very humanity of a man.

Gide's "confidence" in God accompanies a certain sense of contingency or creatureliness, a feeling that is not absent in his writings even when he is least inclined to admit it. One of his more famous questions is: "Is it my fault if your God took such great care to have me born between two stars . . . ?"[69] Though he does not profess to believe in that god, the tenor of the question indicates clearly a sense of dependence. The fact that he is the man he is is not *his* fault, while it must also be noted that what he is, is not his *fault*. Gide never quite overcame a lingering sense of guilt, due partly no doubt to the teaching he received as a boy that man is hopelessly depraved and that there is nothing he can do to work his own salvation. Gide does not always exhibit his religious sense of dependence in connection with the symbol "God" which he uses in a number of meanings. There are certain conditions of existence, or ways of behavior, or projected states of affairs of which he says in earnest that they are God. This is the God whom he accepts. Or, to put it differently, he has no quarrel with theism provided God is described in terms congenial with the preoccupations of his period,[70] and in a way as to avoid idolatry.

The Meanings of "God"

Jean Hytier has observed that as the result of "a kind of stubbornness, Gide has never ceased referring to all the objects of his desire as God."[71] Gide himself admits that he has given the name God to everything he loved, and that he has wanted to love everything.[72] His mother had once described an atheist as a *vilain sot*.[73] To hold on to the word *God* while changing its meaning at every turn was perhaps a way of avoiding being a villainous blockhead. Keeping that word while filling it with varied meanings of one's own has another advantage: with the theist one can say "I believe in God," meaning, with the atheist, that one believes for example in Progress.

Gide's insistence on referring to a future state of affairs—where all the ambiguities of human existence will have been solved—as "God" is a symptom of considerable importance. It must be an unintended acknowledgment that nature, the realm of time, points beyond itself. "Your God" is rejected, yet a divine presence is surreptitiously assured. Sacredness is ascribed to a secular condition by giving it a sacred name. In this case Gide wishes his hearers to attach to "Progress" the emotional reactions that were heretofore reserved to "God." Moreover, the God-Future identification solves neatly the perennial problem of divine immanence and transcendence: the Future is in a sense other than this world and "transcendent," but it is also organically related to the Present and therefore constitutes part of our reality and is "immanent."

There is a series of misty statements made in January, 1916, to the effect that God is not someone to be known, that he must be felt, and that, perhaps, God is love. He writes on January 30:

If I had to formulate a credo, I should say: God is not behind us. He is to come. He must be sought, not at the beginning, but at the end of the evolution. He is terminal and not initial. He is the supreme and final point toward which all nature tends in time. And since time does not exist for Him, it is a matter of indifference to Him whether that evolution of which He is the summit follows or precedes, and whether He determines it by propulsion or attraction.

It is through man that God is molded. That is what I feel and believe and what I understand in the words: "Let man be created in Our Image." What can all the doctrines of evolution do against that thought?

This is the gate through which I enter into the holy place, this is the series of thoughts that lead me back to God, to the Gospels, etc. . . .

Will I some day succeed in setting this forth clearly?

For a long time already I have believed this without knowing it, and now it becomes clear in me through a series of successive illuminations. The reasoning follows.[74]

Gide's credo is of interest because it is not impossible to see in it a hazy anticipation of some more modern trends including the concept of the "God ahead," and the Theology of Hope. It may even constitute a criticism of the belief, elaborated in France by Condorcet and other like-minded students of history, that salvation is a temporal affair and is to be achieved by man himself. The application by Gide of the term "God" to "the end of evolution" is tantamount to admission that evolution is more than a natural process. Before the first paragraph of the passage quoted above comes to an end, eager as he is to subsume time into an eternal order, he reverts to a widely quoted biblical image: God is the end *and* the beginning. He is the alpha and the omega. The only non-biblical concept in this creed is that of evolution. By the end of the second paragraph it too is viewed from a biblical perspective.

So insistently did Gide identify God with the Future in his conscious mind that he occasionally used the concepts interchangeably as in the following entry made in Tunis during the Second World War: "Can there be a more wretched humanity than the one I see here? One wonders what God could ever possibly come forth from these sordid creatures, bent over toward the most immediate satisfactions, tattered, dusty, abject, and forsaken by the future."[75] This is the vantage point from which to understand his famous remark to the effect that God is disappointingly slow in becoming. That God *is* not but *becomes* was a conviction, Gide said, which restored his ethical sense,[76] the implication being that he found in this formula a ground on which religion and morality could be reconciled, or, rather, morality could be given an ultimate, religious support.

In the light of Gide's doctrine of God's gradual realization by man, it should be baffling to read a remark made later, and without intent of correcting himself, that the world is not *as yet* ready "to get along without God."[77] If this is the case, then God or the idea of God does not come into, but vanishes out of, existence gradually. But the contradiction is superficial, and the reason for it not difficult to detect. A pivotal word is used in both instances in two clearly different meanings: in the second instance *God* is "your God." Gide's own God is a promise, never entirely subject to categories of space and time.

God meant to Gide a number of other things, all more or less related to or variants of a state of affairs purged of the vicissitudes of our present existence. Nathanaël—who is, with Ménalque, Gide himself looking upon his pointlessly frustrated youth—is bid not to distinguish between God and his happiness.[78] Alissa in *La Porte étroite* places God and *her* happiness at the same distance from herself.[79] In order to exhaust all the Gidian meanings of *God* one would have to quote the better part of his work. He used it to refer to such concepts as virtue, truth, love, nature, or natural laws, and was himself aware that it served as a handy receptacle for his uncertain metaphysical notions.[80] There is in his thinking an occasional undercurrent of Aristotelianism. God is also substance, and the efficient and final cause of things. "It is much more difficult than one thinks not to believe in God," Gide says in *Les Nouvelles Nourritures*. "The slightest agitation of matter—why should it rise? And toward what?"[81] He will say on another occasion that God *is* not what he creates. He *is* not man. He makes him.[82]

It goes without saying that Gide's more remarkable theological views do not constitute a beginning. That theories which were then in the air —though not visibly so—found their way into his thought is another indication of his *disponibilité,* as well as of his prophetic sensitivity. One certainty remained with him as he kept returning to the problem of God which obsessed him. He made this entry in 1896: "Since there is something, it is God."[83] The argument is of unusual interest in view of a statement made later by an eminent contemporary theologian: "The genuine mystery appears when reason is driven beyond itself to its "ground and abyss," to that which "precedes" reason, to the fact that "being is and non-being is not" (Parmenides), to the original fact *(Ur-Tatsache)* that there is *something* and not *nothing.*"[84]

Tillich calls this the "negative side" of the mystery. Gide had an awareness of it throughout his life. He wrote in 1928: "To say, in *Les Nouvelles Nourritures*: 'Nathanaël, my friend, you are not sufficiently astonished that there is . . . something. And as soon as there is something, it can only be God.' "[85]

In 1947 after repeating the old formulae that "God is virtue," that He "lies ahead," that He depends on, and is achieved through, us, Gide wrote again:

There might very well be nothing; nor anyone. No one to notice that there is nothing, and to consider that natural.

But that there is something, and, whatever it may be, the strange thing! I shall never cease being amazed at this.

Something and not complete nonexistence. It required centuries of centuries to produce that something, to get that, whatever it may be, from chaos. Even more centuries to obtain the least life.[86]

Precision was not one of the virtues of Gide the creative artist, as he abstractly treated metaphysical matters. The point to be retained here is that he could never quite abandon the notion of the Absolute. Toward the reality which does not admit of finitude, definiteness; contains the world; militates against its absurdity and man's loneliness; saves the course of history from being a purposeless, chaotic adventure—toward this reality Gide had an attitude of worship. That genuinely religious attitude will be apparent as the meaning of a pivotal Gidian word is clarified. That word is *Em*.

5

Em.

Emmanuèle and Nathanaël

Em. is an abbreviation of *Emmanuèle,* the name given by Gide in *Les Cahiers d'André Walter* to the young woman with whom the hero of that story is in love. Em. happens also to be the first letter of *Madeleine*—the name of Gide's cousin, whom he married—and of the word *mère.* After *Les Cahiers* Gide seldom referred to Madeleine by her name. He referred to her as Em. for the simple reason, no doubt, that to him she *was* Em., the person depicted in his first creative work. To assume that the use of *Em.* instead of *Madeleine* was a mere convenience would be a gross error. *Em.* had to Gide a complex meaning of its own, and to this complexity contributed his reactions to his mother.

The daughter of a rich man, Gide's mother had married an intellectual of modest means. Her requirements of a moral nature did not make life for Paul Gide, a professor of law, a thing of joy. There are passages in *Si le grain ne meurt* which suggest that Monsieur Gide did not enjoy the companionship of his wife as much as that of "Mademoiselle Anna." This was the manner in which Paul Gide addressed Miss Shackleton, his wife's, and then André's, Scottish nurse. André was eleven years old when his father died. The "meditative, introverted"[1] child now became the sole object of the devotion of his mother, who proceeded with characteristic firmness to bring him as close as possible to her ideal of a virtuous man. The conventional, conservative clothes she selected for him remained in Gide's memory as symbols of the tight rules to which he was subjected. He was not exactly a spoiled child:

. . . I have already said how careful my mother was not to give me more indulgences than other less happily circumstanced children; but she never proposed I should make any change in my habits or break the magic circle of my good fortune. I was well off without knowing it; just as I was French and Protestant without knowing it; outside this magic circle everything seemed foreign to me.[2]

Madame Gide does not impress one with the scope of her learning. She had neither a naturally brilliant mind nor an independent esthetic judgment. She displayed interest in artistic happenings as if in compliance with the fittingness of things, was an occasional commentator on the political developments of the day and a teacher to her son, by word and example, of fundamentalist Christianity.

Gide did disobey this puritanical woman, but not as a matter of course. More often than not disobedience meant wrenchingly acute inner conflict. It was never quite open or defiant. Nor was it ever final, for he always remained with her, and she with him. She was with him as his sense of duty, for example. "I have always loved duty, and it is when I am most free that I feel farthest from happiness," Gide, the reputed hedonist, wrote in 1929. He wrote two years later of the "paradoxical" truth that man's happiness lies not in freedom but in the acceptance of duty and admitted that this was of considerable psychological importance to him.[3] It has been observed that all his women, and only his women, are duty incarnate.[4] They are partially the creation of a man who constantly had the "strange" need of justifying himself.[5]

As the inevitable holder of a position of unique importance in a magic circle in the midst of the real world, Gide's mother turned into something of an idea around which Gide, the sensitive and imaginative inhabitant of that magic circle, wove the fulfillment of his religious requirements. Yet her concrete reality, as a person out there, apart from him, could not be done away with. It was, as such, a regrettable presence. This circumstance accounts for the ambiguity of Gide's attitude toward her.

In *Et nunc manet in te (Madeleine)* Gide tells the story of his equally ambiguous relationship with Madeleine. The book is followed by a Journal in the manner of *La Porte étroite,* an arrangement which is one more evidence of the narrow distance between report and fiction in Gide's writings. The tensions between Jerome and Alissa of *La Porte étroite* are found almost unchanged in *Et nunc manet in te.* The figure of Madeleine traced here is essentially that of Alissa: the same integrity, the same resignation, the same capacity to renounce, the same lack of concern with physical appearance, the same sensitivity and refinement.

Jean Schlumberger, a friend of long standing of the Gides, tries to cor-

rect in his *Madeleine et André Gide* some of the distortions which Gide
has allowed himself in *Et nunc manet in te,* published posthumously.
Schlumberger fails to see a faithful portrait of Madeleine in *Et nunc
manet in te* for understandable reasons. Gide, the creative artist, never
"photographed" his subject. Any good writer could do that. Gide's sub-
jects were, moreover, excuses to draw portraits of himself in the world.
They put forth, directly or indirectly, his moral and religious preferences
or idiosyncrasies. To this rule *Et nunc manet in te* is no exception.

That Gide's life and ideas are functions of his relationship with Em. is
evident. Justin O'Brien rightly observes that "one can only agree with
[Gide's] mature judgment that his pure love for his wife served to divide him more radically than he already was split." At the same time
"Madeleine was necessary to his development. . . . Without her as witness
of his life, he might never have resolved his contradictions in the equilibrium of art." Professor O'Brien goes on to write:

In the large yellow house at Cuverville in which everything shone with polish
and breathed bourgeois virtues, as in the obscure recesses of his mind she
seemed to maintain the systole and diastole rhythm to which he had early
become accustomed.[6]

Madeleine fills in Gide's life the vacancy left by his mother's death.
Thus *Em.* denotes under Gide's pen a composite presence. It is Mme
Gide and Madeleine together, or their identities telescoped into one.
Functionally, Em. is the mother-bride of ancient myths. One need not
subject Gide's writings to a lengthy analysis to arrive at that simple con-
clusion. He says it himself very plainly:

. . . my wife's face often subtly and almost mystically takes the place of my
mother's without really surprising me. The outlines of the faces are not sharp
enough to keep me from shifting from one to the other; my emotion is keen
enough, but its cause is ill-defined. Indeed, the role played by each in my
dreams is about the same: an inhibitory role. And this explains or motivates
the substitution.[7]

The inhibitory role in question must be understood against a background wider than the one which seems to be intended here. The difficulties of Gide with Em. can be traced in the final analysis to the problems
of the nature of her presence. This presence was indispensable to him
and he sought it above all else. At the same time it annoyed him un-
bearably. As he changes his focus Gide sees in Em.'s physical presence

now the sign of her spiritual reality (and then her absence is mourned), now a limited and limiting person (and then he resents her).

It is possible to explain Gide's resentment of Em. in psychological and moral terms. Shying away as he did from heterosexual intimacy, Gide was of the opinion that what he took for chastity in his youth was really homosexuality. It may be, however, that his homosexuality was rooted in turn in circumstances determined by the place that his mother and, by extension, women older than himself occupied in his world. In his projected or attempted intimacies with them repressed incestuous tendencies reduced him to impotence. Speaking of his marriage he writes in *Et nunc manet in te*:

. . . the spiritual force of my love inhibited all carnal desire. For I was elsewhere able to prove that I was not incapable of the impulse (I am speaking of the procreative impulse), but only providing that there was no admixture of the intellectual or the sentimental.[8]

Gide's sexuality and his likes and dislikes in that domain should be a matter of indifference to the world except perhaps for purposes of clinical research. More important from our point of view is the fact that Gide appears to be singularly blind to what is truly the case. Unprejudiced self-examination would have revealed for example that the occasions substantiating the claim made in the above quotation involve, to limit the observation to women, those younger than himself. An Algerian woman, En Barka, is, like his wife, older:

En Barka was much too beautiful . . . ; her very beauty froze me; I felt a kind of admiration for her but not the smallest trace of desire. I came to her as a worshipper without an offering. . . . Caresses, provocations, nothing availed; I was mute, and left her without having been able to give her anything but money.[9]

Unless we assume that hidden associations were at work in Gide, the phrase *"a kind of admiration"* and *worship* remain incomprehensible. Clearly the Arab woman—to whom Gide was no more than another French client—was the occasion of his emotions while the admiration and worship were directed to some other, essentially intangible, object. The worshipful character of this object disarmed Gide. It rid him of, or overcame, his aggressiveness. It produced in him a sort of religious submission. The point must be stressed here that Gide's, as anyone's, relationship with his mother does not entirely explain, but is rather paradigmatic of his attitude toward the reality where he has his being and with which he deals. Justin O'Brien, having pointed out that "Emmanuel is interpreted in the Bible as 'God with us!'" writes in the Introduction to his translation of *Et nunc manet in te*: "Throughout his life his wife appeared to André Gide as his refuge, his anchor to windward, his link with tradition and the past, his protection against everything in himself that he feared, and his possible salvation."[10]

Gide himself was no doubt aware of the connotations that the name has in the Bible where its bearer is a promise of security to Ahaz. While Gide saw Em. as God's presence *in* the world, he referred to himself in the *Nourritures Terrestres* as Nathanaël, a name meaning "God has given (*to* the world)." The motives behind the choice of the name Emmanuèle —pointing as it does to its bearer's power to relieve Gide's solitariness— are further clarified in the following passage from *Les Cahiers,* evocative of a mother figure: "Sleep overcomes me;—lying at your feet, on your knees, oh! I would like to rest my head. . . . To dream—to forget that one is alone . . . Emmanuèle."[11]

Em.'s Two Dimensions

Madeleine as a physically present person confused and embarrassed him nevertheless. The prospect of its possession frightened him, and he was sincere enough to declare it to Madeleine in *Les Cahiers d'André Walter*: ". . . I do not desire you," the hero of that first work declares, "your body embarrasses me and carnal possession frightens me." In *La Porte étroite* Jerome plays with Juliette, Alissa's sister, whereas with Alissa herself the communication, much deeper, is as between André Walter and Emmanuèle—they converse and read together; their physical proximity provides no more than the possibility of a spiritual communion. Jerome, who is said to be in love with a "phantom," deplores "the absurd position of being engaged" to Alissa because society then behaves in a way that encourages their physical intimacy. The lovers resent this reaction to their engagement. When their marriage becomes a possibility, a meeting between them, though eagerly anticipated, results in a fiasco. While they walk by themselves alone, the discomfort of feeling the contact of their damp hands makes them unclasp and let them drop sadly to their sides.

By way of analyzing this situation one may have recourse to the abundance of Freudian images in *La Porte étroite*. Alissa cuts off the heads of faded flowers and picks unripe fruits during a walk with her father, secretly watched by Jerome. On another occasion she and Jerome sit on the edge of an open garden frame through which sprawl huge stalks of cucumber plants, the last fruits of which have been gathered. On the other hand, it is at least amusing to note that in *La Tentative amoureuse,* published in 1893, Luc wishes for love but he too is afraid of carnal possessions. Even though voluptuousness is declared glorious and serene, the hero watches Rachel bathing naked under the leaves near a valley "narrow and tortuous, without a stream, where grow furze and gorse and the wind chases sand." Rarely if ever does one find in Gide's work a favorable reference to a valley. This detail, along with Alissa's cutting off the heads of faded flowers, her picking unripe fruits, as well as the gathering of cucumbers, should arouse the particular interest of those who follow Freud in his interpretation of dreams. As to Alissa's death in *La Porte étroite,* it may well be the secret fulfillment of a wish inasmuch as she represents maternal authority. Nearly all the women of Gide's tales are killed in one way or another. A damaged Gide turns to the female body, declares it uninviting, and takes his revenge.

Such analyses fail to get at the root of the matter. Even if entirely valid, they are but models of a more universal conflict. This conflict is seen in its comprehensiveness in *Le Voyage d'Urien.*

Ellis, the artistic likeness of Em. in that imaginary journey, is seen as through a bifocal lens: Ellis of the Sargossa Sea and Ellis who makes Urien aware, in herself, of the aurora borealis. The former is an obstacle to Urien's most profound yearnings: "Ellis, . . . you are an obstacle to my confusion with God and I will be unable to love you except as melted, you too, in God himself." Then she reappears in the supertemporal world of the Pole. She has now assumed her true self, no longer a mere woman. "By the side of a river one day," Urien tells her, "I thought I had found you anew, but it was only a woman." She had then been reading a book by the author of the theory of windowless monads. Presently she chides Urien for having believed that true communication was at all possible in the phenomenal world of plurality except—and this is *now* manifest— as pilgrims towards God, each following his way but walking towards the same destination: "Urien! Urien, hapless brother! . . . I wait for you beyond Time where the snows are eternal; what we shall have are crowns of snow, no longer of flowers. . . . For each the road is unique and each road leads to God."

The transfigured Ellis bids Urien hold on to a sort of Messianic hope, in accordance with the dominance of the notion of "waiting"[12] throughout Gide's creative work. "My beloved brother, hold fast to Hope." She then takes the road of the seraphim and as she rises to join the choir of angels, rays of the seven mystical gems emanate from her person. The sound from the heavens, Urien's prostration in terror, his waking from the vision and finding his friends asleep also have about them a biblical aura.

Le Voyage d'Urien, a spiritual voyage described physically, is rich in symbolisms of various types. Here too an abundance of images can be seen lending themselves readily to a Freudian analysis, which is not surprising in view of the oft-observed symbolic affinities between sexuality and religion. Yet the main problem of *Le Voyage* is that of time. What the elect—those who reach the Pole—are after is the "faithfulness" of things, namely freedom from their transience. They burn their ship, the symbol of motion, motion itself being, as Aristotle has pointed out, the condition of our concept of time. Gide suggests the confining insularity of time in the names of the Queen and King of the City of Sin along the shores of the Pathetic Ocean, for we may assume that he knew the literal meaning of the name Camaralzaman ("belt of time") that he gave the King. The Queen's name, Haiatalnufus, means, also in Arabic, "life of the individual." Together they represent the condition of man, condemned to death.

The Pathetic Ocean is the sphere of desires never finally satisfied. It stands for the vicious circle of temporality, while the Sargossa Sea is an indictment of time as the instrument of boredom. The realm of timelessness beyond these, represented by the frozen North Sea, appears in itself to be a deadening illusion in the sense that it is not the answer to the human yearning after the ultimate. All that Urien and the odd assortment of companions who have remained with him find is a corpse in a block of ice. It appears to have been the body of a tired man, one who has preceded them here and who has not received the answer to his quest: the piece of paper he holds in his hand is blank.

Yet it is here, in the realm of frozen forms and of no hours that we witness the apotheosis of Ellis. Nor has the voyage been useless from other points of view. Urien and eight others—in the number of the choirs of angels—have reached the Pole. They are serious but not sad, for presumably the dilemma between morality (i.e., a given code of behavior) and sincerity which remained Gide's own life-long problem has been solved in this sphere. The hard trials, Urien informs his companions in what appears to be a sermon, have passed. These trials were twofold: first "the morose banks where we thought we would die of boredom" and secondly "the seashores with forbidden joys." They must consider themselves happy for having known them, for "only through them can people reach here." Law before grace.

"The crowns of snow" to which Ellis invites Urien may not have proved to be to Gide's liking, but the necessity of transcending time and the limitations of reason, as well as the unique possibility of transcending them through Em. were his permanent certainties. In her undesirable phenomenal aspect she was nevertheless the pretext for his self-dedication to what may be described as her form in an immutable, glorious world.

Gide's ambiguity toward Em. as toward Ellis is traceable to the dualism that informs his own temperament and philosophy. His adoration of Em. in the dimension of eternity is hampered by her spatio-temporal limitedness, including her being the embodiment of a prescriptive, fixed code of morality. The ambiguity extends to Cuverville, her domain. There are times when he can write at Cuverville "gaily and easily." More often that place causes him to suffer headaches, dizziness, and torpor, even when the weather—to which Gide was unusually sensitive—is "wonderful, unchanging." Though he never leaves Cuverville, as he says, "without a sort of heartbreak," passages such as the following are not uncommon:

> I am leaving Cuverville tomorrow. The physiological and moral conditions in which I find myself here are most depressing and my work has suffered considerably therefrom.
>
> Those spasms of the esophagus, from which I suffered during my last stay at Cuverville, do not have the terrible *organic* cause that I feared.[13]

At Cuverville he nurtures thoughts that hold him back: "an unaccountable diffidence, modesty, shyness, reticence, laziness, excessive understanding of the *other side,* etc." Gide suffers from these traits of character everywhere, but "it goes without saying that I feel all this especially at Cuverville and when with Em."[14]

In at least one instance Cuverville—the Fongueusemare ("fungus puddle") of *La Porte étroite*—is not merely an extension of, but practically *means* Madeleine:

Alibert told me that he wondered if one ought not to see precaution, prudence on the part of Racine's wife, much rather than the indifference that is generally imputed to her, in her refusal to read or see any play by her husband. . . . Perhaps Alibert outlined that thesis to me only because he was thinking more of Cuverville and of me than of Racine, and perhaps he was attempting, under this pretext, to show me discreetly how capable he was of understanding the modesty and secret wisdom of such a feminine reserve.[15]

Gide went so far as to tell Madeleine that he could no longer live in Normandy because he "rotted" there.[16] He returned to her nevertheless.

Perhaps the most telling instance of Gide's ambiguity towards Madeleine's presence is his marriage to her. Society does not require that a man and woman be married to allow the sort of relationship they maintained after their marriage. One is led to conclude that a certain sacredness attached to Em.'s person—as it did in Gide's eyes to reality at large—[17] that Gide respected that sacredness, and that *he* married her so as to prevent others from violating it. His marriage with Em. is almost an enactment of the "spiritual marriage" of Christian mystics.

Present in Gide's attitude toward Em. are certain modalities of behavior usually found in people's reaction to the object of their worship. Ambiguity is precisely one of these. Rudolf Otto has endeavored to show in *The Idea of the Holy* that religion exists before it is exteriorized and that the external events are excitative objects, the pretexts, as it were, of man's reaction to the Holy. This reaction is ambiguous, being one of terror and attraction.[18] The ambiguity can be traced to the fact that man both yearns for self-offering and resents it. Thus the French word *sacré* has kept the contradictory meanings of *holy* and *accursed*.[19] But even more pertinent perhaps by way of illustrating the religious nature of Gide's ambiguity toward Em. is a perennial ecclesiastical problem which erupted with an unusual force in the eighth century. The Iconoclastic Controversy revolved around the decision of whether or not a "sacred" object can represent an invisible reality without leading to idolatry. Gide's aversion to Em.'s spatio-temporal existence causes him to destroy her in her physical aspect, in effigy, in his various tales.

Again, it is interesting to observe, particularly in view of the occasional identification in Gide's mind of "God" and "Nature," that in his attitude towards Em. there is the sort of ambivalence with which man faces Nature. "Mother Nature" both gives life and kills, and man rebels against and submits to it. We have seen rebellion against and submission to Em. inform Gide's reaction to her. She is, however, more than Nature.

Em. designates in effect not a person, but a personal and living reality which is different from, but which includes Gide.

"Can the Eternal One Be Female?"

Em.'s sacred person marked by the cross is unapproachable. In *La Porte étroite* the last meeting of Jerome and Alissa comes to an end at a small garden door "through which they had come out a little before." She bids good-bye and tells her beloved friend not to come any farther. She looks at him for a moment holding him fast but at arm's length. In her tearful eyes there is an unspeakable love: she is about to withdraw in pursuit of "some better thing!" As the door is shut, the bolt drawn behind her, Jerome, now a prey to the extremest despair, weeps and sobs in the night.

But to have kept her, to have forced the door, to have entered by any means whatever into the house, . . . no, even today, when I look back to the past and live it over again—no, it was not possible to me, and whoever does not understand me here, has understood nothing of me up till now.

Gide never spoke to, or of, Em. easily. Speaking of his relations with his wife he says: "by dint of silence we have almost got to the point of understanding each other."[20] From his *Journal* he suppressed systematically all the passages relating to her, though the *Journal* was blinded as a result. His image is mutilated without the proper references to her. As given in the *Journal* this image presents "in the ardent place of the heart, but a hole."[21] Tact and prudence might have been the reasons for Gide's silence where Madeleine was concerned. He had transcribed the unpublished parts of his *Journal* and "everything concerning that supreme part" of his life "which might explain and throw light upon it."[22] These were published subsequently in *Et nunc manet in te* in which, nevertheless, he cannot overcome his reticence. There was an element of awe in his silence all along. Irresistibly the reader gathers the impression that Em. was taboo: "I have always respected her modesty to such a degree that I almost never take occasion to speak of her in my notebooks and that, even now, I stop."[23]

Nor can one fail to see in Gide's reaction to Em. elements of the worship of the Great Mother, which is a common religious phenomenon. Its modifications have been seen in all cultures from the recurrence of the Madonna and Child theme in art, to the designation of a Mother's Day in the beginning of Spring in the United States. Eugene O'Neill has suggested in *Strange Interlude* that it would have been more logical and satisfying to have imagined life as created in the birth-pain of God the Mother:

Then we would understand why we, Her children, have inherited pain, for we would know that our life's rhythm beats from the great heart, torn with the agony of love and birth. And we would feel that death meant reunion with Her, a passing back into Her substance, blood of Her blood again, peace of Her peace!

If Gide read these lines—which is almost certain—he must have found them profoundly meaningful. In Section VIII of his *Thésée,* when he summarizes his entire theology in a few pages, "a young man of about my own age who seemed in the half-light to be of great beauty," asks, the "half-light" being a pictorial name for mysticism as seen by Gide: "Who came first: man or woman? Can the Eternal One be female? . . . The Kingdom of God is peace. All is absorbed, all is reconciled in the Unique Being."

It is rather as "the Eternal One," as a spiritual presence that Em. is the center of Gide's existence and—to the extent to which he, like Whitman, identified himself with all things that are—the center of reality. He already knew seven years before her death that when that moment came, the knowledge of her being gone would not prevent him from awaiting her. She would, in a sense, still be there. Em. answers an objectless, mystical expectation. Gide writes addressing his words to Ariadne: "Thus you will leave. I shall remain alone awaiting you, though knowing that you are never to come back."[24] *Et nunc manet in te* begins with these words: "Yesterday evening I was thinking of her; I was talking with her, as I often used to do, more easily in imagination than in her presence; when suddenly I said to myself: but she is dead . . ."

Confirming again the fact that the nature of their relationship had hardly undergone any change after Madeleine's death, and that therefore her bodily presence was not a condition of her being there, Gide noted on October 25, 1938:

Everything goes on *as if nothing had happened*—and I too, as if nothing in my life had been changed. This is partly because everything she represented for me subsists untouched by her death. She was a direction of my heart; and already during her lifetime her voice, at times, seemed to me to come from a great distance.[25]

The abstract description of Em. as "direction of my heart" is continued in *Et nunc manet in te*. She is *grâce, douceur, intelligence, bonté*.[26] Em. is spiritually present in Gide's reality as inner directedness, which is of particular interest in view of his impatience with Providence, which is taken by him to be an impossible heavenly correction of all wrongs. Providence may be regarded more accurately as "God's directing activity" which "always creates through the freedom of man and through the spontaneity and structural wholeness of all creatures."[27] This providential role is played by Alissa in *La Porte étroite* with regard to Jerome. Upon shedding her body she becomes an ideal and a power that can integrate Jerome's polarities: her death appears to be her opening up of her real, hidden self to Jerome. He knows her bare soul now that he is acquainted with her intimate journal which she had put in a sealed packet addressed to him. Upon receiving her immaterially in these diaries, he is directed by her from within. He becomes free in the sense in which freedom is defined in two "admirable lines" of John Donne: "Take mee to you, imprison mee, for I/Except you enthrall mee, never shall be free."[28]

Jerome in *La Porte étroite* confides to Juliette that it is to Alissa's memory that he means to remain faithful or rather to her idea of him. If, he says, he married a woman other than Alissa he could only pretend to love her.

"Ah!" [Juliette] said, as though indifferently; then turning her face away from me, she bent it toward the ground, as if looking for something she had lost. "Then you think that one can keep a hopeless love in one's heart for as long as that?"

"Yes, Juliette."

"Hopeless love" in this closing dialogue of the book means a love without a specific object, that is, without an object on which love crystallizes. While Alissa lived, Jerome loved *her*. As a result of her death his heart becomes a loving heart. It is not without symbolic significance that the story ends with a servant bringing "the lamp" into a room where Juliette had collected all of Alissa's furniture. Though Jerome had rejected Juliette before, he thought her, in this room, "very beautiful." The change in the aspect of things was due to Alissa's invisible presence.

Another symbol of inner directedness in Gide's work is Antigone.

Alissa becomes Jerome's "guide" when she can no longer be seen. Oedipus does not see Antigone in a physical sense either. The blind King will go "straight ahead. . . . Henceforward with no roof, no country for my own," caring for all: "Whoever they may be, they are men. I shall be glad to bring them happiness at the price of my sufferings." To this end "you alone shall be my guide," he tells his daughter, another likeness of Em. "I do not see any figure," Gide said, with Antigone in mind, "to which I can better compare her."[29] To advance "straight ahead," without any definite objective is a favorite Gidian aim. He has spoken elsewhere of "a penetration, always simpler, of nature" and of entering "deeper into God."[30]

As a spiritual presence Em. was also the condition of Gide's creativity. He once said that it was for Marc Allégret, "to win his attention, his esteem," that he wrote *Les Faux-Monnayeurs,* just as he wrote all his preceding books, he said, "under the influence of Em. or in the vain hope of convincing her."[31] This was not his opinion some years later:

> Without that Christian formation, without those bonds, without Em., who oriented my pious inclinations, I should not have written *André Walter,* or *L'Immoraliste,* or *La Porte étroite,* or *La Symphonie pastorale,* etc. . . . or even, perhaps, *Les Caves du Vatican* and *Les Faux-Monnayeurs* as a revolt and a protest.[32]

To Em., who made of him a creative person, Gide submitted, offered himself. Similar to the words of medieval lovers are those addressed by Bernard to Laura in *Les Faux-Monnayeurs.* The medieval lover pledged perpetual submission to his lady. Bernard finds that when he is with Laura he has no desires. The freedom for which he longed as the supreme good he uses to bow himself to her devotion. There is an autobiographical element present in these sentiments attributed to Bernard. When he and the angel visit the church of the Sorbonne Bernard cannot pray because he does not believe in any god, but he longs for dedication, for sacrifice. He offers himself—an experience beyond words, which nevertheless is taken up in the organ's song. "You offered yourself in the same way to Laura," says the angel.[33] It is altogether unlikely that "Laura" occurred to Gide at random. It is surely a subtle reference to the role that Petrarch's "guiding star," herself reminiscent of Beatrice, played in that poet's life.[34]

Gide offered himself to Em. creatively through, above all, his letters to her. Madeleine's destruction of these letters caused the greatest grief of his life. What he related to Roger Martin du Gard must be quoted in full:

These letters were the treasure of my life, the best of myself: unquestionably, the best of my writings. Each time I happened to open these packages, I quivered with joy, with pride. In them was all that was purest in my existence, in my heart; never had I written anything more lofty, warmer, more laden with meaning than these letters . . . where were meticulously reflected not only all my thoughts, all my work, but also this love, so precious, which never ceased being in me like a light. It was the intimate diary of my life, it was my very life at its most beautiful, most irreplaceable! I thought about them with confidence in the hours when I doubted of myself, and often I said to myself: "You can die: even if you leave nothing else besides these letters, there is there such a wealth of feeling, of thought, such a profound life, and that under a form so pure, so perfect, that you are sure to survive, sure to awaken in all the adolescents of the future the brotherly thrill that great poets awaken. No matter what you become, and what you do, the immortal work is there!"

And bruskly, there was nothing any more: I was dispossessed of all! Ah, I imagine what a father can feel who comes home and whose wife meets him with the news: "Our child is no more, I have killed him."[35]

It is as if by offering his life to Em. Gide had found his place in a divine economy. He had done what he was destined to do, and lived his days on earth in the assurance of an eternal existence. Madeleine's own explanation of her act was that as she was left alone after her husband's departure with the boy he loved, she felt that her heart was about to cease beating, and that she would die: "I suffered so much. . . . I burned your letters in order to do something. Before destroying them I reread them all, one by one."[36]

The important question is not, of course, why did she do *something?* It is rather, why did she do *this* thing? She did it presumably in order to bring about the results that ensued: she deprived herself of her "most precious belonging" by way of punishing herself, one may conjecture, for failing to cause Gide to be the upright man of her own moral judgment. Her act was simultaneously a punitive measure against Gide himself. Inasmuch as Gide wished to survive on the pedestal of his literary output, his grief is partly accounted for by the loss, with these letters, of the most valuable of his literary creations. Yet had the loss been due to an occurrence beyond control he would not have been inconsolable: "If this loss were even due to some accident, invasion, fire. . . . But that *she* should have done that!"[37] Above all it is her punishment of him that he cannot endure.

Em.'s approval constituted for Gide a final frame of reference in matters of moral behavior. As a student he once asked a friend whether on leaving the lycée he goes down the disreputable Passage du Havre. "Why do you ask?" the friend said. "Suddenly," Gide reports, "I felt overwhelmed by some enormous presence—a religious, a panic terror took hold of me—the same that had come over me at the time of little Emile's death and on the day I had felt myself cut off from humanity."[38] The enormous presence was no doubt that of his mother—or Em. Disobedience evoked images of death and isolation. It would result in something resembling expulsion from Paradise. Gide recognized in 1892, at the age of twenty-three, that the only feminine influence on his "delighted soul" was Em. She, in her capacity as an unmoved mover, had always guided him "toward the highest truths" and had always inclined him "to studious attitudes."[39] She was also the pearl of great price. Not to possess, but to deserve her was the aim of his life.[40] "Work, efforts, pious acts, I offered them all up, mystically, to Alissa," Jerome says, "and, indeed, invented a refinement of virtue by which I often left her in ignorance of what I had done only for her sake."[41] The more profound implications of this last remark can be understood when we recall Gide's insistence, in contrast to the Catholics who expected their reward from God, that virtue is its own reward.

Em. and Gide's Existence

Em. is endowed with metaphysical attributes when she is called upon to dispel the darkness of death. In Gide's *Nouvelles Nourritures* a series of statements about God is interrupted in favor of a description of the Virgin Mary in superhuman terms. The author then bids his interlocutor change the subject.[42] If there is in this passage a condemnation of the mariolatry of popular Roman Catholicism, it is hardly perceptible, while Gide's reticence to talk about the Virgin remains noteworthy. One must suspect a certain association of Mary with Em., a suspicion which is strengthened by his repeatedly expressed wish of having Em. near him at the last hour. Roman Catholics hail the Virgin Mary, and request her invisible presence by their bedside at the dreaded moment of death as an assurance of victory over the powers of darkness and annihilation. Gide's thoughts turn to Em. at times of illness. He writes in his *Journal* on January 4, 1931:

For Em. To dare tell her:

"Have you not understood that I prefer to die anywhere rather than in Paris, and that if I cannot have you beside my bed at my last moment, I prefer not to have anyone?"

In his late fifties he had recalled the walks he had taken in his youth with Em. at La Roque:

The house still slept when we left it. . . . We stepped lightfooted and silent, for fear of startling god or game, rabbit or squirrel or roe-deer, at their play in the glad confidence of the innocent hour, when every morning they create their paradise anew, before man is awake and the day grows drowsy. Pure and dazzling light, in the hour of death, may your remembrance vanquish the shades![43]

Fourteen years later and two years after Madeleine's death Gide wrote that he "should have been quite capable of being 'converted' at the last moment—I mean at the hour of death, in order not to cause her too much suffering."[44]

The love Gide entertained for Em. always had around it a clearly religious aura in every respect, whether *religious* is or is not defined in terms of the fear of death. He declares in *Les Cahiers d'André Walter* that his love for Emmanuèle will grow in the midst of devout prayers.[45] This was the period when his prayer was "like a perceptible motion of the soul towards a deeper penetration into the intimacy of God."[46] It is through Alissa that Jerome hears the Scripture in *La Porte étroite*. In *Si le grain ne meurt*, published in 1926, he compares his love for Em. to the love of God, and recalls it in these terms: "But the Gospels . . . ah! At last I found the reason, the occupation, the inexhaustible spring of love. The feeling I had here made clear to me and at the same time strengthened the feeling I had for Emmanuèle; it did not differ from it. . . ."[47]

In this love Gide found the reconciliation of his polarities, the power wherewith he could overcome his estrangement. Homosexuality, condemned unqualifiedly by Em. for personal as well as moral and religious reasons, was both the cause and the symbol of his estrangement. As was to be expected, he placed the solution of that central drama of his life in a work of art, that is, a world of freedom where Gide could redress at will the undesirable circumstances of his life, and obtain the blessings he wished for. In *Les Faux-Monnayeurs* Edouard records a "visit from

Pauline" shortly after Olivier has come back to life in his studio. Pauline is Edouard's half-sister and the mother of Olivier:

"I am reassured already by knowing Olivier is with you," said Pauline. "I shouldn't nurse him better myself, for I feel that you love him as much as I do."

As she said those last words, she looked at me with an odd insistence. Did I imagine the meaning she seemed to put in her look? I was feeling what one is accustomed to call "a bad conscience" as regards Pauline, and was only able to stammer out something incoherent. I must also say that, sur-saturated as I have been with emotion for the last two days, I had entirely lost command of myself; my confusion must have been very apparent, for she added:

"Your blush is eloquent! . . . My poor dear friend, don't expect reproaches from me. I should reproach you if you didn't love him. . . . Can I see him?"

I took her in to Olivier. Bernard had left the room as he heard us coming.

"How beautiful he is," she murmured, bending over the bed. Then, turning towards me: "You will kiss him from me. I am afraid of waking him."

Pauline is decidedly an extraordinary woman. And today is not the first time that I have begun to think so. But I could not have hoped that she would push comprehension so far.[48]

This is one of the more important pages written by Gide. The reconciliation of Olivier with Edouard represents his reconciliation of himself with himself; the reconciliation of Edouard with Pauline represents his reconciliation of himself with the world, inasmuch as the inner conflict that lies at the basis of all of Gide's work is rooted in the inability of Gide's wife "to understand and accept his sexual orientation."[49]

It is therefore as that through which Gide achieves contact with the external reality that Em. assumes for him a religious significance. Schleiermacher has contended that "both knowledge and activity are a desire to be identified with the Universe through an object," and that this desire is essentially religious.[50] To the extent to which this analysis is accurate Gide's relationship with Em. or rather, his reaction to her presence constitutes a religious state of affairs. Insmuch as Gide's authentic existence was, to use Rimbaud's word, *elsewhere,* Em. was not "this" person but precisely the object through which he identified with the Universe. Schleiermacher has defined religion itself as "an affection, a revelation of the Infinite in the finite, God being seen in it and it in God."[51] Over a century later Paul Tillich wrote in a similarly Augustinian frame of mind that "religion deals with a relation of man to the eternal."[52]

The quest for this relation he called "ultimate concern." He wrote elsewhere that "religion is not only a function of life; it is also the place
where life receives the conqueror of the ambiguities of life, the divine
Spirit."[53] Religion is therefore not only ultimate concern; it is also ultimate fulfillment. To Gide, who did not always believe in a divine Spirit
but was called by Infinity, the name of "the conqueror" was Em. It is
precisely at this point that his humanism transcends itself—or breaks
down. Gide's relationship with his mother and Madeleine does not explain
his religious stance. Rather, his religious awareness of, and his reaction
to, the ground of his existence is driven home to him through the visible
presence of the two women telescoped into one. For a mother is, after all,
the darkness which precedes one's self-conscious, and hence, alienated
existence. She is both the occasion of one's alienation and the visible
instrument of its removal. Through Em. Gide overcomes his alienation.
"In the absence of the pure sound [Em.'s] soul gave forth," it seemed to
him, he "had ceased to hear any but profane sounds, opaque, faint, and
desperate."[54] The opacity of these sounds is of particular interest, for
Gide had a predilection for the transparency of things, a symbol of total
communication.

In Gide's mind the words *Em.* and *God* were sometimes used synonymously. Em. and God assumed the same function in his life and were
interchangeable. There are several passages in *Les Cahiers d'André Walter*
where the Deity on one side and mother-and-Madeleine on the other are
alternatives to the fulfillment of the same need. The following scene occurs shortly after Mme Walter's burial: "Emmanuèle was before me; I
did not look at her, and, in order not to think of her and prevent myself
from dreaming I repeated: 'Since I must lose her, let me at least rediscover thee, my God.' "[55] When Gide's mother died not in fiction but in
real life, Gide's reaction was in keeping with this prayer. It is as if a
closed receptacle had broken and let escape the spirit which would receive Gide himself. He felt himself sink into an overwhelming abyss of
love, sorrow, and liberty. He sought to distribute her things as far as
possible as if anxious to share her revered memory with as large a number of people as possible. Upon her death he experienced "the singular
propensity" of his mind to let itself be dazzled by the sublime.[56] To say
that Madeleine took her place would not be quite accurate. Rather, that
of which the mother was representative now presented itself in the form
of Madeleine: "There was nothing now I could attach myself to but my

love for my cousin; my determination to marry her was the only light left me by which to guide my life. . . . I felt I loved her more than I loved myself."[57] He does not attach himself to his cousin, but to *his love* for his cousin. Madeleine is another object through which that love manifests itself.

The same equivalence of Em. and the Deity is suggested in *L'Immoraliste*. The following dialogue takes place between Michel and Marceline on a Sunday after he has been informed that she had prayed for him during mass that morning:

"You mustn't pray for me, Marceline." . . .
"You will not get well all by yourself, my poor dear," she sighed.
"If so, it can't be helped." Then, seeing how unhappy she looked, I added less roughly:
"You will help me."[58]

"You," that is, instead of God. There is identification of Em. and God in certain propositions where either of these words is the subject or the predicate. He wrote in 1947 that "God is virtue."[59] He had written in *Si le grain ne meurt* that loving Emmanuèle, he loved "virtue itself."[60] But one need not have recourse to such rapprochements to conclude that Em. and God are identified in Gide's mind; he says plainly that it seemed to him that by approaching God he was approaching her.[61] Em.'s religious significance for Gide consists in the circumstance that in and through her he achieves total relatedness.

Gide was dissatisfied in the phenomenal world and yearned for Being as against existence, for reality as against appearance, and for a state of grace as against a state of sin. Jean Delay refers to the incident of Gide's discovery of Madeleine after her detection of her mother's unfaithfulness. That incident, Delay says,

seems to have [for Gide] the value of the passage of the angel establishing a line of demarcation between the "darkness" of his childhood and the radiance of a mystical presence; between the world of blemish and that of grace.[62]

Without Em. Gide had the feeling that he moved in appearances:

Yet however different from me she may have been, it was having known her that made me so often feel like a stranger on this earth, playing the game of life without too much believing in it, for having known through her a less tangible but more genuine reality.[63]

With her he transcended reason and gained an awareness, in spite of reason, of that "secret reality" which he "felt" even though his intelligence "negated" it.[64] Without the assurance of that secret reality the phenomenal world could turn into a frightful quicksand. Gide gives us a glimpse of what life is without Em.:

I was, I still am, like someone sinking into a stinking morass, looking all around him for anything whatever that is fixed and solid of which to catch hold, but dragging with him and pulling into that muddy inferno everything he clutches.[65]

This is equivalent to Fongueusemare (in the literal meaning of the word) without Alissa. The distress is caused not so much by the discontinuation of her companionship as such, as by a sudden loss of moorings, for Em. is the way to the Absolute,[66] and, somewhat in the manner of the Tao,[67] even the Absolute itself. She is the condition of Gide's life and the source of his being: "I cannot imagine myself without her; it seems to me that without her, I would have been *nothing*."[68] Referring to childhood memories, "it is only awakened by my love for her," he says, "that I gained consciousness of being and began truly to exist."[69] He had written elsewhere: "Nothing matters to me any more; I feel myself sometimes detached to such a point from everything, that it seems to me I am already dead and that I lived only through her."[70] Gide has no substantiality of his own in the manner in which this world has no substantiality of *its* own in Augustine's philosophy. It is Em. who lends him his reality. Her loss drives Gide to metaphysical anxiety, for it is clear that the state of dejection described above is not mere mourning over the death of a dearly beloved person. It is akin to what the mystics say occurs in the absence of God. John of the Cross describes it as "abandonment of the spirit in darkness," while Tauler, in words even more strikingly similar to the passage from Gide's *Journal* just quoted, speaks of "a fathomless sinking in a fathomless nothingness."[71]

At the other pole of the nothingness into which Gide sinks without Em. is a state which he perceives as "perfect reintegration."[72] In her all contradictions are resolved, like paths which start at the different sides of a mountain and meet at the summit.[73] His description of her at one time as "the mystical orient of my life"[74] is reminiscent of Plato's comparison to the sun of the Form of the Good which acquired a creative substantiality as it evolved into the ground of Plotinian metaphysics.

Em. is, in sum, the Advaita of Hindu mysticism, the One of Plotinus, which is another way of saying that Gide used that word not so much to refer to a human being as to the otherwise nameless ground of existence. It may even be argued that he preferred *Em.* to an abstract designation of that ground because, as T. H. Greene puts it, "the God of religious worship is never merely the 'ground of all being' but a Person worthy of our reverence, a God who so loves men as to evoke their responsive love."[75]

6

Esthetic-Mystical Theism

Mysticism Condemned

It is frequently necessary to keep in mind Gide's reactions to Em. and to Nature in order to evaluate his propositions containing conventional religious terms. It is against the background of these reactions that we can determine those of his more authentic statements about God. These reactions betray a propensity toward mysticism—which Gide condemns repeatedly. But there is no dilemma. Any sane person would condemn what Gide condemns under that term. What serious students of the subject mean by *mysticism* is something else.

In Gide's mind *mysticism, religion,* and *faith* have uncertain contours; they fuse into each other and are condemned for more or less the same reasons. Opposing mysticism to something he called spirituality, he wrote in 1933: "Many are those who still confuse mysticism and spirituality and who believe that man can but crawl if religion does not support him; who believe that religion alone can keep man from crawling."[1]

Mysticism and *religion* are used here synonymously. Thinking elsewhere of the upbringing of young Jesuits, Gide uses the adjective *mystical* where the adjective *religious* seems to be called for: "Probably nothing distorts more, and more irremediably, that exigent need of exactness than the mystical culture to which those minds were subjected at a still too tender age."[2] Atheism and irreligion can themselves give rise to a sort of mysticism: " 'mysticism' today is on the side of those who profess atheism and irreligion. It is as a religion that the Communist doctrine exalts and feeds the enthusiasm of the young of today."[3] Mysticism is "abdication of the reason," or "of criticism." "I have reason to know," Gide says, that—presupposing and demanding the abdication of reason —"there is no worse enemy than mysticism."[4] The same word is defined again, several years later as "any blind belief."[5] Faith likewise involves "a certain blindness in which the devout soul delights; when it escapes the shackles of reason, it seems to itself to be at its height. It is merely shameless."[6] Edouard in *Les Faux-Monnayeurs* says it more elaborately:

> The deeper the soul plunges into religious devotion, the more it loses all sense of reality, all need, all desire, all love for reality. . . . The dazzling light of their faith blinds them to the surrounding world and to their own selves. As for me, who care for nothing so much as to see the world and myself clearly, I am amazed at the coils of falsehood in which devout persons take delight.[7]

In itself this pronouncement is either tautological ("religious devotion" may *mean* "loss of all sense of reality") or patently erroneous. If "religious devotion" and "reality" carry their generally accepted meanings, then Edouard, or Gide, would find himself in the absurd position of having to admit that all the saints, such men as St. Bernard included, whose souls had surely plunged deep into religious devotion, had lost all sense of reality, all need, all desire, all love for reality. Thomas Aquinas, to cite another example, was certainly a "devout person," yet no one can reasonably claim that he took delight in the coils of falsehood. More likely is the supposition that, in writing as he did, Gide was motivated by a hidden sense of guilt. His puritanical training and anti-romantic temperament combine in causing him to shun a prospect of luxury: the prospect of bathing in a dazzling light. He is "forbidding" himself to be a mystic.

Gide refers to the age we are leaving behind alternately as "mystical" and "mythological." From this age, we are told, we shall awaken into "reality." This reality or "serious epoch" coincides no doubt with the goal of which Oedipus speaks in the play bearing his name. At that time the answer will be "man." To our lingering mythological or mystical "numbness" are due such articles of belief as the Virgin Birth.[8] In the following context the meaning of *mystic* is less clear though it hovers around irrationalism. The conversation occurs in *Les Faux-Monnayeurs* between Dr. Sophraniska and Edouard:

> "You don't seem to believe in the virtue of convictions. . . . I mean in their power as an active principle."
> "You are right," I [i.e., Edouard] said laughing. "I am not a mystic."[9]

Little Boris' "puerile mysticism" as he follows upon Bronja's lead in *Les Faux-Monnayeurs* is pronounced "not very different after all from the one he at first provoked by artifice." It turns him aside, quite as much, "from effort and realization."[10]

Besides carrying such diverse connotations as unreality, puerility, narrow-mindedness, stubbornness, and sloth, *mysticism* may refer to a disposition which scorns order and neatness. Gide finds "mystically" very delicate the distinction in meaning between "Christ died *because* of sinners" and "*for* sinners."[11] A book entitled *Man* elicits from him this criticism:

The lack of composition of this book reflects the mystic disorder of that poor brain [i.e., of Hello]. He is too ready to scorn *reason*, having hardly any himself, and through absurdity he proves its great value despite himself. How could mysticism fail to reject composition?[12]

Gide's own *Cahiers d'André Walter* suffered from mysticism in this very sense. It is only with disciplined effort that Gide emerged from the misty atmosphere where that book was put together. Later it seemed to him that he was won over by reason. It is to the effort involved in clarifying his thought—in drawing clear pictures in his mind, as against the temptation of indulging in "André Walterism"—that he alludes when he writes in 1929 that he can slip into "mystical ideas" as into "old slippers." Though he can "feel at ease in them," he prefers "to go barefoot."[13]

When Gide sees a cause and effect relationship between mysticism and "solitary practices," *mysticism* means, no doubt, "André Walterism."[14] Accordingly, his reaction against "André Walterism" led him to associate anti-mysticism with asceticism, as well as with lean, classical structures. A lack of restraint, indifference to law and order characterized in his mind faith, mysticism, and romanticism alike, the latter being associated in turn with pride and infatuation.[15]

There is no profit in drawing up a complete chart of the shades of meaning attached by Gide to the symbol "mysticism." It was, on the whole, a term of opprobrium. Mysticism was harmful. In his major work on mysticism, *Thésée,* it stands in the way of progress. Theseus believes in progress as one who is on the side of science against religion, religion being for Gide now a blinding light, now "the priest," now a projection, now resignation, now a pie in the sky, and now a response to a dreadful emptiness and tedium of life, and as a synthesis of all these things, an impediment to man's confidence in himself.

But religion also means to Gide love, self-giving, and the expression of the need of adoration which he recognized as dwelling "at the center

of man's heart."[16] We have seen that faith, likewise, besides being assent
to pragmatically unwarranted propositions, "is made of confidence in God
and renunciation of self," and is not to be confused with magic.[17] Mysticism is itself used occasionally to describe a desirable state of affairs
such as the *échanges mystiques* between Lebanon and France.[18] It takes
"a certain dose of mysticism"[19] to go on writing when you know you are
not being listened to, Gide said, and he explained years later that what
urged him to write was his extraordinary, insatiable need to love and be
loved. This was "almost mystical," because he was reconciled to the fact
that it would not be satisfied in his lifetime.[20] Em. herself is described
as "the mystical orient" of his life.

In view of such fluctuations in meaning, compounded by the fluctuat-
ing Gidian reactions to the hazily conceived objects denoted by the words
under consideration, the blanket proposition that Gide rejects mysticism,
religion, and faith cannot be accurate. The fact is that Gide rejects mysticism in a certain sense. He rejects under that symbol or its synonyms,
besides abdication of reason, arbitrary, unwarranted assertions, foggy,
unclear, befuddled, or undisciplined thinking, the domination of society
by a class of people, self-deception, baseless hope, and vacuous promises,
as well as other undesireable behaviors and springs of behaviors. To the
extent to which these things are rejected by every sensible person Gide
is the forceful speaker of important commonplaces. He is far more interesting as one who is a mystic against himself.

At least two more or less paradoxical circumstances may account for
the fact that the term "mysticism" acquired in Gide's mind strong connotations of blame. There is, first, his Protestant ethics of effort. Not to be
a mystic was against the grain; it was the more difficult thing to do, and
a difficult course of behavior was praiseworthy by definition. This was a
precept that Gide adopted early in life and never quite abandoned. And
then there is his perpetual desire to be unlike himself. Upon the further
observation that Gide insisted on a moral, as against a metaphysical, approach to truth and that this is a mystical tendency, the view that his
rambling anti-mysticism is itself an indication of his mysticism in the
proper meaning of this word acquires credibility. The proper meaning
of mysticism will change from observer to observer, but there is a general, if not universal consensus that it refers to an experience—or rather,
experiences of short duration which transcend discursive reason in order
to reach an awareness of the unity of all things, of the self's being taken
up into a reality beyond phenomena. This reconciliation, or even fusion,

of the self with the Other is marked by indescribable joy and peace. In it metaphysical ignorance is overcome. The mystic denies the reality of time. He feels himself flooded by a love of unsuspected intensity.

But mysticism is also the name of a doctrine, namely a philosophical pronouncement to the effect that the reports of the mystics deserve assent, that they must be given credence as valid. Let us call the person who subscribes to this doctrine a mysticist, reserving the term mystic to one who is himself subject to mystical experiences. The principal difficulty with Gide's theism is that he was a mystic, but not always a mysticist. To be sure his mysticism is not the kind envisaged by, for example, H. Delacroix—where the ineffable God is to the God of the Church what intuition is to verbal expression or discourse—but it is mysticism nonetheless. The paradoxical reason for his opposition to mysticism as a doctrine is that being a mystic he was opposed to any doctrine at all, including mysticism as a doctrine. This opposition took on various forms according to his own temperament and in line with the general preferences of his epoch.

From all his reflections on the subject one often gathers the impression that according to Gide a man cannot be a mystic and engage simultaneously in the piecemeal pursuit of scientific knowledge. Mysticism and clarity of thought were opposed in his mind, for he was himself divided between his "German," brooding, metaphysics-oriented temperament and his "French" desire to achieve luminous clarity. He assumed that there is a choice to be made between a mystical attitude on one hand and, on the other, respect for reason and interest in the practical needs of the world. All this is given very clear expression in his *Thésée*. In this same work occurs Gide's most thoughtful statement regarding the nature and aim of mysticism:

Duality is inadmissible. In that case the god himself would be the son. My mind refuses to divide God. If once I allow division, strife begins. Where there are gods, there are wars. There are not gods, but a God. The Kingdom of God is peace. All is absorbed, all is reconciled in the Uniform Being.[21]

These words are spoken by "a young man of about my own age who seemed in the half light to be of great beauty." They do not seem to correspond to the views of Theseus. But one need not assume that Theseus alone is Gide's spokesman in the tale, and that *his* views are definitively Gide's own.

Gide's mysticism was occasionally expressed in more or less conventional terms. In certain of his equivocal statements where his self-confusion with God is suggested, there is a tendency to do away with the awareness of what Evelyn Underhill describes as "the self's continued separation from and incompatibility with that Absolute which it has perceived."[22] That Gide experienced this separation is evident even in his statements where he denies it: "Not admit," he wrote at the age of sixty-two, "that there is no adaptation between the world and me."[23] Consequently, transrational union with the Real[24] continued to be the object of his highest aspiration, his frequent attacks on "mysticism" notwithstanding. And it is good to recall on this occasion that when we are in the presence of two sets of contradictory statements by the same author, one set pointing to mysticism and the other away from it, the former of these statements must be given greater weight because the disposition and willingness to contradict oneself supports *them*.

Gide's mysticism often finds a naturalistic or secular dress, which is in keeping with the fact that his audience was no longer receptive to the words and imagery of a bygone era.

Esthetic Mysticism

Perhaps nowhere has Gide deployed a more strenuous and sustained effort to understand himself—that is, as shown in Chapter 3 above, to find the bases on which relatedness can be achieved—and the nature of the reality to which he must relate than in the central part of *Les Faux-Monnayeurs*. This section of the novel is entitled "Saas-Fée," the name of a small village in the Alpes Valaisannes. A *fée* is a female being endowed with supernatural powers. Gide was certainly sensitive to this detail and may have intended that the title of this central section of his only "novel" carry the faint suggestion of a realm beyond the reach of unaided reason. "Saas-Fée" is placed between the first and third parts of the book, both of which are entitled "Paris." Away from the metropolis where counterfeiters are at work, Saas-Fée brings to mind the "high mountain" of the Transfiguration. Here the problem of the highest good is tackled. In section 3, Part II, Gide raises the problem of how one can endow the temporal process with meaning. How, he asks in effect, can a man raise a barrier against the threat of his gradual annihilation with every passing unit of time.

Tolstoy has asked whether there can be any truth in a world where there is death.[25] Unamuno borrows a related question from a peasant: If there is no immortality, what use is God?[26] Nothingness and meaninglessness are correlative, and since it is only the individual that dies, his absorption into, and self-identification with, the Whole may give him life and meaning simultaneously. It is not surprising therefore that Edouard, as he "explains his theory of the novel," appears to be preoccupied with two questions contending for first position in his mind. One of these is introduced with an example, the discussion between Mithridate and his two sons in Racine. This is a scene in which all fathers and all sons can see themselves, precisely because no fathers and no sons have ever spoken as Racine makes his characters speak here. Edouard draws the conclusion that to localize and to specify is to restrict:

It is true that there is no psychological truth unless it be particular; but on the other hand there is no art unless it be general. The whole problem lies just in that—how to express the general by the particular—how to make the particular express the general.[27]

In terms of art, namely in a sphere where Gide's insights were more accurate and sustained, the above quotation states that the salvation of the individual from meaninglessness and death is through the Whole. Gide, even Gide the individualist, never wavered from this fundamentally mystical principle. Only he conceived the Whole, or visualized it to himself differently at different times. Gide's ambition was to display to the world what he received from the world, without manipulating it for specific, selfish, idolatrous ends. He wished to do so by virtue of his *disponibilité*. To see any one individual should be tantamount to seeing reality. The individual should not selfishly deflect reality in his own self. In the passage quoted Gide is giving expression to that concern: how to express the general by the particular, how to make the particular express the general.

As an artist Edouard wishes to show also his "effort to stylize [reality] into art." The completely "stylized" or ideal reality is not of course a present condition. It is a vision of the future. It is an eschatological expectation. All that can be presently experienced is the *effort* towards it, so that we have, in art, a present fulfillment, namely the particular-universal identification, and a hope, that is, the gradual "stylization" of reality. Eternity and time meet in art. The "please understand" with which Edouard begins the passage is a warning. What is to follow, the implication is, is not to be grasped logically. It is a mystically envisaged endeavor which the speaker is expressing as adequately as he can, without regard to rational sequence.

Underlying Gide's artistic endeavor is the anxiety which attends his awareness of the world's putative absurdity. Generally, the effort to reconcile oneself to oneself and oneself to reality is a response to that anxiety. This anxiety is seen as a tension between "reality" which is the realm of time, and the "ideal reality."[28] In art, that is, in artistic endeavor and experience, one can win that struggle at any one moment. Gide experienced mystical transports largely but not exclusively in the world of art or in an esthetic universe.

The same struggle between reality and the ideal reality is set forth in its moral-religious aspect in the central section of the central part of *Les Faux-Monnayeurs*. Bernard, the alienated, struggling young man who is in search of his place in the world, has a coin which rings true, but is false. "One can almost see through it." It is a fragile thing, made of gilded glass. Bernard, we learn, was about to accept it from a grocer as a genuine ten-franc piece when the latter undeceived him, and sold it to him for five francs. Saas-Fée, which happens to be "at the further end of an *impasse*," is not a place where a false coin can circulate. Honesty itself is transcended here. Bernard shows the false coin to Edouard: ". . . now that you have examined it, give it back to me! I'm sorry that the reality doesn't interest you." The fact is that the reality does interest Edouard and also disturbs him. "That's a pity," quips Bernard and holds on to the false coin. It is to Laura that he hands it in a solemn gesture, and as he does . so we realize that he is finding his genuine identity. The gesture is the enactment of Gide's own declaration that when he stopped looking for himself, he found himself in love. Laura is more than "the ideal reality." She is its mystical "center" and her affinities with Em. are unmistakable: she passes for Edouard's wife. Bernard's words addressed to Laura leave no doubt as to Gide's conviction that the answer to human alienation and falseness, symbolized by Bernard's bastardy and the false coin, is what the mystics call the unitive way:

Let's say [this feeling of mine] isn't love, since you dislike that word; let's call it devotion. It's as though this liberty which seemed to me so infinite, had had limits set to it by your laws. It's as though all the turbulent and unformed things that were stirring within me, were dancing an harmonious round, with you for their centre.[29]

Les Faux-Monnayeurs is in a sense a recapturing of time lost, for it is Gide's self-recreation in a multiplicity of selves from Boris to La Pérouse. Whereas Bernard is reflective, Olivier is emotional, and while they thus have their being one on rather the Apollonian and the other on rather the Dionysian side of the fence of human temperament and behavior, they both agree that life will receive its justification and meaning not in an endeavor to be pursued over a long period of time, but in a single experience akin to a vision. The turbulence he feels within him oppresses Bernard, and his aspiration is to discipline it: "It's like steam inside me; it may whistle as it escapes (that's poetry), put in motion wheels and pistons; or even burst the engine." This bursting of the engine evokes the thought of suicide, but Bernard knows he won't kill himself. But, he says, "I understand Dmitri Karamazof perfectly when he asks his brother if he understands a person killing himself out of enthusiasm, out of sheer excess of life . . . just *bursting.*"

As Bernard speaks these words "an extraordinary radiance" shines "from his whole being." Olivier gazes at him "in a kind of ecstasy." He murmurs:

So do I, . . . I understand killing oneself too; but it would be after having tasted a joy so great, that all one's life to come would seem pale beside it; a joy so great, that it would make one feel: "I have had enough. I am content; never again shall I. . . ."

There is no fundamental difference between the two philosophies: both Bernard and Olivier aim at an ecstatic self-fulfillment. This same disposition remained Gide's own. He always had a nostalgia for the climate of his youth which he characterizes as "mystical and ardent."[30]

A deeper awareness of the genuinely mystical overtones of Bernard's remark on *bursting* is gained from these lines written by Gide in Africa, where there were "no hours," and during a period of his life when he was propelled ahead by an invincible *inquiétude:* "Ah! the sun bakes me, penetrates me, I burst, I melt, I evaporate, become volatilized in the azure."[31] At Droh he once let play within himself "of the shade and the sun the stammering alternation." Then:

Each object lost its lustre, its weight, its reality. I was walking but dreamily.

It seemed to me that I did not see, but I remembered; or rather: I was advancing, not doubting that those things there were real, but that it was I who was seeing them—so thorough was my identification with them.[32]

Gide permanently aspired toward this esthetic mystical experience. He exclaims: "Ah! to be able to tarry here, to escape elsewhere at the same time! Ah! to evaporate, to rid oneself of oneself, and would that a breath of azure, where I would be dissolved, travel. . . . !"[33]

In the following instance sensuous self-diffusion into the Other dovetails imperceptibly into experiences of another order:

. . . Alas, why is not everyone capable of this delightful ecstasy? . . . I felt so glorious that a bit of suffering, I believe, would only have exalted me still further. I supervised everything, I presided over everything, but in an impersonal manner; I forgot myself, I was distracted in a vague sensual delight, losing myself absolutely in it.

Gide surmises that in such a mood—where all return to oneself, all personal consideration is "not only unseemly, but impossible"—all egotism comes to an end making it possible for "all individualism" to triumph. In this state, he goes on to say: "I felt just as capable of the noblest deeds as of the worst, capable of any act whatever. And my mind, as if stupefied, was both unable to measure and unwilling to calculate the consequences."[34] This confidence is of particular interest in view of the fact that one of the characteristics of mysticism is, according to Bertrand Russell, a "belief that all evil is mere appearance," and that, to quote Heraclitus, "to God all things are fair and good and right, but men hold some things wrong and some right."[35] Gide continues: "And my mere presence, everywhere, established among all that I saw, heard, and felt a palpitating harmony that broke down my resistance. I was a part of it."[36]

Ecstasy is traditionally looked upon as a religious-mystical experience. Gide's own ecstasy which begins as an esthetic experience is an expression of a deeper and more comprehensive disposition. We just saw him transcend morality itself. Elsewhere sensuous self-identification with nature gives him the sense of an "infinite *presence*;"[37] "sensual ardor" is for him but the "ridiculous *imitation*" of the fervor of his adolescence;[38] nature, he insists, should not be made into an idol, nor was "Angèle," his audience, to ignore that salvation is not in nature but in love.[39] It is from this perspective that *Les Nourritures Terrestres,* the most elaborate expression of Gide's esthetic mysticism, must be considered.

The freedom that young men and women experienced and still experience upon reading *Les Nourritures Terrestres* is essentially a freedom of submission. Its appeal is religious in the sense that it provides the individual, dangling free of social conventions and hence anxious, with an external reality to which he can attach himself and with which he can literally identify. The Earth is that tangible reality, and the means of self-attachment are the senses. This sensuous alternative to emotional, intellectual, or spiritual attachments was long in the making in Europe.

Among the eighteenth-century authors who prepared the philosophy of *Les Nourritures Terrestres* one may mention J.-J. Rousseau, an outsider who referred to himself as a *"promeneur solitaire"* and wrote his *Confessions* because he was "if not better" than the generality of men, at least "different." Novalis had visualized a world where men, beasts, plants, stones, stars, the elements as well as sounds and colors appeared together as in a single family, acting and conversing in the manner of the components of the same race. Jean Paul opined that when a man is invited to immerse himself in the cosmic ocean to mix freely with flowers and stars, death is defeated. Nietzsche too spoke of bathing or swimming somehow perpetually in clear water or in some other perfect element, transparent and full of brightness. Gide's wish to turn now into a plant and now into a wave or some natural element echoes these expressions of esthetic mysticism. His accepted anticipation of becoming food to worms, the serenity he felt in the presence of animals is reminiscent of Baudelaire's jealousy of the fate of the vilest animals and of Rimbaud's metamorphosis into a bear or a donkey, or into caterpillars. Mallarmé himself wished to escape into matter, away from his human predicament: "Towards thee, I hasten! Give me, o matter/forgetfulness of cruel ideal and of sin." This is, for all intents and purposes, a yearning after death, yet death is transcended because it is accepted voluntarily.[40]

Les Nourritures Terrestres is thus a classical work because it is the *aboutissement* of one mood and the adumbration of another. While it recognizes the senses as reliable instruments wherewith to overcome isolation, it points to their insufficiency and prepares for the Existentialist reconsideration of the problem.

We have already observed that Gide went to Africa, the scene of *Les Nourritures,* not as a tourist, but in search of the golden fleece. He journeyed *"vers cela,"* toward an indefinable something which would bring about the reconciliation of the polarities within him. He writes:

One morning I ventured to take a much longer walk than usual; the country, for all its monotony, had an inexhaustible attraction for me; . . . An azure haze lent distance to the foreground and made every object imponderable, immaterial. I myself, a creature without weight, walked slowly on, like Rinaldo in the garden of Armida, soul and body quivering, dazzled and amazed with a wonder beyond words. I heard, I saw, I breathed as I had never done before; and as the blended stream of sounds, perfumes and colours flooded my empty heart, I felt it dissolve in passionate gratitude.

"Take me, take me body and soul," I cried, sobbing out my worship to some unknown Apollo; "I am thine—obedient, submissive. Let all within me be light! Light and air! My struggle against thee has been vain. But now I know thee. Thy will be done! I resist no longer. I am in thy hands. Take me!"

And so, my face wet with tears, I entered an enchanting universe full of laughter and strangeness.[41]

A less lyrical version of the above occurs in a letter written to "A . . . R . . .":

I no longer exist . . . blessed state; henceforth I am nothing but comprehension, affection, passion, sensation, action even, work to be written and everything else you want—to all this I no longer oppose myself; I no longer oppose myself to myself and it is for this reason that I say that I no longer am.[42]

Of particular interest here is the ease with which Gide identifies "all this" with "myself." This mystical attitude is accentuated in the "Take me!" of the previous passage which he experienced after a near-fatal sickness. It is reminiscent of the cry "Drink my defenseless heart, O all indulgent sun!" of *Les Nouvelles Nourritures*[43] as well as of Olivier's "Take me away!" addressed to Edouard. In yet another and more conventional language Gide will say: "[Lord,] seize a heart that I am incapable of giving you."[44] We have already seen Gide's desire to lose and find himself in the perfect society of the millenium. His repeated attacks on mysticism notwithstanding, Gide reveals his mysticism in still other ways.

Religious Mysticism

The word *mystery* keeps coming under Gide's pen with unusual frequency in his references to external reality. His *Notes d'un Voyage en*

Bretagne is dominated by a sense of the mysteriousness of things which he both seeks and fears.[45] He will note in the course of a journey to the Congo that "nothing is more fetching than the dark mystery of the liquid corridors" of that land. Here the word *fetching* is to be read against the background of a feeling entertained already at a much earlier age, that awareness of mystery is proof of comprehension.[46] Nor is this sense of the mysteriousness of things, of there being a reality *behind* them, awakened in unfamiliar surroundings only. He will feel an "unadulterated awe" not only in front of a cathedral but in the most prosaic surroundings.[47] A sense of mystery attaches also to the object of Edouard's love: everything about Olivier is attractive to him—and mysterious, which is an instance of Edouard's being solicited by strangeness.[48] More generally, Gide will say in his old age that "everything below the surface remains a mystery."[49] It follows that when he tends to ridicule those who behave intellectually as if the world were an enigma of which we had to find the key,[50] the intent is to condemn not the view that the world is a mystery, but the quite different view that the world is a puzzle. The metaphysical anxiety induced by one's existence in the world is not to be confused with one's dismay as one faces a difficult, but in principle at least solvable, problem. Gide was given to the sort of anxiety which we see, for example, in Dostoevsky's *The Possessed,* where Kirillov searches for a justification of his own existence, an anxiety which probably informs all search for justification. He sought transrational relief from this metaphysical anxiety not only in art, pure love, nature, and society but also along Oriental religious paths.

Despite his claim that "*I* no longer exist," Gide, speaking of the "limitless possibilities of acceptance" that he still felt in himself in his later years, said that "they in no wise commit my innermost self." He expected from events "no profound modification of [his] being."[51] The dilemma between, on one hand, an "innermost self" that is indifferent to temporal change and, on the other, an *I* that no longer exists, is reflected not only in the writings of such a recognized mystic as Henry Suso, but also in Upanishadic mysticism. Gide believed in accordance with that mysticism that all individuals were related not so much to each other as to a single center. Moreover his manner of saying that the Great Self ("God") is unknowable was to refer to Him in many, incompatible ways.[52]

There are other uncanny similarities between Gide's broad metaphysical position and certain tenets of Oriental religions, which remind the reader of the Japanese details the Impressionists added to their canvases. Gide took the epigraph of *Les Nourritures Terrestres* from the Koran:

But announce to those who believe and do the things that are right, that for them are gardens 'neath which the rivers flow: So oft as they are fed therefrom with fruit for sustenance, they shall say, "This same was our sustenance of old": And they shall have its like given to them. Therein shall they have wives of perfect purity, and therein shall they abide for ever.[53]

The notion which he sometimes expressed that there is no end to desire, and the state of desirelessness to which he aspired are superficially reminiscent of Buddhism, hiding perhaps, deeper agreements with that world-view at one or two points. After smoking a bit of *kief* (sic) in a café at Blida, "Perhaps," he muses, ". . . did it contribute to the reality of my well-being. This well-being was not at all made of the satisfaction of desires, but of the fading of desire, and of renunciation of everything."[54] There is even an occasional adherence to Buddha's doctrine of "noble silence" as when he avers that a cart of vegetables carries more truth than the most beautiful sentences of Cicero, or in God's claim, as reported by Gide, that the least burgeon, as it develops, explains Himself to Himself better than all the ratiocinations of the theologues.[55]

Gide was not at home in this world. In his essay entitled *Mysticism and Logic,* Bertrand Russell has observed that

All who are capable of absorption in an inward passion must have experienced at times the strange feeling of unreality in common objects, the loss of contact with daily things, in which the solidity of the outer world is lost, and the soul seems, in utter loneliness, to bring forth, out of its own depths, the mad dance of fantastic phantoms which have hitherto appeared as independently real and living.[56]

Gide repeatedly noted his lack of a "certain sense of reality." He wrote on one occasion:

I can be extremely sensitive to the outer world, but I never succeed completely in believing in it. What I am saying has nothing theoretical about it. . . . I can imagine that a very learned doctor would be able to discover that some "internally secreting gland," some "adrenal capsule" is atrophied in me.[57]

The last remarks are indicative of the psychosomatic views which he did not hold in his more serious moments. More interesting is his statement that his failure to believe completely in the outer world has nothing "theoretical" about it. But then it is possible to maintain that Platonistic doubts as to the reality of the phenomenal world are themselves a matter not initially of theory, but of built-in temperament.[58]

Gide speculates that the sense of the exterior world must vary greatly according to the animal species. A cat, he surmises, would not be, upon leaving the dining room, too greatly surprised to find a virgin forest instead of the habitual long room. Would *he* be surprised? He answers that he would, but adds quickly that that is a rationalization: "I can never get over a certain amazement that things are as they are, and if they were suddenly different, it seems to me that that would hardly amaze me any more. The physical world always seems to me a little fantastic."[59]

Amusement is the word that strikes him as adequate to describe his reactions as a young man to the fall of an old coachman, the driver of the carriage in which he was traveling; or to the threats of a gondolier who held him up at midnight in Venice. The term "amusement" has no overtones of insensitivity. It is the reaction of an onlooker to what transpires on a stage, a sort of involvement with built-in distance. Gide saves the coachman from death "taking part in all that as if at a show outside of reality."[60] We may also observe that his lack of a sense of reality served a practical purpose: he wanted to be a writer, and a master had said that a writer-to-be must experience the world as a series of illusions:

But already a certain remark of Flaubert's had given me the cue. . . . It is "advice" that Flaubert is giving to a young man who is planning to write. He says (I do not take responsibility for quoting it exactly): "If the external world has ceased to appear to you as anything but an illusion to be described. . . ." And I do not indulge in metaphysics. I forbid myself to be a mystic, and my intelligence does not give complete assent either to Kant or to Plato. It's something else. I am not worried to know whether or not I believe in the external world: it is the *feeling of reality* that I haven't got. It seems to me that we are all moving about in a fantastic show and that what others call reality, that their external world, has not much more existence than the world of *Les Faux-Monnayeurs* or of *Les Thibault*.[61]

The adjective "complete" in "my intelligence does not give complete assent either to Kant or to Plato" is baffling. What Gide must mean is that he differs from Kant and Plato in *thinking* that the existence of a world of which this one is either the appearance or the imperfect copy is not logically warranted. A temperamental cautiousness, however, an instinctive lack of confidence in his own judgment or his ineradicable mysticism prevent him from seeing that his disagreement is radical and that he should give to Kant or Plato no assent at all in this matter. If Gide is lumping Kant and Plato together as mystics, it would be expected that his "intelligence" enthusiastically balk against them. Yet he forbids himself to follow in their trail. It is odd that a man should forbid himself to be a mystic—that is, commit the moral act of saying to himself "I *must* not be"—when his intelligence has already led him to the conclusion that mysticism is false. The implication once more is that Gide rejected unreasonableness under the label of mysticism, but genuine mysticism he could not quite succeed in casting off, even theoretically. His life in the material reality of the world was not a matter of course. It involved a measure of deliberate effort.[62]

One of the meanings of the proposition: "the material world is an illusion, or does not have a substantiality of its own" is that one must not live in it in earnest, or must not take it seriously. Gide sometimes attributed his lack of a sense of reality to a religious cause, namely to his "detachment" from "this world," which was due, he thought, to his Christian upbringing. He tended as he said to have his authentic existence outside the world of the senses. Desire which belongs in this realm did not interfere with love because it was not important enough to enhance or damage love which belongs in a realm other than that of time.[63] Sensuous reality is the "content" of space. Along with it Gide lacked also the sense of the content of time, namely of history. History was quite unreal to him. The actual history of mankind assumed in his eyes the nature of fiction, and he, as a young creative artist, contemplated writing another.[64]

He was antihistorical by nature, as he says, and under the influence of Mallarmé and "German philosophy," claiming to work "in the absolute," and in reaction against Taine's theories he was completely pushed in the direction of his inclination. A friend had eventually to open his eyes to his almost complete lack of a feeling of historical duration, "so that, . . . reacting against myself, I take care to situate and anchor my thoughts in time." But this resolution, similar to his resolution to inhabit the real world, could not be permanent. As he advanced in years and the world situation deteriorated he longed for "pure and simple contemplation."[65] In line with his contention that *therefores* do not lead to certainty, Gide advocated on the whole a life whose moments would not be linked together horizontally. Time for him was a series of juxtaposed instants, each of which was an escape hatch to eternity. In principle at least, each instant had to acquire its meaning from a vertical dimension of its own, rather than depend on its antecedents and consequents. The repercussion of this approach to time in his art is, as Germaine Brée has observed, that "[Gide] does not, like the ordinary novelist, merely accept as a fact that in a story the time sequence is like the river bed which sustains the flow of a life."[66]

Gide was bound to recognize occasionally that the present inherits its meaning and structure from the past. But the philosophy which most dominantly informs *Les Nourritures Terrestres* remains present throughout his work. It centers around the virtue of forgetting the past-present-future for the sake of the present, and is expressive essentially of a Neo-Platonistic attitude: "Nathanaël, I will speak to you of the *instants.* . . ." Gide does link his philosophy of the full enjoyment of the instant with the fact of death, but gives no evidence of his awareness that the glorification of the instant is an altogether arbitrary device by which to overcome the sense of absurdity which attends the knowledge that at the end of the series of instants, or rather in the course of them, there is annihilation. He concentrates on the power of each instant: "The littlest instant of life is stronger than death and negates it." He continues to speak of instants elsewhere in the same book:

Have you understood of what power is their *presence?* . . . A not sufficiently constant thought of death has not given sufficient value to the littlest instant of your life. . . . And do you fail to understand that each instant would not have taken this admirable lustre if not detached so to say against the very dark background of death?

The thought recurs a few pages later and it is more explicit: "If you knew, eternal idea of appearance, what value the close expectation of death gives to the instant!" As the idea travels through the book it gathers momentum:

We are nothing, Myrtil, but in each instant of life; all the past dies therein before the birth of anything that is to come. Instants! You will understand, Myrtil, of what power is their *presence!* for each instant of our life is essentially irreplaceable: know at times how to concentrate on them uniquely.

From a philosophical standpoint the series of statements quoted is simply inaccurate. The very concept "present" is no more than a function of both "past" and "future." Gide is, to be sure, speaking not of the concept but of the experience of the moment and is actually advocating the enjoyment of it without the concepts of past, present, and future entertained in one's head. It may be argued that one may, indeed, induce oneself to feel the power of the presence of the instant, an experience that can be had either below or above the human predicament: as an animal, perhaps, and at the unitive stage of the mystics. Gide's advocacy of the pure enjoyment of the present moment is a variant of his desire to touch God, to relate to Him, or to Nature, directly. It also runs parallel to the claim that to contradict oneself is to be sincere twice. If we disregard these correspondences and, further, divest the passage quoted of its attractive lyricism, we are left with a rather paltry injunction which Gide probably did not mean: you are walking on wet sand on a pleasantly warm Sunday afternoon, and the thought that the next day you will have to engage in a work not of your choice annoys you. Simply drive it out of your mind! Concentrate on the pleasure of walking, now, on wet sand! The alternative to this artificial determination is to find every moment fascinating, no matter what the occupation at hand—or the lack of it—with the conviction that each moment is impossible to replace. There is of course no logical connection between a moment's being irreplaceable and its not being used for the preparation of another, possible moment. If and when this other moment comes it will also be irreplaceable, and one may enjoy the present moment *because* it is preparing a better one. But Gide's ethic is against that of La Fontaine's *The Grasshopper and The Ant,* since his impatience is with time itself, and hides the profound anxiety of one who is threatened by death. It is, expressed differently, Dylan Thomas' rage against the dying of the light.

The secular glorification of the instant wears a religious dress in *Numquid et tu . . . ?* where it is said that eternity is, or can be made into, a quality of time. Gide was aware of the difference between eternity and everlastingness:

Eternal life is not only to come. It is right now wholly present in us; we live it from the moment that we consent to die to ourselves, to obtain from ourselves this renunciation which permits resurrection in eternity.[67]

Within one or the other of these sets of terms (that of *Les Nourritures Terrestres* and of *Numquid et tu . . . ?*), while expressing his impatience with time, Gide doubted also of his own reality. He remained "tormented, without knowing it, by the need of putting [his reality] to the test." He felt himself "living in the conditional."[68] Part of his torment was due no doubt to his sophistication, to his being an offered man, offered partly to the dominant trends of his times. He did not attune himself intellectually to the feeling that built into the doubt of the reality of this world is the assurance of a reality beyond it. He insisted on the contrary that the only reality was the stuff with which the natural sciences deal:

Nothing is better designed than the study of the natural sciences to cure us of that anguish to which the pursuit of a metaphysical, inaccessible God necessarily leads. . . . Those who strive to see with "the eyes of the soul" are those who have never really known how to observe.[69]

This is a forced note in the generally mystical atmosphere created by Gide's writings. He jotted it down for the benefit of the Catholics, having in mind mainly M. Baumann, a bad observer—or botanist—who described cabbage heads as waving their "hairy leaves."[70] Gide could not tolerate such erroneous descriptions of things, but he nevertheless put the cart before the horse in the quotation just made: he says that the search for God leads to anguish when the plain fact is that it is anguish that leads to the search for God and generally gives God a transcendental status. The fundamental motivation behind Gide's advocacy of the observation of nature is not increase in scientific knowledge or any utilitarian advantage. It is an escape into Nature's faithfulness from the disappointments and ambiguities of daily existence. He did not believe in the existence of matter except as "penetrated" by and "open" to spirit. Nor did he consistently think that a mystical experience can be explained away as an effect of physiological perturbations. Mind is the primary reality. It needs matter, as Edouard says, "in order to bear its witness." He adds, "Hence the mystery of the incarnation."

Gide's horizon was never limited to "this world." Yet he is known in many circles as a humanist. Gaëtan Picon summarizes that estimate of him: "Gide affirms the classical position of humanism: limited to the terrestrial horizon, human life possesses a sufficient meaning."[71] This is clearly a mistake, as it is a mistake to assume that following an evolution Gide abandoned the religious stance of his youth. The mistake is due partly to the assumption that all discourse against "God" is evidence of at least humanism.

A Definitive Meaning of "God"

The variety of meanings with which Gide filled the word *God* itself is not disconcerting, for some of these meanings have greater validity than the rest; or even finality. These meanings can now be determined.

Gide did not find in the work of Henry James "that inexorable cone of shadow where the suffering soul hides himself." Nothing "divine," he said, inhabits that novelist's heroes whom he found "desperately worldly," living only in relation to each other, in function of these relations.[72] This is an instance of Gide's fascination with the problem of man's relationship with God while seeing it as a characteristic of Russian, as distinguished from Western, literature, the latter being concerned mainly with the relationship of men with men.[73]

Gide prayed in the evening one day: "Lord, grant me that I may have need of You tomorrow morning,"[74] a form of request reminiscent of St. Augustine's " 'Anon, anon,' 'presently,' 'leave me but a little.' "[75] But this, presumably, was not Gide's meaning. He explained thirteen years later that that prayer was not "an unconscious confession of indifference, a desire to make God wait, to put Him off till the morrow." It meant merely this:

"My Lord, may my first thought on awaking be for You, as my last thought this evening is for You;" . . . writing "to need You tomorrow morning" in no wise signified that I did not already and immediately feel that *need*.

"At that time," Gide goes on to add, "He used to fill me utterly. For the really devout soul can *the rest* preserve any real value? My need for God has ever been constant."[76]

The proposition "I need God" is intriguing because the verb *need* points to a desire without indicating whether the desire is or is not fulfilled. When I say "I need an automobile" my interlocutor is entitled to infer that I do not own one. But I can also say "I need my automobile," meaning that my ownership of it is no indulgence in luxury. Since Gide needed God, according to his own admission, *while* he was filled with Him utterly, his constant need of Him should point to his constant awareness of His needed presence. The same conclusion can be drawn from the first three sentences of *Les Nourritures Terrestres*. The first and third of these sentences constitute a paradox, while the second repeats that same paradox more succinctly: "Each creature indicates God, none reveals Him." Gide gave expression to the horns of this same dilemma at wide intervals. He wrote in *Les Nourritures* that God is that which is before us; he announced years later that "the thinking creature with himself alone as an end suffers from an abominable void."[77] The theological implication of these seemingly contradictory sayings is not that Nature is God, or that God *is* not, but that God is hidden. He is the secret reality.

"Now," Luther had said, "God in His own nature and majesty is to be left alone; in this regard, we have nothing to do with Him, nor does He wish us to deal with Him. We have to do with Him as clothed and displayed in His Word, by which He presents Himself to us. That is His glory and beauty, in which the Psalmist proclaims Him to be clothed."[78] *Les Nourritures Terrestres* belongs in this theology. Gide was never certain that he had ceased believing in what he called "the immanent omnipresence [of Christ],"[79] a description which rephrases Luther's theory of the ubiquity of Christ. When in Gide's shifting and peculiar terminology *God* meant nature itself, He not only ceased being the ultimate reality, but a new meaning was promptly attached to the word *Christ* and the formula "God = nature, Christ = supernature" promulgated, as if to ascertain the fact that nature is not absolute but contingent.[80]

Gide was drawn to what he vaguely referred to as "beyond," without believing in personal immortality. His mature conviction that "it is essential to be able to find happiness *beyond*," only repeats a declaration made thirty-one years earlier that it was impossible for him *not* to conceive a higher unity presiding over the struggling forces of, and division in, nature.[81]

Happiness lies in a recognition of agreement rather than of strife. And even if each of the forces of nature in turn struggled against all the others, it would be impossible for me not to conceive a higher unity presiding over that very struggle, starting-point of every division, in which each soul can take refuge for its own well-being.[82]

The search for the meaning of things beyond history was the manner in which Gide reacted to human anxiety. "Man has done nothing," he writes, quoting Dostoevsky's Kirillov, "but invent God in order to go on living and not kill himself: there's the summary of universal history up till now."[83] He writes more or less on his own behalf more succinctly that God is "but a projection of . . . [an] inner fervor."[84]

These statements have no logical validity: the fact that God does respond to an inner fervor is no proof of his nonexistence; that he quenches a spiritual thirst neither proves nor disproves that he is an imaginary device fabricated by men for the very purpose of satisfying themselves. Such statements display the correlation in the speaker's own mind between the absurd precariousness of life and the determination to anchor it on eternal Being. Why should a man invent God otherwise?

Gide's own implicit objection is invariably to the same misdeed: to conceive of God as another object, to "invent" God as one invents a tool for a specific need. It is for this reason that were it not for "that damned question of belief" (meaning here that which makes one say, for example, "the unicorn exists"), his assent to Catholicism *and* Protestantism would not have been beyond the realm of possibility. His reason bristles against such a faith. Many serious believers—and their number has kept increasing since Gide wrote these lines—would understand and support him in this protest.

An entry made in his *Journal* in 1931 further illustrates the manner in which Gide confesses his faith while presuming to attack faith. He writes:

. . . we do not adore the same God. And the only one in which I can believe, diffuse in nature, I am willing to grant them that he no longer deserves the name of God. In order to be seen by us, he does not ask for faith, but merely for attention. His mystery is all the greater for being in no way supernatural.[85]

Supernatural in Gide's mind again carries the connotation "hovering over nature," and this he cannot of course accept. On the other hand, "diffuse *in* nature" means "other than nature" and the difference between the two images of "over" and "in" is negligible, as long as God is, as Gide confesses, an object of "attention" and adoration. The following entry of 1941 could have been written by any recognized mystic:

I ought to confess honestly that I have ceased to know just what that image hides. In this case it is less a matter of a situation than of a spiritual state. One cannot get closer to what is everywhere. It is much rather a question of a transparency of the soul that allows us to feel Him. The majority of men do not know that *state of communion;* but it brings the soul, the entire being, such a delightful felicity that the soul is inconsolable after once having known it and then allowed it to slip away.

This is partly what makes me, without believing in any definite God, really enjoy only the company of pious souls.

Quietism? No; but constantly in a state of effort and stretched toward something indefinable and adorable, toward a higher condition in which the individual is lost and absorbed—to which I see no other name to give but the very name of God.[86]

This is not a stray, solitary saying. Gide often expressed in his own terms the Plotinian flight of the alone to the Alone. He had written in 1897: "If you wanted, if you knew, Myrtil, in this instant, no longer with a wife and children, you would be alone before God on earth."[87] And in 1928:

I must accept the fact that my path takes me away from those toward whom my heart inclines; and even recognize that it is my path from this: that it isolates me. If I were truly capable of prayer, I should cry out to God: Permit me to need only You.[88]

"If I were truly capable of prayer" is a remnant from his deliberate though unsuccessful opposition to mysticism. The passage itself is a prayer. After awakening to his obligations toward society Gide modified his mysticism by giving an added name to the Absolute. He called it "prolix humanity": "God holds me; I hold him; we are. But in thinking this, I am but one with all of creation; I melt and am absorbed in prolix humanity."[89]

"Prolix humanity" may mean mankind in its ongoing *élan*. Gide is avoiding supernaturalism, yet he is acknowledging it unawares through the use of the word *creation* which evidently implies a Creator. This ostensibly humanistic, but fundamentally theistic, declaration is made in *Les Nouvelles Nourritures*. The reader of this book is informed moreover that God dwells not in the object but in love, and that salvation or self-discovery is in love, which is a roundabout way of saying that salvation is in God. The humanism of *Les Nouvelles Nourritures* is entirely super-ficial. We have seen that Gide's moral sense was restored upon his realization that God was becoming. He writes:

No impiety or presumption in this thought, for I was convinced at one and the same time that God was achieved only by man and through man, but that if man led to God, creation, in order to lead to man, started from God; so that the divine had its place at both ends, at the start and at the point of arrival, and that the start had been solely in order to arrive at God. This bivalvular thought reassured me and I was unwilling to dissociate one from the other: God creating man in order to be created by him; God the end of

man; chaos raised up by God to the level of man and then man raising himself up to the level of God. To accept but one of them: what fear, what
obligation! To accept but the other: what self-satisfaction! It ceased to be a
matter of obeying God, but rather of instilling life into him, of falling in love
with him, of demanding him of oneself through love and of achieving him
through virtue.[90]

It is pointless to ask Gide to be more precise regarding the manner in
which a creature can create his creator, to mention but one of the host of
difficulties raised by this religious and metaphysical discursion. It is pointless to do so, because in attacking muddle-headedness in others Gide was
attacking a shortcoming or temptation of his own, and because the passage quoted, at once clear and obscure, is characteristically mystical. Gide
persistently refused to separate the life of man from the life of God, a
position which constitutes the tone of his entire opus. This is now explained in moral terms in a context where God appears to be the ground
of all existence, all in all, the alpha and the omega, and love. God is
creative power. He keeps the world together and propels it toward a
future perfection. This God always had a place in the innermost recesses
of Gide's being.

The Devil

Gide's concept of the Devil was, of necessity, a function of his concept
of God. The Devil is an agent of disruption. The logic of the Gidian
notion of the Devil is thus quite simple and entirely in agreement with
his therapeutic theory of art: being very much aware of his inner polarities he reasoned at first, and for a long time, that someone or something,
namely "the Devil," must do the polarizing. It then occurred to him that
the polarities may be there without such a mover. The Devil in Gide is
an agency of disruption even when he is made to be responsible for progress. Among an abundance of declarations to this effect, three rather
famous Gidian statements may be cited:

"There is no work of art without collaboration of the demon." This is
a good example of a sentence where an effective but misleading image
prevents accuracy. The word *collaboration* is enough to convey the image
of a co-author (hence the demon is thought of as someone) sitting alongside Gide at his desk and working with him. Gide has expressed the idea

elsewhere, without this image. Art for him is, among other things, an activity induced by inner polarities and contributing to their reconciliation. The meaning of the above quotation thus becomes clear. When there are no polarities, namely no "demon," there is no work of art.[91]

A second significant context where we are faced with the Devil is the *Journal des Faux-Monnayeurs*. Gide writes:

> *The treatise on the nonexistence of the Devil.* The more we deny him, the more reality we give him. The Devil is affirmed in our negation. . . .
>
> Of [the various characters] I should like one character (the Devil) to circulate incognito throughout the entire book, his reality growing stronger the less the other characters believe in him. This is the distinguishing feature of the devil, whose introductory motif is: "Why should you be afraid of me? You know very well I don't exist."[92]

The title of the novel—*Counterfeiters*—clarifies the meaning of the phrase "the Devil circulates incognito throughout the entire book." The novel is about a society where there are no genuine ties among people. Gide came to see eventually that the Devil was a mythical person created as a picturesque description of motor principles behind undesirable states of affairs. The more he is denied the more real he becomes, for those forces in society which bring about disruption will become greater and do more damage as they are covered up or ignored, metaphysics itself being a way of covering up with ponderous discourse the real causes of the human predicament. The Devil inhabits, as Dostoevsky has said, the region of the intellect: such questions as What is man? Whence does he come? and the like, if asked in the abstract, are promptings of the Devil.[93] Besides, reason, when it prides itself and has the temerity to answer the ultimate question, gets in the way of the mystic embrace, for it separates from the knower the thing known. Thus does the Devil do his disruptive work.

There is also the Gidian recognition of the demonic element in man:

> Vincent [of *Les Faux-Monnayeurs*] . . . lets himself be permeated by the diabolic spirit. He imagines he is becoming the Devil; it is when things go best for him that he feels the most damned. . . .
>
> He knows that in gaining the world he is losing his own soul.

In the story Vincent appears to be in the wrong profession: a physician who should be occupying a chair of comparative biology. This is the first sign of the disharmony within his being. A brilliant conversationalist, he is insensitive and morally irresponsible. He goes to Africa not, like Gide himself, "toward *that*," but after Lady Griffith. She in turn is a pure sensualist, has fortune, intelligence, beauty, but no soul. Vincent goes into the wilderness and finds not the way to salvation. He becomes a victim of the Prince of this world. His drowning of Lady Griffith in the jungles of Africa may be construed as an act of revolt against his own depravity. It is a crime all the same, made even more reprehensible by the circumstance that it is committed by ruse. His freedom and spontaneity appeal to the novelist who creates the world where Vincent has his being, but since Vincent has neither law nor master nor scruples, he is the novelist's despair. The Devil who is the agency of his disruption and estrangement is the same Devil whose name is Legion and who also estranges Saul, one of the most tragic characters created by Gide.

Saul, a ruler of Israel, wants and tries to pray but fails every time. The reason is given early in the first scene of the play. Genuine prayer was for Gide a state of being where there is no awareness of any obstacle between himself and reality at large. Saul, surrounded by demons, is an encaged, lonely man. That in Gide's mind the concepts of disruption, estrangement, and the Devil are the same is further evident from a remark in *Si le grain ne meurt*: ". . . decidedly the devil was on the watch for me; the shades of night were gathering thick and fast and no sign gave warning there was any rift through which a ray of light might reach me." Toward the end of that same book Gide held the Devil responsible for his being rent asunder, flesh on one side and spirit on the other, and for being torn from Em. altogether.[94]

There is, finally, the paradox of the Devil being a power contributing to progress, as observed by Justin O'Brien. Having noted Gide's agreement with Blake's proposition that "Without Contraries is no progression," Professor O'Brien writes:

Gide's interest in the Devil parallels his interest in Prometheus; more sophisticated and more subtle in its expression, it replaces that earlier interest. Perhaps because he had early traced a suggestive parallel between Prometheus and Christ, he hesitated to draw another one between Prometheus and Satan, those two arch unsubmissive spirits who both symbolized progress in his mind.[95]

A good summary by Gide himself of his views on God and the Devil is this: "When I say: the Evil one, I know what that expression designates just as clearly as I know what is designated by the word *God*. I draw his outline by the deficiency of each virtue."[96] Saint Augustine had written in *The City of God* that evil "is a name for nothing but the want of good."[97]

Gide's philosophy of religion is in line with that Augustinian theory of good and evil. He regretted the opacity of matter. While matter was thus a principle of distance, two spirits such as his own and Em.'s had the potentiality of commingling. The miracle was that matter could become a vehicle of spiritual communion: "matter is infinitely porous to spirit, accepter of all the laws, obedient, transparent from one end to the other." Again: "That matter should be penetrable and ductile and open to spirit; that spirit should join up with matter to the point of being undistinguishable from it—I am quite willing to call religious my wonder before that."[98]

We have had occasion to see that Gide was not unconditionally opposed to the mystery—or concept—of the Incarnation. The remark just quoted is itself almost a paraphrase of John 1:14: "And the Word became flesh and dwelt among us." Yet those critics who make of him a simple humanist and an unqualified advocate of progress and scientism are not to be blamed. Gide did his very best to confuse everyone. He refused to define himself. To define is to set limits. It is to isolate. Above all Gide wished not to *isolate* things, not to isolate himself.[99]

7

Gide's Morality

"Good," Naturalness, Passivity

On the whole Gide's morality is beyond good and evil; he belongs to a school which claims that what the generality of men recognize at any one time as "good" or "bad" is not good or bad absolutely. One must not conform to what others say is good, or to what they have built into idols. This ethics is essentially a protest against limited and limiting prescriptions. Gide also appears to condemn the view that pleasure is bad because it is pleasurable, or that it must not be enjoyed for its own sake. Whether the intrinsic goodness of pleasure was a Gidian conviction is doubtful. He was certainly no hedonist.

Gide's intense concern with morality is apparent in his repeated, though not uncontradicted, claim that of all his books *Corydon* is the most important. It is in this book that he presents his most sustained theory of the good life, though his motivation for writing it is not to solve a philosophical problem. What urges him on is missionary zeal. "I have persuaded myself," he says, "that this book, however subversive it may seem, is directed only against falsehood," and he is ready to sacrifice himself so that truth may prevail.

Corydon is more the documented presentation of a case than a creative work. Even then it is written in the manner of a Gidian novel: the reader is there to behold not the final product of a thinking process but the process itself. Having said "gravely" that he will not publish the book, Corydon, whom we observe writing *Corydon,* considers the necessity of martyrdom. He then hesitates a moment, and says finally: "Perhaps I shall not withhold [publication]."

The completed book may not be the successful "defense" of homosexuality it purports to be. The grounds on which Gide advocates its "goodness" provide nevertheless the most certain clues as to what he means by *good*. His theory of morality can confidently be extracted from this book. *Corydon* is composed of four Dialogues, the first of which is an introduction to the other three. In the short foreword to the second Dialogue the plan of the defense is announced. The material is divided into three parts: the first will consider homosexuality from the point of view of natural history; the second will discuss it as seen in history, literature and the arts; the third will look at it from the point of view of sociology and morality.

Having read the book composed according to this outline, the reader will conclude with Corydon—so Gide hopes, at any rate—(a) that homosexuality is natural; (b) that it contributes to the creation of beauty; and (c) that it is conducive to strength as well as to such virtues as bravery, honor, sobriety, and chastity. It follows that a given behavior deserves praise and not blame when it conforms to nature, improves the world esthetically, and is useful to society. Of these, "naturalness" is Gide's most comprehensive ethical concept. It covers his reputed sensualism, his opposition to family and "cause," his *disponibilité,* his theory of the *acte gratuit,* his peculiar brand of "individualism," his indecision between freedom and determinism, his "sincerity," as well as his occasional advocacy of a morality of abnegation. The ethics of conformity to nature is in keeping with Gide's passivity, which is his fundamental temperamental trait. His homosexuality is itself an instance of this passivity.

No doubt the problem of interpersonal communication is a complex one. Yet it is roughly correct to say that every human encounter is initially a conflict which can be solved in only one of three ways: as a man is faced with another being he may either eliminate his own resistance to the other, seek to eliminate the other's resistance, or establish a fair give-and-take. While Gide, like the generality of men, aspired toward the third of these, he adopted in his fiction the second alternative where the No-sayer is eliminated in the person of a woman often modeled after mother-and-Madeleine the Puritan. In real life Gide had recourse to the first alternative more often than not. He was passive. He resisted certain pressures with tenacity, yet he was always on the defensive. He was almost always ready to abandon his stand in favor of the opponent's. His thought often proceeded in function of someone else's, a propensity which he analyzes as due to his desire of being in sympathy with the rest of the world.[1] He was helplessly inclined to hand himself over to friend and foe alike.[2] He also informs us that his "only care was to reveal [others' thoughts] to them."[3]

Gide, who had "the least pugnacious temperament" and was "not at all revolutionary," was not a man of initiative except in the field of literature. When he wrote in *La Tentative amoureuse* (*The Attempt at Love*) that Luc dared nothing, he was, as usual, describing himself.[4] Bernard of *Les Faux-Monnayeurs* is not an aggressive person, though this must not be taken to mean that he lacked courage. Having left the house where he grew up, the only decision of any consequence that he makes is to defy ordinary decency. He steals Edouard's luggage under completely safe circumstances and reads the owner's personal papers. His leaving the house is essentially an act of faith, a willingness to abandon himself to the influences that might be coming his way. He does *not* join a cause, but we do not see him engage in any act of daring. Gide himself, at the age of forty-five, during a most critical shortage of manpower in France could not find for himself an employment commensurate with his competence.

There is a revealing detail in *Si le grain ne meurt* that indicates his lack of initiative even as a schoolboy. Gide recalls that as a youth he decided, he did not know exactly why, to leave the Ecole Alsacienne for the Lycée Henri IV. Then he gives a more elaborate account of the same change:

The Ecole Alsacienne, though excellent in the lower classes, was supposed at that time to be less good in the higher. *Rhétorique* did at a pinch, but my mother was advised that it would be better for me to attend my *philosophie* at one of the regular *lycées* and she decided on the Lycée Henri IV. I myself, however, had resolved to prepare my next examinations alone or with the help of a few private lessons.[5]

Informed of this detail, the reader of the autobiography no longer wonders why young Gide did not know the reason for his decision to change schools. The decision simply was not *his*.

Gide speaks of the small shadow cast by his person in *Les Nourritures Terrestres* and observes that all happiness is fortuitous.[6] "Everything that one prescribes and *wishes* to obtain is constraint," he writes decades later as he observes the filming of natives in Chad. "It would be of greater value, often, to pluck the happy offerings of chance."[7] As a rule he let time solve his problems. When Ali, his little guide, flings himself down a sandhill, naked, Gide "waits," and the boy takes the initiative, where-upon Gide makes one of his better known observations:

I waited! I wonder today at my fortitude. . . . But was it really curiosity that held me back? I am not sure. The secret motive of our acts—I mean of the most decisive ones—escapes us; and not only in memory but at the very moment of their occurrence.[8]

This is not an isolated instance. At Biskra his mother sees Meriem leave, at dawn, the premises occupied by Gide and his friend Paul. "It was obvious a woman had come from Paul's room," he writes. "It was certain my mother had seen her, had understood. . . . What could I do but wait? I waited."[9] Like Bernard of *Les Faux-Monnayeurs* he knew what he did not want[10] and waited for events to pull him out of unde-sirable situations. His relationship with his wife is a case in point. Crisis after crisis occurred. No explanation, no frank discussion between hus-band and wife ever took place. A solution of a sort came only with Madeleine's death in 1938.

Gide became a person of political importance with his condemnation of abuses in the French colonies of Africa upon his return from a jour-ney to the Congo in 1925. The entire episode of his protests against the exploitation of the Negroes is limited to the exchange of a few letters. Promises were made to ameliorate the situation, by way of calming ruffled sensibilities. No steps of any importance were taken, and no per-son in authority was unduly disturbed over the artist's deprecations. Gide himself had not proposed any change in the system. He had invited the white men in charge in Africa to be more human within that system, for he was still under the impression, at the time, that inner dispositions can assure the welfare of all, regardless of the shape of the social struc-ture.[11]

Gide was not always willing to admit that at the time of his first jour-ney to Africa, when he raised no problems of social justice at all, he was concerned with himself only. He writes:

If I had kept a journal during my first trips to Algeria as I did daily in the Congo, most likely I should have spoken of the business of the Gafsa phos-phates, which I was then able to follow closely, of the withdrawal of the white Father after the death of Cardinal Lavigerie, and especially of the arrival of barrels of absinthe to break down the natives, and of the expropriation of the Arabs by the device of the Cazenave bank according to a monstrous method that I would probably have exposed.[12]

This piece of *apologia pro vita sua* written at the height of Gide's Communistic sympathies is pathetic, and invalid. He is saying, in effect, that had he written on a piece of paper the information he had in his head, he would have protested. The fact is that even after his experiences in the Congo there remains an element of unreality about Gide's concern for the welfare of the natives. He suffers in his heart with a detached, abstract sentimentality. He does not appear to be concerned with *these* people and their children. He is not engaged actively in the amelioration of their lot. He is a compassionate soul, an observer, for whom the living and their offspring are no more concrete than the dead. R. Martin du Gard reports Gide's uncontrollable sobs upon hearing that a native African tribe had been destroyed by white men—twenty-four years earlier.[13] Clearly the men of this tribe had as much substantiality as Agamemnon, whose fate also caused him to sob uncontrollably.

Men of action led him when he raised his voice against concrete, present injustice. André Malraux was with him, for example, when the liberation of Georges Dimitrov, in one case, and that of Ernest Thaelmann, on another, were at issue.[14] He was "pushed" into his most noteworthy act of *engagement,* namely his open, temporary espousal of the Communist cause. He writes:

Emotionally, temperamentally, intellectually, I have always been a Communist. But I was afraid of my own thought and, in my writings, strove more to hide than to express it. I listened too much to others and gave them more credence than I did myself, as much through sympathy as through lack of self-assurance, through incurable modesty, through fear of "being entirely of my own opinion." Events over yonder have taken this in hand and I am grateful to them for pushing me to it.[15]

Gide seemed to be acting on his own initiative and against the advice of many when he declared his disappointment with communism in *Le Retour de l'U.R.S.S.,* and in the subsequent *Retouches* to it. But then he was back safely in his native non-Communist land. Another more important venture had been the publication of *Corydon.* Here too Gide's well-being or literary fame was not threatened. In writing the essay Gide was under the impression that he was rendering an invaluable service to mankind. The common acceptance of uranism was indispensable if the fabric of society was not to collapse.[16] The book seemed to acquire in Gide's eyes the stature of a messianic message; it is as if he expected the world to be divided into two camps upon its reception: those for and those against it. When he was informed of a request to publish it in New York, he was "very amused to see that America is the first to declare herself."[17] Yet it is doubtful whether Gide would have published that work had not Freud's authority supported him.[18]

The printing of part of the book in 1911 and its general distribution thirteen years later were acts of courage nevertheless. The paradox is that Gide is most aggressive as he declares to the world the principal symptom of his passivity. People given to homosexuality, he himself admits, may have developed that inclination as a consequence of being "disconcerted and repelled by the mystery of another sex."[19] He says elsewhere that we owe our "respect" for women to homosexuality.[20]

Gide was *anti*-fascist; *anti*-Stalinist. Such negative activities as *désoccidentaliser, décatholiciser, déciviliser* have been attributed to him.[21] He was prone to define himself in negative terms. He thought in the last years of his life that it was "essential—not to be this or that, but—to be."[22] Since it is ordinarily impossible to *be* without being this or that, Gide's opinion of what is essential must be taken to indicate a refusal to live in time and space, perhaps a wish—to use the phrase of William James —to be "grasped and held by a superior power," superior, that is, to the phenomenal world. James called this state of affairs Passivity and made of it the fourth mark of mysticism.[23] Withal Gide did not lack fervor, or what another prominent student of mysticism called "initiative on the soul's part." Gide called it *passion*.[24]

Transparency

He had another name for genuine mystical passivity of which his passivity in the world was a symptom. He called it *disponibilité* and meant by it an ideal akin to Keats' "negative capability," or Wordsworth's "wise passiveness" defined by the philosophical critic William Barrett as "the inflow of feelings from an enveloping nature."[25] *Disponibilité* denotes a religious-moral obligation to be available or open to any experience that outer reality may bring or suggest: the truth, or a truth, might reveal itself tomorrow, and one must keep in readiness for it, with the consequence that one will perpetually keep oneself in abeyance. Rimbaud erate Dionysian abandonment to every possibility of sensual and emo-also comes to mind in this connection. He was convinced "that a delib-

tional experience can lead, like a kind of inverted fakirism, to the knowledge and expression of an essential Reality behind all appearances."[26] Some such aim may have led Gide to his famous precept: "To assume the largest possible measure of humanity."[27] The following passage constitutes a good Gidian definition of that ideal: "Nathanaël, let each expectation, in you, be not even a desire—but simply a disposition to receive.—Await all things that come to you; but desire only what comes to you.—Desire only what you have." The thought is subsequently amplified:

My soul was the open inn at the crossroad; he who wished to enter, entered. I made myself ductile, in a friendly way, available through all my senses, attentive, a listener until I had not *one* personal thought, captor of all emotion passing by, and so slight was my reaction to things that rather than protest against anything, I no longer held anything as evil.[28]

Of particular interest in this passage is the word *attentive* in view of Gide's conviction that God needs not faith but attention. The injunction: "Await all things that come to you" is impossible to obey because one can only wait—in the ordinary meaning of *wait*—for a *known* entity; nor can one desire only what one has, for the simple reason that one does not desire what one already has. Gide's meaning is that one must make of receptiveness a principle of life: not only must one be willing to give assent to any occurrence whatever, but one must go a step further and *wish* for anything at all, simultaneously generating within oneself the conviction that whatever one now has or whatever experiences one is now undergoing are or have been the result of such a wish. It is to the psychological state where one wills any experience at all—to that unreserved suspenseful commingling of the entire person with the totality of things —that Gide gave the name *ferveur*. It is a sort of enthusiasm in the etymological meaning of the word.

It must be added that Gide was not uncritical of the ideal of *disponibilité*, though it remained with him all his life. One cannot admit into one's lifeboat *all* the shipwrecked, and if it is to remain afloat, some hands reaching for it must be ruthlessly severed.[29] This haunting, bloody image was his criticism of that ideal. The very savagery of the image is an indication of the violence with which he reacted to his own limitedness as "this" individual, or to the regrettable impossibility of being *disponible* entirely.

It was necessary to dwell on Gide's mystical passivity for a correct reappraisal of his reputed sensualism. The suggestion that Gide was strictly sensualist "at least" at the time of *Les Nourritures Terrestres,* is made for example by Archambault.[30] Gide appears to be a better critic of his own work when he writes that not even hedonism can be extracted from *Les Nourritures Terrestres.* What he looked for through the pages of that book was life "in the third person."[31] However, if sensualism is the ethical doctrine that gratification of the senses is the highest good, Gide was not a sensualist. Such Gidian statements that may lead to the conclusion that he was a sensualist turn out to hide, upon closer examination, an advocacy of the view that true felicity is beyond physical pleasure.

Gide has argued in *Corydon* that what is known as "sexual instinct" does not exist. He presents with considerable self-gratulation as "his" original theory the view that what the male animal seeks is pleasure and not necessarily the consummation of desire with an individual of the opposite sex.[32] This theory—whether valid or not—ought not to lead to the conclusion that Gide attributed a certain finality to the pleasure principle. Rather, he was of the more or less paradoxical opinion that indulgence in pleasure is good because desire, standing as it does in the way of more valuable experiences, is bad. The thing to do is to be rid of desire, and such means of being rid of it as do not harm anyone can be adopted with impunity. The entirety of Gide's ethics consists in putting the flesh out of the way: he tried *silencing* the flesh until about the time of his first trip to Africa, and when this means did not prove efficacious he advocated *indulgence* as a means toward the same end. A given pleasurable experience, Gide says in effect, is not, because of the sheer accident of its being pleasurable, to be condemned. It does not deserve blame. The underlying philosophy of *Les Nourritures Terrestres* is that pleasure is natural, and its indulgence is the manner in which one opens up and enters into existential contact with reality, whereas its repression is a result of human decrees; when bottlenecked, it turns the individual upon himself and alienates him.

This is not sensualism. Gide knew with Freud that desires may be satisfied unconditionally only where a man is by himself—as in the paradise of *Les Nourritures Terrestres.* It is perhaps the memory of that theoretical exaltation and its transposition to a Plotinian level that made him observe later in life that "the only salvation is in solitude."[33] But unbridled sensual satisfaction is foolishness for a social being as demonstrated in the sorry destiny of Saul, the head of a commonwealth.

The basic trouble with the proposition that desires must be satisfied as a means of being rid of them is of course that desire is a temporal, this-worldly impulse and cannot be finally vanquished until one transcends temporality altogether.[34] Gide looked upon pleasure as the physically felt accompaniment of freedom. From other vantage points he condemned it. Great souls cannot stop at pleasure, for the Idea must use them, he said. At a more mature age he saw in the sense of duty the distinguishing mark of a moral being capable of transcending materiality and connected it with happiness.[35] The occasional reconciliation in his writings of duty with pleasure can be accounted for partly by the fact that like many other words *pleasure* had peculiar meanings for him depending on the role which it played in his scheme of things and of which he happened to be thinking at the moment. Thus pleasure makes the blade of grass grow, it prepares the corolla for the kisses of sunbeams.[36] In his poetic way Gide is here attributing to pleasure functions that are sometimes attributed to God or to such motor principles as nisus and *élan vital*. Likewise, when he presents *volupté* as the criterion of the perfection of an act, or as the decisively affirmative factor in moral choice, he is advocating self-abandonment to a metaphysical absolute.[37]

Pleasure is used in other contexts with other connotations. Here is a good deal of Existentialism given in a nutshell:

All choice is frightening, when one thinks of it; frightening a liberty that a duty no longer guides.—It is a path to elect in a country which is unknown on all sides, where each one makes *his* discovery and, observe it well, makes it only for himself. . . . the country exists only as it is formed gradually by our approach and the countryside around arranges itself little by little before our walk.[38]

And yet, wherever Nathanaël goes he will meet "God" who is already there. *Volupté* or *pleasure* appears to accompany the process of bringing oneself into existence in accordance with an already given dynamic Presence. *Pleasure* is also a cosmic aim. While it is toward pleasure that all nature's efforts tend, it is simultaneously a means to an end. It is perhaps the consciousness of being subjected to an appointed destiny, as

when the butterfly escapes from the prison of the chrysalis. This last
image suggests the sort of liberation which "Fabrice" experienced with
young "Michel" at his side.[39]

There is always a trace of bravura in Gide's elaborations with regard
to the permissibility of pleasure when the word is used to mean sensual
titillation, and is not a function of more inclusive human aims. He himself, "spiritualistic to an unbelievable degree,"[40] did not indulge in
pleasure as frequently as certain of his confessions might lead one to
suppose.[41] Edouard on his way to Paris from England notes how short he
has been on pleasure and proposes to go to a house of ill-fame as soon as
he arrives in the capital. The proposal does not appear to have been
carried out. The fact is that Gide never quite overcame a sense of guilt
attendant upon indulgence in pleasure for the sake of pleasure, and his
condemnation of it is not restricted to the period of *Numquid et
tu . . . ?*[42] A close reading of some of the most salacious passages of *Si
le grain ne meurt* and *Ainsi soit-il* will further support the contention
that while Gide knew intellectually that desire in itself is not an unclean
thing, he satisfied it not for its own sake but in order to gain spiritual
freedom, in the manner of one who turns away from an alluring but
basically unwanted sight at which he has looked only to be rid of a
pestering curiosity. These passages must be read against the background
of an important declaration made in *Les Nourritures Terrestres*:

For, what one deprives oneself of today, they used to read to me in the Gospel,
later one rediscovers a hundredfold. . . . Ah! what should I do with more
good things than my desire can apprehend?—for I have already known
luxurious pleasures so strong that a little more and I would no longer have
been able to taste them.[43]

While he abides by his determination not to continue to read the Bible,
Gide could probably cite from memory the verse to which allusion is
made: "And everyone who has left houses or brothers or sisters or father
or mother or children or lands, for my name's sake, will receive a
hundredfold, and inherit eternal life."[44] He is in agreement with the
principle of renunciation set forth in this verse, but not with the purpose
for which renunciation is enjoined, for he does not believe in immortality.
The promise *as promise* is pointless, he feels, for he knows that he has
already reached the maximum he can enjoy. He, in the manner of Blake,
in his poem "Eternity," kissed the joy as it flew and lived "in eternity's

sun rise." Any hypothetical value beyond that would be tantamount to pouring more than a gallon of water in a one-gallon receptacle. The extra bliss would be a waste. The hidden meaning of "luxurious pleasures so strong that a little more and I would no longer have been able to taste them" is revealed in the last pages of *Si le grain ne meurt*.

It is during the "ecstasy" with Mohammed, Gide informs us, that he found his normal "nature." He appears to be in agreement with Aristophanes' analysis given in mythical dress in the *Symposium* that men and women are born with sexual propensities which are to be recognized as essentially different on the basis of the object to which these propensities are directed. But our interest must center on the ethical aspect of the problem, namely on the value attached to sensual pleasure. The passage where the story of the ecstasy with Mohammed is told in great detail leads, when read attentively, to conclusions other than the ones Gide seems to wish to suggest.

In the first place, Oscar Wilde, who made the ecstasy of that night possible for Gide and whom Gide generally respects, is here cast practically in the role of Satan. Bigger than Gide, he bends, and his "huge hand" clutches young Gide's shoulder as claws clutch a prey; his "interminable, uncontrollable, insolent laugh" increases as Gide becomes more disconcerted, and reverberates through the evening. One need not read the image of Mephistopheles into the text. Gide volunteers the information that "it was the amusement of a child and a devil." It was the work of the "Adversary," and though Gide "had already triumphed *in my imagination* and *my thoughts* over all my scruples," he felt he was "vanquished." He had pronounced the crucial *yes,* but he still did not wish to show the violence of his desire, not even to Wilde, a reluctance which can only mean that he wished this desire were not there in the first place. The night with Mohammed was preceded by a period of excessive self-gratification. In it, "in excess itself," he was seeking "escape." He hoped "to come out into the fresh air *on the other side,* to wear out *my demon* (I recognize his wile), when it was only myself I wore out, expending myself crazily to the point of utter exhaustion, to the verge of imbecility, of madness."

The phrase to be retained is "utter exhaustion," in contrast with his ostensibly unbounded joy with Mohammed. As one reads on, one sees that the ineffable ecstasy with his partner in pleasure did not at all constitute a climax. It is episodic, incidental. It was a means to an end. One is neither revolted nor scandalized, but rather moved to pity as one observes young André Gide being taken in by his own words and mistaking for "passionate jubilation" and "ecstasy" the stubborn fury with which he was trying to get even with his "demon." He was actually inflicting upon himself a punishment of sorts, and was far from that contented state where D. H. Lawrence's gamekeeper, for example, finds himself after his intimacies with Lady Chatterley. "Glutted and exhausted as I was, I had no rest nor respite till I had pushed exhaustion further still." He was always "obliged afterwards, and in solitude," as he continues to inform us in *Si le grain ne meurt,* "to labor after that total exhaustion which alone afforded me respite, and which I obtained at no less cost." As one peers below the surface of his confession, one sees that his end in view was not at all the enjoyment of the senses. What he was after was exhaustion, for through exhaustion the solid flesh loses at last its "weight."

When Gide gets up with the first glimmer of dawn and runs without any specific destination in mind, his joyfulness is analyzed as "a kind of lightness of body and soul,"[45] which brings to mind St. Augustine's ideal of incorporeality. This is the end in view. It is essentially the same as the one described in terms of melting into and merging with surrounding nature. "This is why my most perfect memories of sensual delight are those enveloped in a landscape which absorbs it and in which I seem to be swallowed up. In the . . . transports with Mala, it is not only the beautiful swooning body of the child I see again, but the whole mysterious and fearful surrounding of the equatorial forest."[46] Earlier, Gide remembered "one delicious evening" with a young Italian boatman, "when my rapture was encompassed by the shining of the moon, the misty magic of the lake, the moist perfumes breathing from its shores."[47] To dissolve the body as an obstacle, or to use it as a means of immersion into the surrounding reality, to achieve that "more hidden voluptuousness" is what Gide looks for, beyond "the voluptuousness of the flesh."[48] He wishes to wear his senses out so as to achieve transparency, namely a condition where he—like a pane of glass which is there (to the sense of touch) and yet not there (to the sense of sight)—will have solved the problem of his existence in the world, the impossible problem of being one with all of reality, without ceasing to be oneself: "My senses were worn out to the point of transparency, and when I went down in the morning toward the town, the azure of the sky entered into me."[49]

Bernard's Ascent

There lurks a measure of sophistry in the claim that desires must be eliminated, through satisfaction, so as to neutralize the body as an obstacle between the self and reality. Since there is no immediately apparent reason why enjoyment should not be wanted for its own sake, its status as a means to some end other than itself becomes dubious. Yet the generally austere tenor of Gide's moral prescriptions within the framework of his impatience with time itself lends further support to the view that he was not a sensualist, and that the conclusion that the nearest thing to a message in Gide is "perhaps a refined hedonism, the exaltation of desire,"[50] is to be attributed to an unduly hurried reading of his texts. Roughly in line with Descartes' philosophy, Gide may have refused to believe that some of the young men he dealt with had souls, as he implicitly refused to believe in Madeleine's body. The fact remains that all visible things lead him beyond themselves, "to that *other* world."[51] The horizontal dimension of existence is a stepping-stone from which to leap on to the vertical dimension of being. By the same token the only injunction which would summarize his message with a measure of adequacy is: step beyond that which you have or which is given. His long battle with Barrès over *déracinement* and the imperative of surpassing oneself *(dépassement de soi)* are instances of that religious-moral preference. What underlines the dynamism of this ethics is that in accordance with his anti-idolatry, Gide does not define the aim or destination of the strenuous journey of life. Very early in his writing career he had already said that man must not localize his duty or affection.[52]

Speaking of one of the principal characters of his only novel, Gide wrote to Charles Du Bos: "I should like to show in my Bernard a lofty and noble nature, and who nevertheless goes forward in life without a goal, for whom the goal should be no other than the very act of living."[53] This is, with its Existentialistic overtones, not a new outlook, but a new emphasis. One thinks of the birds of the air and the lilies of the field which Jesus invited his hearers to imitate. They too have no purpose but life itself. The remedy against the anxiety of advancing toward no particular aim is built into the Christian morality, for life here is life within God's purpose, even if that purpose is unknown to man. Gide has no remedy against the anxiety of going without going anywhere, except the gratuitous affirmation that to do so is good. It is nevertheless worthy of note that in *his* real world, namely in the world of art, to be without a destination is to be unhinged.[54] In 1932 he greets with an "indescribable satisfaction" the Communist invitation to build, according to given patterns, tomorrow's society: "To cease advancing aimlessly and to head toward something . . . what an indescribable satisfaction!"[55] This is nevertheless idolatry, and Gide could not but turn away from it in the end. His opposition to the family has similar roots. He "hated"[56] that institution. His repeated readings of the Gospels failed to show a single word of Christ that strengthened or even authorized the family and marriage. Along with institutional religion, he regarded it as an impediment to progress. His low regard for "causes"—his self-dedication to the "cause" of homosexuality notwithstanding—is illustrated by his treatment of the pitifully gullible Fleurissoire in *Les Caves du Vatican,* and by Bernard's refusal to sign a pledge. Family, church, and "cause" are limiting things. They constitute at least a partial diversion of a man's loyalty to God himself. St. Antony also hated these things in a sense, for without that disposition he would not have gone to Africa. Gide's journey to the same country may well have had the same essential motivation.[58]

The playful boy in Gide had no taste for choices, for a life of tension and of ambiguity. Besides, a choice is also a limitation, as he was well aware. It is a deviation from the Whole, inasmuch as each choice closes the door to a thousand possibilities. He found himself in a paradox where the very avoidance of choices causes one to be threatened by them constantly: he sought not to choose so as to remain free, but freedom is a sought-after condition only because it affords the possibility to choose or facilitates the act of choice. As late as 1932 Gide was repeating, as valid, a statement he had made in *Les Nourritures Terrestres*:

> "*Determinatio est negatio.*" This formula of Spinoza, furnished me by a note in the fourth volume of Karl Marx's *Capital* (p. 49) could be applied as an additional contribution to my sentence in *Les Nourritures Terrestres*: "choosing seemed to me not so much selecting, as rejecting what I did not select."[59]

It is impossible to avoid the tension of freedom. With deliberate self-maintenance in a situation of freedom goes the simultaneous wish to be relieved from it. "Is this what I ought to be doing now?" is an anxiety-inducing question because it is raised by the fact that man's days are numbered: there is time to realize only *some* of the possibilities open to oneself. It is anxiety-inducing also because a man is condemned to ignorance as to whether the choice he makes of the use of this ephemeral and irreplaceable moment is the one that ought to be made. One way of eliminating the tension of freedom is to deny its reality. On the whole Gide does not profess belief in free will. His views in this respect are summarized in his description of man as "a willing marionette," a phrase which he clarified nearly thirty years later: "man is never free; but the simplest and most honest thing is to act as if he were."[60] What *is*, Gide claimed over and over again, is what ought to have been—a pronouncement which does not accord with his reputed individualism, but then Gide's individualism is not what is ordinarily understood by that term. His determinism was not a position arrived at philosophically. It is possible to say, loosely, that he uses the adjective *willing (volontaire)* as in the phrase just mentioned, or in "my little voluntary monad has cast this body upon the dust of sunbathed roads,"[61] meaning not *free,* but endowed with the sense or feeling of freedom, and he follows Leibniz in insisting that what is is the best available. One might as well entertain this notion when one cannot improve the otherwise undesirable situation in which one finds oneself. There is therefore room in human life for this sort of consolatory determinism, and Gide holds it.[62]

In the meantime the fact of freedom directs Gide, as it does Berdyaev, to the unfathomable foundation of his existence, and while he dreads it, he is also fascinated by it. His fascination with bastards—men of unknown origin who commit "gratuitous" acts which have their origin in invisible depths—may be an indication of the religious appeal that freedom holds for him. The problem then is: how can one preserve one's "freedom" and, simultaneously, be rid of the anxiety that attends it?

Reference to an Absolute eases the anxiety of freedom, and where the theist enjoins obedience to the will of God, Gide speaks of one's "natural" propensities, of one's "inclinations," concepts which imply the *givenness* of the general pattern of behavior which one ought to follow. An "outlaw" (like himself), Gide declared, "can accept being placed on the Index, and put to shame by the human laws and conventions of his time and country; but cannot accept to live outside the bounds of Nature."[63] The meaning of "bounds of Nature" is as uncertain as that of "will of God," and subject to infiltration by the preferences of him who uses the phrase. Gide himself spoke of *normal* homosexuals,[64] thereby excluding the others, rather arbitrarily, from the area enclosed by the "bounds of Nature." All that can be retained from his stance therefore is his feeling of moral dependence on Nature, with the understanding that the word *Nature* is an undefinable entity, conveniently postulated to serve as an absolute. Gide's feeling of creatureliness is evident also in his emphasis on *waiting,* for he who waits betrays his deep conviction that he cannot be his own savior. It is within this framework that one must consider Edouard's famous advice to Bernard, to which we turn.

To the counsel, "Follow your inclination" the objection can immediately be raised: are we, then, animals? Gide's answer is that animals do not, figuratively speaking, go uphill. Men must. When an inclination does not lead up hill it must presumably be resisted. But when can a course of action be said to be leading "up hill"? Since a great variety of answers can be given to this question, Edouard's advice: "It's a good thing to follow one's inclination, provided it leads up hill" is something of a blank. Gide's own interpretation of it may be seen in the behavior of Bernard, who "accepts" the advice.

Bernard's career had begun in *Les Faux-Monnayeurs* with his revolt against his family when he discovered that it was a nest of lies. He did not really belong to it; he leaves it. Chapter XIV of the novel is the account of a *rite de passage* presented as a wrestling match. The struggle with the Angel that takes place during the night inevitably reminds the reader of the combat at Peniel when Jacob, the son of Isaac, gained awareness—following a moment of solitude—of a mysterious supernatural reality which he fought but of which he sought and obtained the blessing. Though Bernard, unlike Jacob, does not ask his angel to stay and bless him, he is nevertheless converted to a new standard of morality.

An indication of this change is that after the departure of the angel his reaction to two women friends changes radically. Sarah, a granddaughter of the principal of the school where Bernard has his room, had been to England where she had acquired a taste for total liberty. She was now determined "to grant herself every licence, to dare all." Rachel, her sister, carries—harassed by never-ending work and financial demands —a large load of the responsibility of keeping the place together. Bernard and Sarah had met for the first time at a riotous dinner party, and become intimate a few hours later. Now, as Bernard leaves his room, he meets Rachel in the passage:

"I want to speak to you," she said. Her voice was so sad that Bernard understood at once what it was she had to say to him. He answered nothing, bowed his head, and in his great pity for Rachel suddenly began to hate Sarah and to loathe the pleasure he took with her.[65]

This "hatred" as well as his rejection of family and party ties is a function of Bernard's discovery of the spiritual dimension of existence through his acquaintance with Laura, Sarah's sister. It is this acquaintance which prepares his reconciliation with Monsieur Profitendieu who, he had discovered, was not his natural father. Whether this man is or is not his father is no longer a decisive factor regulating Bernard's reaction. He returns to him because, seen from a spiritual vantage point, blood ties lose their relevance. The obligation of a constant ascent to higher spheres without ignoring the circumstances which must condition the ascent is in keeping with what we may describe as Gide's "theory of the eagle." Both the theory of the gratuitous or motiveless act and such ethical views as Gide expressed using the symbol of the eagle are further indications of the non-horizontal, mystical bases of his morality.

"Individualism"

The *acte gratuit,* which is as Jean Hytier puts it "an act that is unthinkable, save in theory,"[66] is anticipated by Fichte's "free act without rational ground,"[67] possibly even by Meister Eckhart's "disinterest."[68] It is another facet of Gide's impatience with time or his unwillingness to make choices, his refusal to be determined by society or the horizontal dimension of existence; it is rooted in his desire to be *disponible* and fervent, and, no less than all his other major convictions, is present in *Les Cahiers d'André Walter*: "The will that is reasoned becomes thereby sicklier: let action be spontaneous."[69] It is significant, moreover, that though Gide did not rule out the possibility of *good* gratuitous acts,[70] the most notorious gratuitous act, described in *Les Caves du Vatican,* is a murder. That incident may well be interpreted as a parable of man's utter or inevitable depravity. The act may have been unmotivated, in the sense of not being calculated to lead to a *specific* advantage accruing to Lafcadio; it was not, nevertheless, committed without reason, and Gide himself did not "perhaps . . . believe in [disinterestedness] either."[71] Nor is Lafcadio's hidden motivation impossible to detect. The scene of the following quotation is a compartment in a train. Fleurissoire, a weak, gullible man dedicated to a phony cause, enters the compartment and sits opposite Lafcadio—a young, energetic man who makes demands on himself but has no respect whatever for the established code of morality, and for whom nothing is sacred. He turns up the brim of his hat and begins to consider Fleurissoire with apathy and apparent indifference:

"What is there in common between me and that squalid little rat?" reflected he. "He seems to fancy himself too. What is he smiling at me like that for? Does he imagine I'm going to embrace him? Is it possible that there exist women who fondle old men? No doubt he'd be exceedingly astonished to know that I can read writing or print with perfect fluency, upside down . . . all for the love of art. Cadio, my dear boy, the problem is this: to impinge on that fellow's fate . . . but how? Oh! I'll offer him a cachou. Whether he accepts or not, I shall at any rate hear in what language.

"Grazio! Grazio!" said Fleurissoire as he refused.

"Nothing doing with the old dromedary. Let's go to sleep," went on Lafcadio to himself, and pulling the brim of his hat down over his eyes, he tried to spin a dream out of one of his youthful memories.[72]

It is immediately clear that the problem is one of relatedness. It is created upon Fleurissoire's entering the compartment, for now Lafcadio is no longer surrounded by things only: he is in the presence of another human being. His first impulse or attempted solution to the problem is recorded in the passage quoted: he tries to establish a relationship where he will play the dominant role. Fleurissoire refuses to be on the receiving end of things vis-à-vis Lafcadio, and the latter's strategy of dominance fails. The second solution is to withdraw from the scene altogether. He tries to spin a dream. But this is impossible: he could not sleep. Human environment will not let one be: "if I were to take a peep at him through my eyelids, I should see him looking at me," Lafcadio muses. Other people will keep doing things and even when they mean well they will keep importuning one. Fleurissoire fiddles with the electric light in the compartment. He cuts a ridiculous figure and is, at that moment, mankind's last remnant in Lafcadio's self-centered world.

Lafcadio turned on the light. The train at that moment was running alongside a bank, which could be seen through the window, illuminated by the light cast upon it from one after another of the compartments of the train; a procession of brilliant squares was thus formed which danced along beside the railroad and suffered, each one in its turn, the same distortions, according to the irregularities of the ground. In the middle of one of these squares danced Fleurissoire's grotesque shadow; the others were empty.

"Who would see?" thought Lafcadio.

Lafcadio hurls Fleurissoire out of the train to his death, taking elaborate precautions not to be caught. It was not an impulsive crime. A crime without a motive is, paradoxically, what he *intends* to commit. He does not realize that the desire to be the author of a motiveless crime is itself a motive.

It's not so much about events that I'm curious, as about myself. There's many a man thinks he's capable of anything, who draws back when it comes to the point. . . . What a gulf between the imagination and the deed![73]

Lafcadio wishes to bridge the distance between freedom and limitation, for the gulf between the imagination and the deed is precisely an aspect of that distance. Confronted with a problem of relatedness, he is unable to solve it in a manner satisfactory to both. He is utterly incapable of putting himself in Fleurissoire's stead; he is compelled to reduce him to the status of a thing. His act is therefore the act of absolute self-centeredness, as distinguished from selfish—what he, or Gide, would call "motivated"—crimes. It is demonic in the sense that it is the wrong, destructive solution to the problem of interpersonal relationship.

Lafcadio is an alienated man with a vengeance. Conventional morality, grown vapid in his eyes, can no longer sustain him. He kills Fleurissoire, this product and servant of a phony morality, as an angry child breaks an object that will not function. His murder is not unrelated to Michel's profound indifference to Marceline's fate in *L'Immoraliste*. He is Nathanaël grown aware of the problem of other people's presence. His crime is, to use traditional Christian terminology, the story not of *a* sin, but a parabolic description of *the* ("original") sin in which Gide did not formally believe.

In the same area of the doctrine of human depravity belongs Gide's repeated opposition to Pascal's celebrated statement that the ego is hateful.[74] Close scrutiny shows that Gide is opposed neither to the idea nor even, in this case, to the words of Pascal. Pascal *and* Gide together are in agreement with those who uphold the doctrine of the original sin. They both regret the fact, in Gide's words, that "every mind makes itself a centre, and one always thinks the world is grouped about oneself—"[75] This is precisely what Gide means by "interested" in his phrase: "the interested people are alone hateful."[76] Thus the agreement on this point between Pascal and Gide is complete. The stipulation that one must feed one's "eagle" with one's liver is Gide's manner of saying that repudiation of egocentricity should not entail unfaithfulness to oneself.

The world of *Prométhée mal enchaîné,* where the symbol of the liver-fed eagle occurs, is a world at least seemingly absurd. Prometheus, who is everyman, or mankind, must achieve meaning in this meaningless world. This consists in self-realization of which the Promethean eagle is the symbol and instrument. The philosophical premise on which the theory is built is that the "common man" does not exist. That which is possessed by Prometheus, and no one else, is his eagle, and everyone has an eagle of his own. Everyone has a unique potential self. A man's duty is to see this potential self, and then cover the distance between it and the self given in the here-and-now. Prometheus is confronted with the choice of selling, strangling, or taming his eagle. He opts for the third alternative, because he does not wish either to dishonor, or to be untrue to, himself. "Conscience" does not exhaust the symbolism of the eagle. It is also civilization, belief in progress, man's *raison d'être.* In a word, the eagle is the idea which must consume man and by which man must be consumed willingly.

Gide had looked upon humanity as the "staging of ideas on earth."[77] In *Le Prométhée* the same notion in almost the same words occurs, with one difference: *ideas* is replaced by *eagles.* The history of men, we read here, is the history of eagles.[78] The entire book is the dramatization of another early entry in his *Journal*: "Make a rule of paying attention in each creature only to the unique and different element, of which the common matter is merely the too massive support."[79] Gide causes Prometheus to eat his eagle in the end, suggesting that his ideal must serve to invigorate and sustain him, and not vice versa, a variant of the dictum that the Sabbath is made for man, and not man for the Sabbath.

An austere version of the rather humorous *Prométhée* is *Philoctète ou le Traité des trois morales (Philoctetes or the Treatise on the Three Theories of Conduct),* dedicated to a professional philosopher, Marcel Drouin, who remained a friend of Gide until his death in 1946. There are here three dramatis personae with three different attitudes toward life, but only two moralities: the morality of Ulysses and that of Philoctetes. The object of Ulysses' devotion is definite, namely Greece or, more generally, the nation or fatherland. It therefore leads to the evils of casuistry and compromise. The timeworn phrase "the end justifies the means" puts in a nutshell the sort of morality Gide is describing through Ulysses. The imperfection of his morality is to be ascribed not to the object itself of Ulysses' final loyalty, but to the circumstance that that object is finite. Philoctetes is not opposed to devotion. His devotion is indeterminate. It is, one might claim, to the nameless God beyond God, the ineffable "something above the gods" of the quotation below. He seeks the removal of all idols from between himself and the ground of his being. He says to Neoptolemus, a young observer whom he cannot win over but who, by the end of the dramatic poem, is no longer faithful to Ulysses:

[Devote oneself] to the gods. . . . But the truth is, Neoptolemus, there is something above the gods. . . .
There is—(*Taking his head in his hands, overcome*) I don't know any longer. I don't know. . . . Ah! Ah, oneself! . . . I don't know how to say it any longer.[80]

A long series of Gidian pronouncements in the vein of this "oneself!" has inevitably led to the conclusion that Gide's morality is a morality of individualism.[81] But to say that the morality of Gide is a morality of individualism is not to say much, for the simple reason that the meaning of "individualism" is disappointingly vague. The boundary between individualism and its opposite is as impossible to trace as the boundary between *here* and *there* or *now* and *then,* even though the concepts here, there, now, and then are quite clear and distinct. Even within this range, however, it should be impossible to reconcile individualism and a totalitarian system. Gide, feeling free, he says, to use certain words without regard to their dictionary meaning, reconciles individualism and communism. When these are "properly understood," that is, as he understands them himself, they are not "essentially irreconcilable." It is certain, he says, that he does not see "an equalitarian communism"; not a uniformity of qualities, a standardization which is impossible and hardly desirable, but "an equality of conditions only at the outset." Communism also means to him an internationalization of economic interests coinciding with "the happily irreducible differences among cultures and traditions." Communism is a symphony where each musician plays his own instrument and follows his own score. It is the ship *Argo* where there was no private property perhaps, but which was guided by "a single will, common to all," while each member of the crew had a function of his own. Gide goes on to write:

And since I believe, furthermore, that the personality never asserts itself more than by renouncing itself, it seems to me that . . . and that the only ones who can worry about communism are the indecisive personalities, or those who think they can assert themselves only at the expense of others.[82]

These are not the thoughts of a youthful idealist. Gide was sixty-four years of age when he wrote them down. He was then under the impression that he had at last awakened to the importance of social issues, and felt no doubt that he was making personal, if not original and valid, pronouncements about communism. But the statement has in fact nothing to do with communism. It is of interest to us for other reasons. Plato and St. Paul seem to be the sources of his inspiration, but they would both find a truncated version of their own programs in Gide's vision of the ideal society. Plato would be puzzled by the fact that Gide's orchestra has no conductor; Paul would question the possibility of the *Argo's* crew being governed by "a single will, common to all," without the location of that will in one other specifiable body. The question of the failure of the orchestra without a conductor, or of the sinking of the boat without a captain does not arise in Gide's mind, because his impression that he is writing about communism *against* others who are not Communists is an illusion. He is describing a utopia—which the world has really no reason to refuse—where everyone becomes who everyone is, with the result that a beautiful symphony is heard and the ship of the commonwealth sails smoothly along.

In the midst of his putative interest in social issues Gide remained a mystic: his dominant desire is always to be in creviceless communion with the depths of reality. His statement quoted above that "the personality never asserts itself more than by renouncing itself" does by no means stand alone. It is one of his most consistently held convictions. He is irresistibly driven to that idea in every conceivable connection. It is expressed on one occasion as follows:

I have realized the profound truth of the words: "whosoever shall seek to save his life shall lose it." To be sure, it is in perfect abnegation that individualism triumphs, and self-renunciation is the summit of self-assertion.[83]

He paraphrased the Bible to say "that the fruit, unless it falls and dies, cannot assure new blossoms."[84] John 12:24 reads: "Truly, truly, I say to you, unless a grain of wheat falls into the earth and dies, it remains alone; but if it dies, it bears much fruit." Gide used part of this verse as a title for his autobiography. He wrote late in life that we all belong to the whole.[85] He had written in 1929, reflecting on a study by M. Belgion on himself:

... today we rate humanity much too high; that man is not interesting, important, worthy to be adored, for his own sake; that what invites humanity to progress is precisely not to consider itself (and its comfort and the satisfaction of its desires) as an end, but rather as a means through which to achieve and realize something.[86]

This passage further proves that progress for Gide was a religious event. His individualism—when the word is not used to mean religious commitment—must be reduced to rebellion against bourgeois mores or hypocrisy: "How can one fail to be an individualist amid the conventions of a bourgeois society?"[87] and one would be hard put to find a writer of significance who is *not* an individualist in this sense.

There is yet another meaning in which Gide would call himself an individualist: he claimed that "each" is more precious than "all,"[88] and that God is to be realized through individuals. More interesting than the precise meaning of *God* in such a familiar Gidian context is the affinity between his observation and the views of such non-naturalists as Berdyaev, Buber, and Maritain that "the person is an actual spiritual category bound to God; it is the image of God in man. . . . It is the ultimate value in ethics, the divine purpose in each concrete human being." On the other hand, a remark by Paul Tillich gives the clue to Gide's ambiguity about individualism. "No individual exists," as Tillich puts it, "without participation, and no personal being exists without communal being."[89] As to the last words of Gide's lecture pronounced in Beirut and Brussels in 1946 that "the world shall be saved by some individuals,"[90] it is no improvement on Isaiah's doctrine of the remnant.

In sum Gide's position is that if everyone is actively true to his genuine self, society itself will reach the possible limit of its freedom. It is because this view stands on deeply religious convictions that he could fall into startling exaggerations and reconcile his individualism—as Calvin did his freedom in God—with the strictest regimentation, with an altogether autocratic political system. He wrote in 1918:

I consider liberty as a fearful and disastrous thing that one must try to reduce or suppress in oneself first—and even, if one can, in others. The frightening thing is imposed slavery, to which no consent is required; the excellent thing is self-imposed slavery; and for lack of something better: the slavery to which one submits. Oh, voluntary servitude![91]

It goes without saying that if one man is entitled to reduce or suppress liberty in others, some people will have to suffer "imposed slavery"; Gide admits the frightfulness of that condition but does not appear unsettled by it. Thirteen years later he was faced with an actual situation testing his theory:

I must explain myself to Salvemini: despite my admiration for the young hero's deed, I lack something: belief in liberty. It is most difficult for me to bring my own thought to light. The notion of liberty, as it is taught us, seems to me singularly false and pernicious. And if I approve the Soviet constraint, I must likewise approve the Fascist discipline. I am more and more inclined to believe that the idea of liberty is but a snare.[92]

Gide's individualism never quite indicated ordinary freedom, and it meant doing as one pleases even less. Occasional cases of sheer indulgence are distorted affirmations of his desire to free himself of himself. If achievement and *mesure* had not in fact had the upper hand in his moral preferences, he evidently would not have been the productive artist whose art was meant to be imitated by life.

In Gide's conclusive view individualism is dialectical. It must lead to "banality"[93] through a process reminiscent of Nietzsche's third metamorphosis: from the lion who gives a holy Nay even unto duty, into a child, the giver of the holy Yea.[94] Gide was a young man when Jean-Marie Guyau published his *Esquisse d'une morale sans obligation, ni sanction*. The basis of morality, Guyau argues, is the most intense, the richest, the fullest life possible only to conclude, anticipating Gide, that "individual life must spread itself for and in others and, if need be, give itself."[95] While an heir to this morality with neither obligation nor sanction, Gide foresaw a time when *ethical* problems would interest "only a few timid souls."[96] This is the time when men and women will have realized the inherent harmony between their will and what may be termed the universal will, or God.

Sincerity and Effort, or Joyful Work

Gide's insistence on sincerity, as distinct from honesty (*probité*), itself points to a situation where the ego does not interpose itself between the individual and the whole, for only then is his existence authentic. Gide was particularly weary of the hypocrisy of hiding pride in humility. Eventually he detested humility, wherever met, for he took it time after time to be a disguise for pride, a notion which fails to make the simple distinction between those who practice humility on one hand, and those, on the other, who are humble, while there can be no doubt that there are people of both sorts.

Moral sincerity characterizes the man who responds uncalculatingly to an appeal. Bernard's question, "if *I* don't do it, who will? If I don't do it at once, when shall I?"[97] echoes the advice given to Nathanaël to the effect that he should make of himself the most irreplaceable of beings. It is rooted in the Reformation, specifically Puritan, conviction that each individual has his own responsibility under God,[98] and is reminiscent of the manner in which Isaiah answered the call of the Lord.[99] Perhaps, as in the case of a vocation, one does not *decide* to be sincere. Gide used the concept of sincerity largely in connection with art. He also thought of it in connection with Bartholomew's being met by Christ:

A man "in whom is no guile." I know no other which, more than this word of the Gospel, has dominated my life. It seems to me pretentious to say so. But, young as I then was, yes, that is what I inscribed in my mind. It seems to me today that "sincerity" and the effort to achieve it *in oneself* are contained therein.[100]

As a principle of conduct Gide's sincerity appears almost to be built on the Upanishadic claim that "thou art it," Upanishadic teaching having itself been a reaction against Vedic formalism. He wrote in 1923:

. . . to act according to the greatest sincerity, implied a resolution, a perspicacity, an effort that strained my whole will, so that I never seemed more moral to myself than at the time when I had decided to cease being moral; I mean: to be moral henceforth only in my own way. And I came to understand that perfect sincerity, the kind that, in my opinion, leads to the most valor and greatest dignity, sincerity not only of the act itself but of the motive, can be achieved only through the most constant, but also the least bitter, effort, only with the clearest vision (I mean: the least suspect of self-satisfaction), and the most irony.[101]

This confirms, in yet another remarkable example of Gide's consistency with himself below the surface, what he had written some thirty years earlier:

I am torn by a conflict between the rules of morality and the rules of sincerity.

Morality consists in substituting for the natural creature (the old Adam) a fiction that you prefer. But then you are no longer sincere. The old Adam is the sincere man.[102]

One must recall that Adam was the completely integrated man. There was no distance between him and God. If we assume that speech and self-consciousness are correlated, this statement by Gide acquires additional meaning: "It is important to observe that this concern [of being sincere] inhabits and can only inhabit those who have *nothing to say.* Let those who can understand why."[103] Sincerity is, in the final analysis, an almost mystical experience, the authentic life that few can know:

There is a profound sincerity much harder to achieve and much rarer than simply that of expression. Some people go through life without ever experiencing a really sincere feeling; they do not even know what it is. They imagine they love, hate, suffer; their very death is an imitation.[104]

Behind Gide's indomitable optimism—he regarded every pessimist as a personal enemy[105]—behind his determination never to despair, there is the religious awareness that the roots of his total existence extend beyond what is available to the senses. He was always under the impression that he achieved happiness with great ease, and that joy and bliss were natural to him, though he occasionally did look upon life as a long interval of disquietude, torment, insoluble questions,[106] and often referred to the anxiety born of freedom. Those evils which could not be removed he overcame through the eminently Christian virtue of renunciation, with a childlike faith or, to use his word, *attention.* Against a second set of evils which were either imaginary or removable he advocated hard work, patient investigation of causes, and discipline. Here the virtue par excellence is effort. While the fundamental virtues governing social relationships are *probité,* and justice, effort is necessary to register advances.

Occasionally Gide seems to be arguing that effort is a criterion of good-ness. Both in *Les Cahiers d'André Walter* and in *La Porte étroite* effort appears at any rate to be the condition of virtue. But this is a negative effort: the effort not to do what the body demands. It is self-evident, otherwise, that effort, as such, is neither good nor bad, or at least neither useful nor harmful. Its utilitarian value is determined by the object to which it is directed, a point which Gide eventually recognized. Thus Bernard does not like "difficulty for its own sake."[107]

It may be argued that the negative effort of *Les Cahiers* (1891) and the effort advocated in *Thésée* (1946) are different in nature. The latter is positive; its object can, moreover, be defined without recourse to super-naturalism. The effort of Theseus towards noble causes and the weal of mankind will, if successful, achieve three things: the earth will be purged of tyrants, bandits, and monsters; byroads will no longer be dangerous; the skies will be cleared. To interpret the parable: we must work toward a world where freedom and security coincide, while religious beliefs vanish. The principal beliefs that will vanish are evidently those in "your God," immortality, disembodied souls, a cosmic purpose. Yet if theism is, as the dictionary defines the term, "Belief in the existence of one God who is viewed as the creative source of man, the world, and value and who transcends and yet is immanent in the world," then many a theist would have no difficulty in going along with Theseus' program. Nor would anyone object to the view that work towards psychological and material welfare must be done with joy.

Gide agreed with Dostoevsky that veritable happiness consists in "excessive work, *con amore*." One of his own many formulations of the same view is: "The first condition of happiness is that man may take joy in his work. There is no real joy in rest, in leisure, unless joyful work precedes it." [108] Through work, it must be observed, one fills with mean-ing extended time, while joy renders each instant of it valuable in itself.

Is there a state more desirable than happiness? The insistent advocacy by Gide of such traditionally other-worldly virtues as abnegation and renunciation will not allow the critic to conclude that happiness was for Gide the highest good. Beyond happiness there is what he called "perfect felicity." He found perfect felicity in the world of art:

It is raining pitchforks. Closeted in the greenhouse with Goethe's poems, surrounded by golden yellow calceolaries, without fever, without anxieties, without desires, I enjoy a PERFECT FELICITY.[109]

This was in 1905. We have seen Gide use nearly the same phrase for the description in traditional terms of a mystical experience in 1941. To feel God in a *state of communion* was a "delightful felicity," and on any less exalted level the soul was inconsolable.[110] The idea or disposition described in both passages, one written in his middle age, the other in his old age, is identical with what he had written in his youth: "the soul at rest worshipped and no longer looked at things." Then decades later in the midst of his most vehement denials of God he wrote, "There is a certain way of negating God that approaches adoration."[111] As distinguished from adoration, happiness could mark only the upper limit of what Gide called "constancy and friendship" in his last creative work. Even the most anti-mystical of his heroes, Theseus, could not stop at that level. He must go beyond "a certain point," and beyond it, he is made to say, "one can only go forward alone"—a declaration of considerable importance pointing to the fact that Oedipus and Theseus in *Thésée* do not so much represent opposite viewpoints as translate the same fundamental stance. Theseus' journey forward must be understood in terms of Gide's declaration that aloneness is the condition of being in the truth.[112] His lifelong determination to leave the familiar and go beyond as well as his emphasis on renunciation show the kinship of his soul to the Traveler of Aziz, the Sufi. The remotest aim of the Traveler is beyond reach, for his journey "to God" does not come to an end upon reaching God, but continues "in" Him. Though the mysterious Traveler "has fraternal love for his fellow-pilgrims, detachment from wayside allurements, untiring perseverance on the road, he is still encumbered and weakened by unnecessary luggage. The second state of his journey, therefore, is initiated ... by a casting off of his burden: a total self-renouncement."[113] This is precisely Gide's "triumph of individualism" and the condition of his "delightful felicity."

Notes

Chapter 1

1. Jacques Schiffrin, ed., *Les Personnes du Drame* (New York: Pantheon Books, 1945), 150.

2. Francis Brown, ed., *Highlights of Modern Literature* (New York: New American Library, 1954), 126.

3. *The Journals of André Gide*, trans. Justin O'Brien (New York: Alfred A. Knopf, Inc., 1949), III, 366 (cited hereafter as *J*).

4. *So Be It*, trans. Justin O'Brien (New York: Alfred A. Knopf, Inc., 1959), 4.

5. *J*, III, 26, 108.

6. "Les Cahiers," *Oeuvres Complètes*, I, 54 (cited hereafter as *OC*).

7. *Ibid.*

8. See "La Querelle du Peuplier," *OC*, IV, 405.

9. See *J*, II, 123.

10. It must be noted, however, that Ramon Fernandez's purpose in writing his book was to help Gide think better! (*André Gide*, 13, 25).

11. Paul Tillich, *Systematic Theology* (Chicago: University of Chicago Press, 1951), I, 81.

12. See Raymond Colin, "Literature and Philosophy" in *University of Buffalo Studies*, Vol. 23, No. 2 (Sept. 1956).

13. *J*, II, 404.

14. *Ibid.*

15. "Lettres à Angèle," *OC*, III, 180.

16. *J*, II, 367.

17. "Lettres à Angèle," *OC*, III, 180.

18. *Les Nouvelles Nourritures*, 116.

19. See "Les Cahiers," *OC*, I, 54.

20. See "De l'influence en littérature," *OC*, III, 251 ff.

21. "Le Voyage d'Urien," *OC*, I, 282; "Isabelle," *OC*, VI, 219; "Le Retour de l'Enfant prodigue," *OC*, V, 5; *Strait is the Gate*, trans. Dorothy Bussy (New York: Vintage Books, 1959), 25; *The Counterfeiters* with Journal of "The Counterfeiters," trans. Dorothy Bussy and Justin O'Brien (New York: Alfred A. Knopf, Inc., 1927), 160 (cited hereafter as *CWJ*).

22. "Les Cahiers," *OC*, I, 112.

23. *J*, II, 342 f.

24. Thus Jean Hytier, who bases his brilliant study of Gide on this formula, engages nevertheless in a detailed analysis of the *acte gratuit* which is not properly speaking an esthetic concern. See his *André Gide*, trans. Richard Howard (Garden City, N.Y.: Doubleday

Anchor, 1962), 7 *et passim*. The meaning of *esthetic* is notoriously nebulous. It is particularly difficult to cling to "the esthetic point of view" for long in an examination of Gide's work.

25. *J*, I, 35.

26. *CWJ*, 221.

27. *Ibid.*, 271; *J*, II, 324.

28. *Le Théâtre Complet d'André Gide* (Paris: Ides et Calendes, 1947), I, 183.

29. *J*, IV, 275.

30. *CWJ*, 262.

31. *Ibid.*, 346.

32. *Les Nourritures Terrestres* (Paris: Gallimard, 1944), 207.

33. *Divers* (Paris: Librairie Gallimard, 1931), 26. Cf. *Sutra of Wei Lang* where the sixth patriarch says: "If I tell you that I have a system of Law to transmit to others I am cheating you. What I do to my disciples is to liberate them from their own bondage with such devices as the case may need" (Christmas Humphreys, *Buddhism* [Penguin Books, 1952], 183).

34. "A Propos des Déracinés," *OC*, II, 441.

35. *Pretexts*, ed. Justin O'Brien (New York: World Publishing Co., 1959), 75 ff.

36. *J*, I, 80. Gide is not certain whether rarity precedes excellence or vice versa: "Were a miracle to produce in our woods some astounding orchid, a thousand hands would stretch out to tear it up, to destroy it. If the bluebird happens to fly past, every gun is sighted; and then people are amazed that it is rare!" (*J*, I, 262).

37. *CWJ*, 393; *J*, II, 104–105.

38. *OC*, I, 110; *OC*, IX, 371–72; *Les Nourritures Terrestres*, 15.

39. See E. R. Dodds, *The Greeks and the Irrational* (Boston: Beacon Press, 1957), 135.

40. F. H. Bradley writes: "The positive relation of every appearance as an adjective to Reality, and the presence of Reality among its appearances in different degrees and with diverse values—this double truth we have found to be the centre of philosophy" (*Appearance and Reality* [Oxford: Clarendon Press, 1930], 488).

41. *J*, III, 287, 237.

42. E.g., in *Les Faux-Monnayeurs* the letters to Bernard's mother revealing as they do the truth about her and, simultaneously, the secret of his origins, are found in a box placed in the drawer of a console-table: to get at the letters Bernard had to pry open its top. Along the same pattern the truth about Edouard, namely his diary, is found in a suitcase; Edouard in turn finds the name (or the identity) of his nephew in a satchel, in a scene of recognition; in *Les Caves du Vatican* Julius de Baraglioul, on an errand to meet Lafcadio, finds the latter's diary in an unlocked drawer prior to meeting him in person; the student in *Isabelle* knows Isabelle's secret before meeting her in person: it was hidden in a letter behind a wall panel on which he had proceeded to carve her name. In *La Porte étroite* Jerome receives Alissa's diary in a sealed packet.

43. "Les Cahiers," *OC*, I, 50.

44. *J*, IV, 301–302.

45. Alfred North Whitehead, *Religion in the Making* (New York: Macmillan Co., 1926), 15.

46. *If It Die*, trans. Dorothy Bussy (New York: Random House, Inc., 1935), 109. Gide never overcame the feeling of not being like others. His only "novel," written in his fifties, reveals his fascination with a news story that appeared in the *Journal de Rouen* (June 5, 1909): Nény of the Lycée at Clermont-Ferrand was driven to suicide by a band of students who accused him of not resembling them. See Jean Delay, *La Jeunesse d'André Gide*, T 215 ff.

47. *If It Die*, 153.

48. Simone de Beauvoir, *The Prime of Life*, trans. Peter Green (New York: World Publishing Co., 1962), 10.

49. Georges Sorel, *De l'utilité du Pragmatisme* (Paris: Librairie des sciences politiques et sociales, 1921), 451.

50. *J*, III, 234.

51. See *Les Nourritures Terrestres*, 15; and "Considérations," *OC*, IX, 153.

52. See Gilbert Murray, *Five Stages of Greek Religion* (Garden City, N.Y.: Doubleday & Co., 1955), 119–65; and Sidney Hook, *The Quest for Being* (New York: Dell Publishing Co., 1963), 73.

53. Evelyn Underhill, *Mysticism* (New York: A Meridian Book, 1955), 453.

54. *J*, III, 166.

55. Henri Brémond, *Prière et Poésie* (Paris: B. Grasset, 1926).

56. "Les Cahiers," *OC*, I, 73.

57. See *J*, III, 166; and "The Antichrist," *The Complete Works of Friedrich Nietzsche*, ed. Dr. Oscar Levy (New York: Russell & Russell, Inc., 1964), XVI, 210. Georges Bataille is of the opinion, nevertheless, that Nietzsche's jealousy of Christ betrays his inability to admit that he, Nietzsche, was a mere man, whereas Gide was "altogether at the opposite side of such an unreasonable anguish" ("Nietzsche et Jésus selon Gide et Jaspers" in *Critique*, VI, No. 42, Nov. 1950, 99–114).

58. Jean Guitton equates the Gidian instant with religious "salvation" and mentions in this connection Simone Weil to whom he attributes Catharistic tendencies. See his "André Gide et l'éternel présent," in *La Table Ronde*, 175–77.

59. Marcel Schwob, *Le Vrai drame d'André Gide*, 72; cf. Teilhard de Chardin, *Hymne de l'Univers* (Paris: Editions du Seuil, 1961), 82, 105.

60. Weil, *La connaissance surnaturelle*, 28; Dietrich Bonhoeffer, *Prisoner for God*, trans. R. H. Fuller (New York: Macmillan Co., 1954), 164. Cf. *J*, II, 425; *J*, IV, 278, 301–302; *So Be It*, 154.

61. Paul Tillich, *The Shaking of the Foundations* (New York: Charles Scribner's Sons, 1948), 57.

Chapter 2

1. Rom. 2:22.

2. Rom. 10:10.

3. Rom. 12:11.

4. As in the case of Bernard, who must follow his inclination provided it leads uphill. See *CWJ*, 327. Another advocate of the duty of making oneself irreplaceable, Miguel de Unamuno, places it within a religious context: "Act so that in your own judgment and in the judgment of others you may merit eternity, and so that you may become irreplaceable, act so that you may not merit death." (*Tragic Sense of Life*, trans. J. E. Crawford Flitch [New York: Dover Publications, 1954], 262).

5. Rom. 14:12; I Cor. 7:17.

6. Phil. 1:8.

7. The aim of Paul's exhortation is active preparation for the Kingdom of God as in Eph. 5:16 and Col. 4:5. A similar notion is not foreign to Gide as he exalts effort. See Chapt. 7.

8. Cf. *J*, I, 261, 297.

9. *J*. III, 30, 31. (See nevertheless Chapt. 4 below, n. 59).

10. *J*, II, 403, Cf. *OC*, XIV, 401, n. 2.

11. *J*, III, 281.

12. Cf., e.g., *J*, III, 162.

13. Rom. 5:1.

14. "Dostoievsky," *OC*, V, 70.

15. *Les Nouvelles Nourritures*, 52.

16. Cf. I Cor. 1:10 ff.

17. "Pages retrouvées," NRF, XXXII, 501 quoted by Justin O'Brien in *Portrait of André Gide* (New York: Alfred A. Knopf, Inc., 1953), 210.

18. *J*, II, 173.

19. The issue of the Old vs. the New Adam is related to Gide's problem of self-knowledge or self-discovery and will be dealt with in Chapt. 3. Paul condemns homosexuality in Rom. 1:26 and I Cor. 6:9.

20. Cf. Jean Schlumberger, *Madeleine et André Gide* (Paris: Gallimard, 1956), 247.

21. *J*, *I*, 190, 217.

22. *Martin Luther*, ed. John Dillenberger (Garden City, N.Y.: Doubleday Anchor, 1961), 18.

23. The verse quoted is from John 9:41 where it is not given by the Evangelist the meaning attributed to it by Gide. See, for example, G. H. C. MacGregor, *The Gospel of John* (New York: Harper & Brothers, 1928), 231.

24. Rom. 6:4.

25. O'Brien, *Portrait*, 223.

26. *Ibid.* It may be noted that the Pastor is also criticized in this novel by his son for choosing what pleases him out of the Christian doctrine. This was the criticism leveled against Gide by his Catholic friends. The Pastor's son turns to Catholicism in the novel.

27. "Lettres," *OC*, XIV, 408. Cf. John Dillenberger and Claude Welch, *Protestant Christianity* (New York: Charles Scribner's Sons, 1954), 46.

28. "Dostoievsky," *OC*, XI, 208–209. For love of nature in the Renaissance, see Jacob Burckhardt, *The Civilization of the Renaissance in Italy*, trans. S. C. C. Middlemore (New York: Harper & Brothers, 1958), II, 295 ff.

29. *If It Die*, 177.

30. *J*, IV, 244 *et passim*.

31. *If It Die*, 241. The rapprochement in Gide's mind between classicism and health is one of his ideas to be traced to Goethe: "I call the classic HEALTHY, the romantic SICKLY" (*Conversations with Eckermann* [Washington & London: M. Walter Dunne, 1901], April 2, 1829, 302).

32. *J*, I, 319.

33. Etienne Gilson, "L'Itinéraire d'Henri Bergson," *Les Nouvelles Littéraires* (25 janvier 1962), No. 1795, 1.

34. *If It Die*, 305.

35. *J*, II, 206.

36. *J*, III, 370.

37. See *J*, III, 231.

38. See Gordon Wright, *The Reshaping of French Democracy* (New York: Reynal & Hitchcock, 1948), 138, 199.

39. *J*, III, 128.

40. *J*, III, 372.

41. *J*, II, 339.

42. *J*, III, 48.

43. *J*, II, 117.

44. *Et Nunc Manet in te*, 113. Cf. *J*, II, 381.

45. *J*, III, 237. Cf. *J*, II, 330.

46. *J*, IV, 281; *Corydon* (New York: Noonday Press, 1961), 157. In the last letter his mother received from him before her death (1895) Gide had written: "For months I have studied only *Life*, that of others and my own, and the mere fact of seeing more mystery in it is a proof to me that I always understand it better" (Delay, II, 493).

47. *J*, III, 109. Gide was equally impatient with that proverbially heavy book, Karl Marx's *Das Kapital*. See *J*, III, 375.

48. For the official text which condemns and orders into the Index of Prohibited Books "all the works of André Gide" (May 24, 1952), as well as for the reasons given therefor see *Prétexte*, No. 2 (November 1952).

49. *J*, III, 373; and cf. p. 76: "But I note with curiosity that not one of my shortcomings would find encouragement in Catholicism; quite the contrary, only my good qualities would, and doubtless the best ones (or so it seems to me this evening)—. . . ."

50. *J*, III, 408, 409.

51. "Lettres à Angèle," *OC*, III, 233, 235.

52. *J*, III, 270.

53. "El Hadj," *OC*, III, 77 ff.

54. *J*, III, 259.

55. *Ibid.*, 231.

56. Cf. Frederick C. Grant, "The Gospel for an Age of Anxiety," *Advance* (December 22, 1952), 20.

57. *J*, III, 226.

58. *J*, III, 33.

59. *Ibid.*, 237. Cf. *Robert* (Paris: Gallimard, 1930), 40, 41.

60. Matt. 22:30.

61. Luke 9:58.

62. *Oedipus and Theseus*, 42.

63. *Feuillets d'Automne*, 242. See also *Attendu que* . . . , 225 ff; and *J*, II, 251.

64. *J*, III, 244.

65. Harold March, *Gide and the Hound of Heaven* (Philadelphia: University of Pennsylvania Press, 1952), 16.

66. "L'évolution du Théâtre," *OC*, IV, 215 f.

67. *J*, III, 33.

68. *J*, III, 392.

69. Henri Peyre, "André Gide: Martyr and Hero of Sincerity," *Literature and Sincerity* (New Haven, Conn.: Yale University Press, 1963), 276–305.

70. T. S. Eliot, *On Poetry and Poets* (New York: Farrar, Straus and Cudahy, 1957), 22, 23.

71. Matt. 13:34.

72. "De l'importance du public," *OC*, IV, 192.

73. On Gide's bafflement with regard to the word *sincere*, see also *CWJ*, 64.

74. "Caractères," *OC*, XII, 7.

75. *J*, III, 145; "Journal," *OC*, VI, 406.

76. Weil, *La Pesanteur*, 156: "Superimposed readings: to read necessity behind sensation, to read order behind necessity, to read God behind order."

77. E. F. Scott, "The Ethics of the Gospels," *The Evolution of Ethics*, ed. Elias Hershey Sneath (New Haven, Conn.: Yale University Press, 1927), 288.

78. "Les Limites de l'Art," *OC*, III, 407.

79. "Quelques livres," *OC*, III, 418. See *OC*, VIII, 484.

80. Paul Tillich, "Being and Love," *Four Existentialist Theologians*, selected by Will Herberg (Garden City, N.Y.: Doubleday Anchor, 1958), 304.

81. *J*, III, 57–58.

82. "Le Voyage au Congo," *OC*, XIII, 106.

Chapter 3

1. Acts 2:2.

2. Nearly twenty years later echoing the *dénûment* sought by the Prodigal, Gide was writing in his own name: "I hope to acquire ever more poverty. (Paradox). In destitution lies salvation" (*J*, II, 386).

3. Cf. "Les Cahiers," *OC*, I, 144: "Oh! to curl up near you, to sit at your feet, in your enveloping warmth, my head on your knees, in the deep fold of your robe, and feel on my forehead the sweetness of your soft breath."

4. Cf. C. G. Jung, *Modern Man in Search of a Soul*, trans. W. S. Dell and Gary F. Baynes (New York: Harcourt, Brace & Co., 1933), 264.

5. O'Brien, *Portrait*, 208.

6. Kierkegaard has expressed this same concern in Christian terms: "The Christian heroism (and perhaps it is rarely to be seen) is to venture wholly to be oneself, as an individual man, this definite individual man, alone before the face of God, . . ." he writes in the Preface to *The Sickness unto Death*. Nietzsche asks in *The Joyful Wisdom*: "What saith thy conscience?" and the answer is "Thou shalt become what Thou art" (Vol. X, 209).

7. *J*, I, 10.

8. *Gide vivant*, ed. Colin-Simard (Amiot-Dumont, 1952), 54.

9. De Beauvoir, *The Prime of Life*, 292.

10. *J*, II, 414.

11. *J*, III, 334.

12. "Le Renoncement au Voyage," *OC*, III, 303. This passage can be read more profitably in terms of what Gide wrote later in *Les Nouvelles Nourritures*: "God dwells not in the object, but in love" (27).

13. *J*, I, 413.

14. *J*, III, 261.

15. *J*, I, 7–8; *J*, II, 342.

16. *J*, I, 19. *The Immoralist* (trans. Dorothy Bussy), 43, 44. Both Victor Poucel (*Etudes*, 24) and Martin Turnell (in *Nobel Prize Winners*, 80) say that the Immoralist's life becomes a search for the authentic being, "the Old Man" for whom the Gospels had no use.

17. *J*, II, 409.

18. *Les Nouvelles Nourritures*, 115.

19. *Ibid.*, 113.

20. *Ibid.*, 114.

21. *OC*, IV, 548.

22. "Dostoievsky," *OC*, XI, 161.

23. Etienne Gilson, *The Christian Philosophy of Saint Augustine*, trans. L. E. M. Lynch (New York: Random House, 1960), Foreword by Pontifical Institute of Mediaeval Studies (Toronto, December, 1959), 3.

24. "Feuillets," *OC*, XIII, 433. Cf. *J*, I, 29.

25. Arthur Rimbaud, *Oeuvres* (Paris: Mercure de France, 1924), "Une Saison en enfer," 265, 305.

26. *Ibid.*, "Bateau Ivre," 90; *Peer Gynt*, V. xi.

27. *J*, II, 299, 355.

28. *CWJ*, 52.

29. Cf. *Les Nouvelles Nourritures*, 98–99.

30. The Greeks had seen an affinity between health and "self-knowledge"; the etymological meaning of salvation is health, and a healthy person is precisely a person who is in a harmonious relationship with the environment, or "reality." In self-knowledge as a mystical concern the discovery of the "unspoiled self" and direct communion with God (a Gidian ideal) coincide: "To clear away the rubbish-heap so that he may get down to this treasure-house is from one point of view the initial task of the contemplative. This clearing away is the first part of 'introversion': that journey inwards to his own centre where, stripped of all his cleverness and merit, reduced to his 'nothingness,' he can 'meet God without intermediary' " (Underhill, *Mysticism*, 312).

31. *J*, III, 304.

32. Cf. *Les Nourritures Terrestres*, 168; and Rimbaud, "Bateau Ivre," 85: "Lighter than a cork I danced upon the waves."

33. *Strait is the Gate*, 36.

34. *J*, II, 301.

35. Nietzsche, "Ecce Homo," XVII, 81.

36. *J*, I, 18.

37. Cf. *J*, II, 255.

38. *CWJ*, 375.

39. See Turnell, *Nobel*, 82 f.; Jacques Lévy, *Journal et Correspondance*.

40. *Timaeus* 29e–30b.

41. *CWJ*, 243, 292.

42. *Ibid.*, 172. Gide gave a graphic illustration of this concept to Roger Martin du Gard to whom *Les Faux-Monnayeurs* is dedicated (Roger Martin du Gard, *Notes sur André Gide*, [Gallimard, 1951], 36 f).

43. *CWJ*, 173.

44. Du Gard, *Notes*, 40–41.

45. *CWJ*, 173–74.

46. *Ibid.*, 200.

47. At the age of twenty-four Gide had had "an ambitious plan," which he thought he ought to have carried out before letting it be devoured by his scruples. It was to write an imaginary history of the world, in order "to prove" that "mankind might have had a different history. . . . and nevertheless remained human" (*If It Die*, 242–43). He was to present lines common to all the countries in a particular history which, needless to say, had to be tailored to fit a preconceived philosophy of history. The hidden assumption here is that there is something behind, or at the center of, our history—as it has in fact unfolded itself—and the latter is merely one of the many possible manifestations of *that*.

48. *J*, II, 246.

49. *Les Nouvelles Nourritures*, 20.

50. Gide agrees with Keats: "It is a wretched thing to confess; but is a very fact that not one word I ever utter can be taken for granted as an opinion growing out of my identical nature—how can it, when I have no nature?" (*J*, II, 327, n. 18.). Cf. Gide's "théorie d'impersonnalité" as developed in a letter to François-Paul Alibert. See Schlumberger, *Madeleine*, 171. Gide had maintained earlier "that an artist needs this: a special world of which he alone has the key . . . everything in him should be or seem new, seen

through a powerfully coloring idiosyncrasy. He must have a personal philosophy, aesthetics, and ethics;" (*J*, I, 77).

51. *If It Die*, 168–69.

52. "Feuillets," *OC*, XV, 512.

53. Georgio de Santillana, *The Age of Adventure*, The Renaissance Philosophers (New York: Mentor Books, 1956), 236.

54. *If It Die*, 193–94.

55. *J*, I, 170.

56. *J*, III, 381.

57. *So Be It*, 81.

58. *J*, III, 243.

59. *Ibid.*, 275.

60. *J*, I, 3; *J*, II, 209; *If It Die*, 262; du Gard, *Notes*, 77.

61. *J*, III, 247.

62. *J*, I, 51. On the other hand, as he notes thirty-eight years later, when Rome does *not* recall Stendhal it fails to fascinate him though "more glorious . . . than yesterday; as exalting as possible" (*J*, III, 291).

63. *CWJ*, 183.

64. *If It Die*, 243.

65. *Ibid.*, 257.

66. *Ibid.*, 258.

67. *The Immoralist*, 132.

68. "Le Retour du Tchad," *OC*, XIV, 143.

69. *J*, III, 134.

70. *J*, II, 270.

71. *J*, III, 244.

72. *J*, IV, 300.

73. *Ibid.*, 107.

74. "Les Cahiers," *OC*, I, 51: "To write . . . what?—I am happy." Cf. *J*, II, 211: "Never did I *feel* younger and happier than last month!—to such a point that I was unable to write anything about it. I could only have stammered."

75. *J*, IV, 203.

76. "The most beautiful things are those that madness prompts and reason writes" (*J*, I, 38).

77. *J*, II, 343.

78. *J*, I, 25.

79. *J*, III, 32–33.

80. Cf. *J*, IV, 53.

81. *J*, II, 153.

82. "Emmanuel Signoret," *OC*, IV, 176; "Le Renoncement au Voyage," *OC*, IV, 273.

83. *J*, II, 306.

84. Cf. *J*, III, 107.

85. *J*, II, 392.

86. Martin-Chauffier, the editor of Gide's *Oeuvres Complètes*, makes this comment on Edouard's pronouncement: "One must understand what the meaning of the word 'novelist' that Edouard uses is in order to define his situation before men. It does not at all signify that Edouard looks upon men as does a novelist, but that he looks upon men as a novelist looks upon his heroes" (*OC*, XII, viii).

Chapter 4

1. *J*, II, 374.
2. "Lettre à Monsieur Deherme," *OC*, VI, 470.
3. *Strait is the Gate*, 50.
4. *CWJ*, 192–93.
5. *Strait is the Gate*, 144.
6. See O'Brien, *Portrait*, 216.
7. Gide has claimed that Alissa is not Madeleine. Professor O'Brien grants the validity of the claim but points out that Madeleine *became* Alissa in the course of time and that here, once more, life seemed to imitate art. Whatever the case, the near identity of the two women is unmistakable (*ibid.*, 215, 216). In the opinion of Wallace Fowlie "[Alissa] is, without a question, a faithful portrait of [Gide's] wife" (*Clowns and Angels*, 32).
8. Schlumberger, *Madeleine*, 23.
9. *Ibid.*, 46, 62.
10. *Ibid.*, 29.
11. *Ibid.*, 34.
12. *Ibid.*
13. *Ibid.*, 99. The same tergiversation is seen in her entry for October 8, 1891: "I am terrified of feeling more clearly than ever how close I am, soul and mind, to you—how I belong to you. To forget! To live no longer with the constant thought of you—Oh! When will that be?"
14. *Ibid.*, 62–63.
15. *Ibid.*, 43, 62 (emphasis added).
16. *Ibid.*, 61, 54–55.
17. *Ibid.*, 102, 117.
18. *J*, II, 421.
19. *If It Die*, 171–72.
20. *CWJ*, 95, 96.
21. *Ibid.*, 218, 221.
22. *Les Caves du Vatican* (Paris: Gallimard, 1922), 30, 31; *J*, II, 290.
23. Catharine H. Savage, *André Gide: L'Evolution de sa pensée religieuse*, 79. Cf. Van Meter Ames, *André Gide*, Chapt. II, "From Puritan to Pagan."
24. "Les Cahiers," *OC*, I, 61.
25. *J*, I, 20.
26. *Ibid.*, 23.
27. *Ibid.*, 41.
28. *Ibid.*, 39–40, 42.
29. "Le Retour du Tchad," *OC*, XIV, 156.
30. *J*, III, 359.
31. *J*, I, 72.
32. *Les Nourritures Terrestres*, 44, 45.
33. *J*, II, 177.
34. *Ibid.*, 122.
35. For a defense of the thesis that for Bonhoeffer God is "*super*natural, not belonging to the universe within man's comprehension," see Kenneth Hamilton, *God is Dead: The Anatomy of a Slogan* (Grand Rapids, Mich.: William B. Eerdmans Publishing Co., 1966), 38.

36. *J*, III, 394.

37. *Attendu que . . .* , 232 f.

38. *J*, III, 202.

39. *Ibid.*, 259.

40. *J*, II, 109.

41. *J*, III, 268.

42. Walter Rauschenbusch had written that "the perfect social order is the highest good" and had given his assent to Emile de Laveleye to the effect that "there is a social order which is the best. Necessarily it is not always the present order. Else why should we seek to change the latter? But it is that order which ought to exist to realize the greatest good for humanity. God knows it and wills it. It is for man to discover and establish it" (*The Social Principles of Jesus* [New York: Association Press, 1916], 63). Leo XIII had also found intolerable "the state of things now obtaining" and had "clearly" seen in 1891 "that some opportune remedy must be found quickly for the misery and wretchedness pressing so unjustly on the majority of the working class: . . ." (*The Church Speaks to the Modern World, The Social Teachings of Leo XIII*, ed. Etienne Gilson [Garden City, N.Y.: Doubleday Image Books, 1954], 205, 206).

43. *Les Nouvelles Nourritures*, 141, 160.

44. *J*, IV, 48 (emphasis added).

45. *So Be It*, 152.

46. *J*, II, 375.

47. "Lettre à E . . . R . . . ," *OC*, II, 485.

48. *J*, I, 19.

49. *J*, III, 274. Gide sometimes refers to himself as X, and M is the initial of his cousin's name. See Chapt. 5.

50. *If It Die*, 239.

51. *J*, I, 40, 42.

52. It is his adherence to this notion that probably accounts for his attributing to Fouillée some reflections on Protestantism written in fact by Emile Faguet. See *J*, I, 77–78. Cf. "Lettres à Angèle," *OC*, III, 233–34.

53. *J*, I, 72.

54. *J*, II, 415–16.

55. *J*, IV, 278.

56. *J*, I, 40.

57. *J*, III, 202.

58. Cf. his entry concerning a sentence of his *Amyntas*: "I address my devotion this morning to the Saharan Apollo, whom I see, with golden hair, black limbs, and porcelain eyes" (*J*, III, 103).

59. *J*, III, 165.

60. Amos N. Wilder, "The New Quest for the Historical Jesus," *Christianity and Crisis*, Vol. XXII, No. 23 (Jan. 7, 1963), 248.

61. *J*, I, 40, 72.

62. *J*, II, 183. Cf. Underhill, *Mysticism*, 306: "Mystical prayer, or 'orison'—the term which I propose for the sake of clearness to use here—has nothing in common with petition. It is not articulate; it has no forms. 'It is,' says 'The Mirror of St. Edmund,' 'naught else but yearning of soul.' "

63. Cf. *J*, IV, 105: ". . . it may be said that prayer creates God."

64. *J*, II, 340.

65. *J*, III, 287.

66. "Les Cahiers," *OC*, I, 53.

67. *Ibid.*, 112.

68. *J*, II, 177; "Considérations sur la Mythologie grecque," *OC*, IX, 149.

69. *J*, III, 84.

70. Cf. *J*, IV, 281.

71. Hytier, *André Gide*, 19.

72. Cf. *Les Nourritures Terrestres*, 46.

73. *Si Le Grain ne Meurt* (Paris: Gallimard, 1952), 108.

74. *J*, II, 122.

75. *J*, IV, 206.

76. *Ibid.*, 113, 114.

77. *So Be It*, 154.

78. *Les Nourritures Terrestres*, 43.

79. "Teach me to put off my happiness, to place it as far away from me as Thou art" (*Strait is the Gate*, 127).

80. *Les Nouvelles Nourritures*, 78 f.

81. *Ibid.*, 71.

82. Robert Mallet, *Une Mort Ambiguë*, 57.

83. *J*, I, 72.

84. Tillich, *Systematic Theology*, I, 110; cf. Martin Heidegger, *An Introduction to Metaphysics* (Garden City, N.Y.: Doubleday & Co., 1961), 1 f.

85. *J*, III, 16.

86. *J*, IV, 275, 278.

Chapter 5

1. *J*, I, 298.

2. *If It Die*, 148.

3. *J*, III, 38; Preface, A. de Saint-Exupéry, *Vol de nuit*, 11.

4. Albert Thibaudet, "André Gide," *Revue de Paris*, 748.

5. Jean Lambert, *Gide Familier*, 24. J. Lambert is the husband of Catherine, Gide's daughter born out of wedlock.

6. O'Brien, *Portrait*, 270–71.

7. *So Be It*, 106. Gide has also reported similar behaviors of his mother on one hand, and wife on the other: they both felt duty bound to offer their services to neighbors in distress at the cost of considerable risk or damage to themselves. See *If It Die*, 135, and *Et nunc manet in te*, 59. Gide liked reading aloud not only to Madeleine but also to his mother. See *If It Die*, 164.

8. *Madeleine*, trans. Justin O'Brien (New York: Alfred A. Knopf, Inc., 1952), 20.

9. *If It Die*, 261.

10. *Madeleine*, xiv.

11. "Les Cahiers," *OC*, I, 109.

12. Indicative of the eschatological connotations of "waiting" in Gide's mind is a casual entry in his *Journal* where he finds the Spanish language beautiful because it "confuses waiting and hope" (*J*, III, 234).

13. *J*, II, 391, 268, 321, 198, 263, 412 (emphasis added). Gide attributes the indisposition and his spells of insomnia to certain ill-regulated reflexes.

14. *J*, III, 101, 102.

15. *J*, II, 420–21.

16. See Schlumberger, *Madeleine*, 192.

17. Mallet, *Une Mort*, 49, 50.

18. Rudolph Otto, *The Idea of the Holy*, trans. John W. Harvey (London: Oxford University Press, 1957), Chapt. XIV.

19. Jane Harrison observes that being cursed was a way of being offered: "the person cursed or bound down was in some sense a gift or sacrifice to the gods of cursing, the underworld gods: the man stained by blood is 'consecrate' (*Kathieromenos*) to the Erinyes" (*Prolegomena to the Study of Greek Religion* [Cambridge: Cambridge University Press, 1922], 141.

20. *J*, III, 308; *Et Nunc*, 20 *et passim*.

21. *J*, III, 413.

22. *J*, IV, 184.

23. *Madeleine*, 63. Cf. *J*, I, 320.

24. *J*, III, 205.

25. *J*, III, 408.

26. *Et Nunc*, 8.

27. Tillich, *Systematic Theology*, I, 266.

28. *J*, II, 272.

29. *Madeleine*, 53.

30. *Les Nourritures Terrestres*, 77; *Si le grain ne meurt*, 215.

31. *J*, III, 15.

32. *Ibid.*, 167.

33. *CWJ*, 182–83, 320.

34. O'Brien, *Portrait*, 53 *et passim*.

35. Schlumberger, *Madeleine*, 191–92. Cf. *Et Nunc*, 79, 80.

36. *Madeleine*, 62.

37. *Ibid.*, 60, 61. Cf. Schlumberger, *Madeleine*, 206.

38. *If It Die*, 159.

39. *J*, I, 19.

40. *Strait is the Gate*, 20.

41. *Ibid.*

42. *Les Nouvelles Nourritures*, 82 f.

43. *If It Die*, 174–75.

44. *J*, IV, 12.

45. "Les Cahiers," *OC*, I, 110.

46. *If It Die*, 179.

47. *Ibid.*, 178.

48. *CWJ*, 294. One may observe an uncanny similarity between the tone of this passage and, in C. G. Jung's view, the eschatological expectation of the author of the Apocalypse: "There shall be no more sin, no more repression, no more disharmony with oneself, no guilt, no fear of death and no pain of separation, because through the marriage of the Lamb the son is united with the mother-bride and the ultimate bliss is attained" (*Symbols of Transformation* [New York: Harper & Brothers, 1962], I, 223).

49. O'Brien, *Portrait*, 250.

50. Friedrich Schleiermacher, *On Religion*, trans. John Oman (New York: Frederick Ungar Publishing Co., 1955), 37, 48.

51. *Ibid.*, 28.

52. Paul Tillich, *The Religious Situation*, trans. H. Richard Niebuhr (New York: Meridian Books, 1956), 36.

53. Paul Tillich, *The Protestant Era*, trans. James Luther Adams (Chicago: University of Chicago Press, 1948), 58; *Systematic Theology*, II, 80.

54. *Madeleine*, 54.

55. "Les Cahiers," *OC*, I, 30.

56. *If It Die*, 309.

57. *Ibid.*, 310.

58. *The Immoralist*, 25, 26.

59. *J*, IV, 277.

60. *If It Die*, 310.

61. *Madeleine*, 11.

62. Delay, *La Jeunesse*, 301.

63. *Madeleine*, 54.

64. *Ibid.*

65. *J*, III, 394. Cf. *Madeleine*, 85.

66. *Et Nunc*, 107: "Thinking, this morning, of how little I am worth without her, gauging the little virtue of my heart, I came to understand better that necessity for intermediaries between man and God, for intercessors against whom Protestantism rebels so violently."

67. Cf. G. Bounoure in *Souvenirs Littéraires*, 19.

68. *Et Nunc*, 102.

69. *Ibid.*, 16; Cf. *CWJ*, 63.

70. *Ibid.*, 104, 105.

71. Underhill, *Mysticism*, 391, 400.

72. *J*, II, 175.

73. Cf. *Strait is the Gate*, 101.

74. *Si le grain ne meurt*, 128.

75. Theodore M. Greene, "Christianity and Its Secular Alternatives," *The Christian Answer*, ed. Henry P. Van Dusen (New York: Charles Scribner's Sons, 1948), 78.

Chapter 6

1. *J*, III, 256. Cf. p. 373.

2. *Ibid.*, 278.

3. *Ibid.*, 281.

4. *J*, II, 421; *J*, III, 281.

5. *J*, III, 166.

6. *Ibid.*, 38.

7. *CWJ*, 97. Cf. 392–93.

8. *J*, II, 417; *J*, III, 252, 265; *Oedipus and Theseus*, 26 ff.: "They also say that Semele, who was Cadmus' daughter, and a mortal, carried Bacchus the god within her womb." There is no doubt that the reference is to the credal "born of the Virgin Mary." Cf. *J*, IV, 203.

9. *CWJ*, 179.

10. *Ibid.*, 194.

11. *J*, III, 30, 31.

12. *Ibid.*, 47.

13. *Ibid.*, 60.

14. *Ibid.*, 24.

15. "Réponse à une Enquête," *OC*, X, 25–26.

16. *Ibid.*, 236.

17. *Ibid.*, 48.

18. *Souvenirs Littéraires*, 21.

19. *J*, II, 205.

20. *J*, IV, 295.

21. *Oedipus and Theseus*, 79.

22. Underhill, *Mysticism*, 381. Cf. *J*, II, 395, where Gide will identify his duties toward God with those toward himself. In another effort to be one with the Absolute—within a secular frame of mind—he will write: "the important thing is to recognize oneself especially in the best and to stay on the side of *God*" (*J*, IV, 139).

23. *J*, III, 170.

24. For a striking description of Gide in an ecstatic state within an esthetically defined universe, see du Gard, *Notes*, 54–55.

25. André Breton, *Les Pas Perdus* (Paris: Gallimard, 1924), 8.

26. Unamuno, *Tragic Sense*, 5.

27. *CWJ*, 172.

28. *Ibid.*, 174.

29. *Ibid.*, 183. In order to receive the full impact of the word *devotion*, as used by Gide, the passage quoted must be read against this entry in his *Journal* for April 23, 1932: "That *state of devotion* in which feelings and thoughts, in which the whole being is oriented and subordinated—I now know it anew as in the time of my youth. Is not my present conviction comparable to *faith*?" (*J*, III, 232).

30. *J*, III, 167.

31. "Mopsus," *OC*, III, 7.

32. "Le Renoncement au Voyage," *OC*, IV, 328.

33. *Ibid.*, 339.

34. *J*, I, 82.

35. Bertrand Russell, *Mysticism and Logic* (Garden City, N.Y.: Doubleday Anchor Books, 1957), 3, 10.

36. *J*, I, 82.

37. *Les Nourritures Terrestres*, 18.

38. *J*, III, 167 (emphasis added).

39. "Lettres à Angèle," *OC*, III, 164.

40. See Michel Carrouges, *La Mystique du Surhomme* (Paris: Gallimard, 1948), 44, 74, 85, 155 ff.

41. *If It Die*, 261–62.

42. "Lettres," *OC*, II, 481.

43. *Les Nouvelles Nourritures*, 18.

44. *CWJ*, 280; *J*, II, 181.

45. "Notes d'un Voyage en Bretagne," *OC*, I, 10.

46. "Voyage au Congo," *OC*, XIII, 121.

47. *J*, II, 354.

48. *CWJ*, 90. Cf. *If It Die*, 256.

49. *So Be It*, 53.

50. *J*, II, 355.

51. *J*, IV, 45, 222.

52. A. C. Bouquet, *Comparative Religion* (Penguin Books, 1941), 99.

53. *The Koran*, trans. J. M. Rodwell, Sura II (XCI), v. 23.

54. "Le Renoncement au Voyage," *OC*, IV, 286. Cf. Henri Massis, *Jugements* (Paris: Librairie Plon, 1929), 63.

55. "Réflexions sur l'Allemagne," *OC*, IX, 111; *Les Nouvelles Nourritures*, 76. Cf. *J*, III, 53: "of how many labyrinthine problems is not the most modest flower the natural solution? And the mysterious relationships of its forms, its color, its scent?"

56. Russell, *Mysticism*, 8.

57. *J*, II, 363. Students of Pierre Janet might interpret the symptom in question in terms of psychasthenia. But Gide's lack of a sense of reality must not be considered outside the context of his religious convictions and of the other aspects of his personality.

58. F. Sierksama reports that the Aukauer Bush Negroes are convinced that it is impossible to visualize the true appearance of a god, that absolute truth and beauty cannot be expressed in a mere image and that the purpose of an image is only to denote in the simplest terms the existence of the deity it represents. In contrast, "it is not too much of an exaggeration to say that in Egypt the image *is* the man or god it represents." (*The Gods as We Shape Them* [London: Routledge and Kegan Paul, 1960], 152, 177). From the former of these attitudes it should not be difficult to arrive at "a certain sense of unreality." Gide would have found fascinating the following answer given by a boy, eleven years old, to the question: What Do You Wish? "I wish that I could wake up. This world is only a dream. If you knew what life is like in the real place, this would seem unreal to you, too. In the real place, people are made, not born. The child grows up, and, if, after living a few hundred years, you're tired of life, you just lie down, and you're gone. If you want something, you have it, poof! Hate, or anything but love, is unheard of. Sometime I'll wake up" (*New York Times Magazine*, November 25, 1962, 70). The Aukauer Bush Negroes and this boy may be described as "Platonists" who know not Plato.

59. *J*, II, 364.

60. *Ibid.*

61. *Ibid.*, 365.

62. *J*, II, 408.

63. *J*, III, 57. Gide identifies the realms of time and of the senses when he writes of Stendhal's Octave, for example, that "his love is of those over which time holds no sway" ("Préface à Armance," *OC*, XI, 75).

64. *If It Die*, 242–43.

65. *J*, III, 312; *J*, IV, 35.

66. Germaine Brée, "Time Sequences and Consequences in the Gidian World," *Yale French Studies*, No. 7, 53.

67. *J*, II, 172–73.

68. *J*, III, 117.

69. "Journal," *OC*, XV, 390.

70. *J*, I, 330.

71. Gaëtan Picon, *Panorama de la Nouvelle Littérature française* (Paris: Gallimard, 1951), 23.

72. "Lettre à C. du B.," *OC*, X, 548.

73. "Dostoievsky," *OC*, XI, 149.

74. *J*, II, 182.

75. *The Confessions of St. Augustine*, trans. Edward B. Pusey, D.D. (New York: Random House, 1949), 154.

76. *J*, III, 83.

77. *Les Nourritures Terrestres*, 15; *J*, III, 158.

78. *Martin Luther*, ed. Dillenberger, 191.

79. *J*, III, 258.

80. *Ibid.*, 36.

81. *J*, II, 404.

82. *J*, I, 72.

83. "Dostoievsky," *OC*, XI, 301.

84. *J*, III, 85.

85. *Ibid.*, 164. Cf. *J*, IV, 11.

86. *J*, IV, 82–83.

87. *Les Nourritures Terrestres*, 85.

88. *J*, III, 15.

89. *Les Nouvelles Nourritures*, 79–80.

90. *J*, IV, 113–14.

91. "Dostoievsky," *OC*, XI, 280.

92. *CWJ*, 384, 385, 386.

93. "Dostoievsky," *OC*, XI, 267.

94. *If It Die*, 99. Cf. *ibid.*, 240 and *J*, II, 183: "It is at the joints of our love that the Evil One attacks us."

95. O'Brien, *Portrait*, 290, 297.

96. *J*, II, 189.

97. Saint Augustine, *The City of God*, trans. Marcus Dods, D.D. (New York: Random House, 1950), 365.

98. *Les Nourritures Terrestres*, 149; *Les Nouvelles Nourritures*, 71. The word *dispose* in the French original seems to be the feminine form of *dispos*, and an adjective. *Dispos* is used as a masculine adjective only, but Littré regrets that restriction, and Gide may well have taken the liberty of breaking the rule. Dorothy Bussy translates as if Gide had written "dispose *de* l'esprit," whereas the text is "dispose *à* l'esprit" which may also mean of course "makes [us] receptive to spirit."

99. *J*, II, 415.

Chapter 7

1. Cf. *Attendu que* . . . , 225; "Chroniques de l'Ermitage," *OC*, IV, 384: *J*, II, 400–401.

2. *J*, I, 212.

3. *J*, II, 352.

4. "La Tentative amoureuse," *OC*, I, 227. Cf. *J*, II, 352; and *J*, IV, 243: "I no longer even know whether or not I should still like to begin my life over again; or else, I should do so with a little more daring in affirmation."

5. *If It Die*, 186, 199.

6. *Les Nourritures Terrestres*, 42.

7. The success of the film is his immediate concern here, but the remark obviously has a wider application.

8. *If It Die*, 251.

9. *Ibid.*, 261.

10. *CWJ*, 251.

11. See *J*, III, 334.

12. *J*, III, 258–59.

13. Martin du Gard, *Notes*, 89–90.

14. André Gide, *Littérature Engagée*, ed. Yvonne Davet (Paris, Gallimard, 1950), 40 f, 113 f.

15. *J*, III, 225.

16. *Ibid.*, 117.

17. *J*, II, 357.

18. Cf. *ibid.*, 299, 320.

19. *Corydon* (English trans.), 115.

20. *Ibid.*, 141. As if to support the contention that homosexuality is a way of withdrawing within one's own camp, an expert, G. W. Allport, has written that "with half of mankind [i.e., his own sex] the male may feel an in-group solidarity, with the other half, an irreconcilable conflict" (*The Nature of Prejudice* [Cambridge, Mass.: Addison-Wesley Publishing Co., 1954], 33).

21. O'Brien, *Portrait*, 332; Léon Pierre-Quint, *André Gide*, 528; Ramon Fernandez, *André Gide*, 235.

22. *J*, IV, 270.

23. William James, *The Varieties of Religious Experience* (New York: Random House, 1902), 372.

24. Baron Friedrich von Hügel, *The Mystical Element of Religion as Studied in Saint Catherine of Genoa and Her Friends* (London: J. M. Dent & Sons, 1923), II, 143. Gide, as he said to a German, would rather cause others to act than act himself ("Conversations avec un Allemand," *OC*, IX, 142). He would rather ask questions, he said in another context, than say yes or no. Yet he declared immediately after this latter observation: ". . . I do not care to have people believe that I have been passive. Passion has spared me passivity" (Mallet, *Une Mort*, 58). It is fair to assume that Gide uses here *passive* to mean *indifferent* which he was not, and the passion of which he speaks and passivity are not mutually exclusive as he implies.

25. William Barrett, *What is Existentialism?* (New York: Grove Press, 1964), 36.

26. *The Poetry of France*, Intro. & Notes by Alan M. Boase (London: Methuen & Co. Ltd., 1952), p. 1.

27. *Les Nourritures Terrestres*, 20.

28. *Ibid.*, 30, 77–78.

29. *CWJ*, 57.

30. Paul Archambault, *Humanité d'André Gide* (Bloud & Gay, 1946), 84.

31. "Lettre à A . . . R . . . ," *OC*, II, 481 f.

32. *Corydon* (English trans.), 44 f.

33. "Feuillets," *OC*, XIII, 412.

34. *Les Nourritures Terrestres*, 111: "Alas! Alas! I know how to prolong my suffering; but my pleasure I do not know how to tame it." Cf. Epicurus, *Principal Doctrines*, XX.

35. "Lettre à A . . . R . . . ," *OC*, II, 482. *J*, IV, 271–72: "The feeling of *duty* confers a sort of benediction on every deed accomplished; one feels like a moral being; one escapes the law of gravity; profound satisfaction (and yet without any pride) that I owe perhaps to my Protestant heredity, but that doesn't matter. And all that, without any need of turning to mysticism, remains human (in me at least). Amazing aptitude for happiness."

36. *Les Nouvelles Nourritures*, 97.

37. *Les Nourritures Terrestres*, 41.

38. *Ibid.*, 14.

39. *J*, II, 209.

40. *J*, IV, 298.

41. Cf. Göran Schildt, *Gide et l'Homme*.

42. *J*, II, 117.

43. *Les Nourritures Terrestres*, 194.

44. Matt. 19:29.

45. *If It Die*, 286 ff (emphases added). See *J*, III, 53: "I have often experienced the fact

that my brain is never more lucid, more open, more joyful, and more alert than when, the night before, I have mortally overstrained my flesh."

46. *So Be It*, 126–27.

47. *If It Die*, 288.

48. *Les Nourritures Terrestres*, 198.

49. *Ibid.*, 199.

50. W. A. Nitze and E. P. Dargan, *A History of French Literature* (New York: Henry Holt & Co., 1955), 738.

51. *Les Nourritures Terrestres*, 137.

52. *J*, I, 78.

53. Archambault, *Humanité*, 213.

54. "De l'Importance du Public," *OC*, IV, 187.

55. *J*, III, 225.

56. *Les Nourritures Terrestres*, 79.

57. *J*, I, 78.

58. The similarity of motive behind the two journeys becomes more interesting as we note a detail reported by Saint Athanasius: the Devil in order to seduce Antony assumes the form of a woman. He fails. Then, as the ultimate in temptation, he takes the form of a native boy (*Life of Saint Antony*, Chapts. V, VI).

59. *J*, III, 237.

60. *J*, I, 75; *J*, II, 377.

61. "Notes d'un Voyage en Bretagne," *OC*, I, 11.

62. *Les Nourritures Terrestres*, 90–91: " 'Events,' Josèphe resumed, 'have made use of me in a way that I did not consent to.'—'So much the worse!' resumed Ménalque. 'I prefer to tell myself that what is not, is that which could not be.' "

63. *Corydon* (English trans.), 46. It is readily seen that this is a version of the classical distinction between *nomos* (law) and *physis* (nature).

64. *Corydon*, 145.

65. *CWJ*, 324.

66. Hytier, *André Gide*, 94. "Act without motive" is indeed meaningful only if we are to stop at the surface of such behaviors as were observed, for example, by a policeman: " 'Murder without Motive'—the phrase used by a Houston police official to describe the local situation—occurs widely in Texas, as it did in San Angelo in November, 1959, when a twenty-two-year-old former WAF shot her daddy to death, as she later told police, 'for the hell of it.' Just two years earlier, a sixty-six-year-old native of Houston was playing dominoes with a friend half his age when an argument arose, and the elder man took out a .38 Colt revolver and shot his opponent between the eyes. 'I didn't have anything against the boy,' the hot-tempered player told the police. 'I just killed him. That's all' " (John Bainbridge, "The Super-American State," *The New Yorker*, April 22, 1961, 93).

67. W. Windelband, *A History of Philosophy* (New York: Macmillan Co., 1921), 605 f.

68. *Meister Eckhart*, trans. Raymond B. Blakney (New York: Harper & Brothers, 1957), 82 ff. Eckhart would say, the translator comments, that "no one can be truly interested in anything until he is disinterested" (316). There is a parallel here between this paradox and Gide's view of individualism.

69. "Les Cahiers," *OC*, I, 31.

70. Mallet, *Une Mort*, 94 f.

71. *J*, II, 398. Eight years earlier Gide was speaking of the "theory of the gratuitous and *unmotivated* action" (*CWJ*, 379).

72. *Lafcadio's Adventures*, trans. Dorothy Bussy (New York: Vintage Books, 1953), 181.

73. *Ibid.*, 185–86.

74. *J*, I, 74: " 'The ego is hateful,' you say. Not mine. I should have liked it in another; . . ." It is odd if this is the case that Gide should remember nothing from his childhood "that was not ugly, dark and deceitful" (*If It Die*, 4). Cf. "Lettres à Angèle," *OC*, III, 181.

75. *If It Die*, 214.

76. "Lettre à A . . . R . . . ," *OC*, II, 482.

77. *J*, I, 75.

78. "Le Prométhée mal enchaîné," *OC*, III, 134.

79. *J*, I, 72.

80. André Gide, "Philoctetes," *My Theater*, trans. Jackson Mathews (New York: Alfred A. Knopf, Inc., 1952), III. ii, p. 151.

81. See, e.g., Lawrence Thomas, *André Gide: The Ethic of the Artist*, 1 *et passim*.

82. *J*, III, 279.

83. *J*, II, 129. To give one more example: He wrote in a *billet* to Angèle that the triumph of individualism and that of classicism coincide: ". . . the triumph of individualism is in renunciation to individuality" ("Billets à Angèle," *OC*, XI, 36).

84. *J*, III, 32.

85. *J*, IV, 67–68.

86. *J*, III, 79.

87. *J*, III, 230.

88. "Préface à Armance," *OC*, XI, 81, n. 2.

89. See *Four Existentialist Theologians*, ed. Herberg, 9–10.

90. *Souvenirs Littéraires*, 59.

91. *J*, II, 245.

92. *J*, III, 196.

93. "Billets à Angèle," *OC*, XI, 36. Gide expressed this idea several times. Another formulation is as follows: "A great man has only one care: to become as human as possible —I'd say rather: TO BECOME BANAL" ("De l'Influence en Littérature," *OC*, III, 262).

94. *Thus Spake Zarathustra*, Part I, Sec. 1.

95. Jean Marie Guyau, *Esquisse d'une Morale sans obligation, ni sanction* (Paris: Félix Alcan, 1896), 246.

96. *J*, III, 216.

97. *CWJ*, 51.

98. Dillenberger and Welch, *Protestant Christianity*, 104.

99. Isa. 6:8.

100. *J*, III, 182.

101. *J*, II, 342.

102. *J*, I, 19.

103. "Quelques livres," *OC*, III, 421.

104. *J*, III, 168–69.

105. *Ibid.*, 262.

106. *J*, IV, 139; "Préface à Armance," *OC*, XI, 83.

107. *CWJ*, 251.

108. "Dostoievsky," *OC*, XI, 167; *J*, III, 328.

109. *J*, I, 140.

110. *J*, IV, 82–83.

111. "Notes d'un Voyage en Bretagne," *OC*, I, 15; *J*, III, 375.

112. *Oedipus and Theseus*, 101; "Journal Sans Dates," *OC*, VI, 37.

113. Underhill, *Mysticism*, 130.

Bibliography

Works by André Gide

With dates of original publication. The place of publication is Paris, unless otherwise indicated.

Les Cahiers d'André Walter. Librairie Académique Didier-Perrin et Cie, 1891.

Le Traité du Narcisse. Théorie du Symbole. Librairie de L'Art indépendant (LAI), 1891.

Les Poésies d'André Walter. LAI, 1892.

Le Voyage d'Urien. LAI, 1893.

La Tentative amoureuse. LAI, 1893.

Paludes. LAI, 1895.

Réflexions sur quelques points de littérature et de morale. Mercure de France (MF), 1897.

Les Nourritures Terrestres. MF, 1897.

Le Prométhée mal enchaîné. MF, 1899.

Philoctéte and *El Hadj* (with *Le Traité du Narcisse* and *La Tentative amoureuse*). MF, 1899.

Feuilles de route. Bruxelles: Printed by N. Vandersypen, 1899.

Lettres à Angèle. MF, 1900.

Le Roi Candaule. Revue Blanche, 1901.

L'Immoraliste. MF, 1902.

Saül. MF, 1903.

Prétextes. MF, 1903.

Amyntas: Mopsus; Feuilles de route; De Biskra à Touggourt; Le Renoncement au Voyage. MF, 1906.

Le Retour de l'enfant prodigue. "Vers et Prose," 1907.

La Porte étroite. MF, 1909.

Oscar Wilde. MF, 1910.

Nouveaux Prétextes. MF, 1911.

C.R.D.N. (Corydon). Bruges: Printed by St. Catherine Press Ltd., 1911.

Isabelle. Nouvelle Revue Française (NRF), 1911.

Bethsabé. Bibliothèque de l'Occident, 1912.

Souvenirs de la Cour d'Assises. NRF, 1914.

Les Caves du Vatican, 2 vols. NRF, 1914.

La Symphonie pastorale. NRF, 1919.

Si le grain ne meurt. Bruges: Printed by St. Catherine Press Ltd., 1920.

Numquid et tu . . . ? Bruges: Printed by St. Catherine Press, Ltd., 1922.

Dostoievsky. Plon-Nourrit et Cie, 1923.

Incidences. NRF, 1924.

Les Faux-Monnayeurs. NRF, 1926.

Le Journal des Faux-Monnayeurs. Editions Eos, 1926.

Voyage au Congo. NRF, 1927.

Le Retour du Tchad. NRF, 1928.

L'Ecole des femmes. NRF, 1929.

Suivant Montaigne. NRF, 1929.

Essai sur Montaigne. Editions de la Pléiade, 1929.

Dictées. NRF, 1929.

Un esprit non prévenu. Editions Kra, 1929.

Robert. NRF, 1930.

La Séquestrée de Poitiers. Gallimard, 1930.

L'Affaire Redureau with *Faits divers.* Gallimard, 1930.

Divers. NRF, 1931.

Oedipe. Editions de la Pléiade, 1931.

Goethe. NRF, 1932.

Perséphone. Gallimard, 1934.

Les Nouvelles Nourritures. Gallimard, 1935.

Geneviève ou la Confidence inachevée. Gallimard, 1936.

Retour de l'U.R.S.S. Gallimard, 1936.

Retouches à mon "Retour de l'U.R.S.S." Gallimard, 1937.

Notes sur Chopin. Bruxelles: Revue Internationale de Musique, 1938.

Journal 1889–1939. NRF, 1939.

Découvrons Henri Michaux. Gallimard, 1941.

Théâtre: Saül, Le Roi Candaule, Oedipe, Perséphone, and *Le Treizième arbre.* Gallimard, 1942.

Interviews Imaginaires. Yverdon et Lausanne: Editions de Haut Pays, 1943.

Interviews Imaginaires. La Délivrance de Tunis. New York: Editions Jacques Schiffrin, 1943.

Attendu que . . . Alger: Charlot, 1943.

Thésée. New York: Jacques Schiffrin, 1946.

Souvenirs Littéraires et Problèmes Actuels avec deux présentations de G. Bounoure. Beyrouth: Les Lettres Françaises, 1946.

Et nunc manet in te. Neuchâtel: Richard Heyd, 1947.

Paul Valéry. Domat, 1947.

Correspondance (with Francis Jammes). Pref. and notes by R. Mallet. Gallimard, 1948.

Feuillets d'automne. MF, 1949.

Correspondance (with Paul Claudel). Gallimard, 1949.

Journal 1942–1949. Gallimard, 1950.

Lettres de Charles Du Bos et Réponse d'André Gide. Intro. by Juliette Charles-Du Bos. Editions Corrêa, 1950.

Littérature engagée. Intro. and notes by Yvonne Davet. Gallimard, 1950.

Ainsi soit-il ou les Jeux sont faits. Gallimard, 1952.

Correspondance (with Paul Valéry). Pref. and notes by R. Mallet. Gallimard, 1955.

Oeuvres Complètes. 15 v. NRF, 1933–39.

Selected Prefaces and Articles

Introduction to R. Tagore's *Gitanjali (l'Offrande lyrique).* NRF, 1914.

Introduction to Baudelaire's *Les Fleurs du Mal.* Ed. Pelletan, R. Heller, 1917.

Preface to *Lettres du lieutenant de vaisseau Dupouey.* NRF, 1922.

Foreword to Pushkin's *Queen of Spades (La Dame de Pique).* J. Schiffrin et Cie, 1923.

Introduction to Wm. Blake's *The Marriage of Heaven and Hell (Le Mariage du ciel et de l'enfer).* C. Aveline, 1923.

Preface to Saint-Exupéry's *Vol de nuit.* Gallimard, 1931.

Preface to Thomas Mann's *Achtung Europa! (Avertissement à l'Europe).* Gallimard, 1937.

Preface to Yvon's *L'U.R.S.S. telle qu'elle est.* Gallimard, 1938.

Prefatory notes to H. Fielding's *Tom Jones.* Gallimard, 1938.

Preface to *Les Pages immortelles de Montaigne.* Editions Corrêa, 1939.

Introduction to the *Theatre* of Goethe. NRF, La Pléiade, 1942.

Preface to *Ecrivains américains d'aujourd'hui.* Genève: Ed. du Continent, 1944.

Prefatory letter to *Hamlet.* New York: Jacques Schiffrin, 1944.

Preface to *Poussin.* Le Divan, 1945.

Introduction to *Jeunesse d'Europe* by Jacques de Launay and Claude Murat. France-Empire, 1948.

Preface to Marcel Drouin's *La Sagesse de Goethe.* Gallimard, 1949.

"Printemps" in *La Guirlande des années.* Flammarion, 1951.

Translations Used

The Correspondence between Paul Claudel and André Gide. Boston: Beacon Press, 1964.

The Counterfeiters with Journal of "The Counterfeiters," trans. Dorothy Bussy and Justin O'Brien. New York: Alfred A. Knopf, 1957.

The Fruits of the Earth, trans. Dorothy Bussy. New York: Alfred A. Knopf, 1957.

If It Die, trans. Dorothy Bussy. New York: Random House, 1935.

The Immoralist, trans. Dorothy Bussy. New York: Vintage, 1959.

The Journals of André Gide, trans. Justin O'Brien. 4 vols. New York: Alfred A. Knopf, 1949.

Lafcadio's Adventures, trans. Dorothy Bussy. New York: Vintage, 1953.

Madeleine (Et nunc manet in te), trans. Justin O'Brien. New York: Alfred A. Knopf, 1952.

Pretexts: Reflections on Literature and Morality, ed. Justin O'Brien, New York: Dell Publishing Co., 1964.

So Be It, trans. Justin O'Brien. New York: Alfred A. Knopf, 1959.

Strait is the Gate, trans. Dorothy Bussy. New York: Vintage, 1959.

My Theater, trans. Jackson Mathews. New York: Alfred A. Knopf, 1952.

Two Legends: Oedipus and Theseus, trans. John Russell. New York: Vintage, 1958.

Works on Gide

Albérès, René-Marill. *L'Odyssée d'André Gide.* La Nouvelle Edition, 1951.

Ames, Van Meter. *André Gide.* Norfolk, Conn.: New Directions, 1947.

Amoudru, Bernard. *De Bourget à Gide: Amour et Famille.* Editions Familiales de France, 1946.

André Gide et notre temps. Gallimard, 1935.

Archambault, Paul. *Humanité d'André Gide.* Bloud & Gay, 1946.

Barjon, Louis. *Gide et Saint-Exupéry: Dialogue des deux ferveurs.* Routes & Jalons, 1952.

Beaunier, André. *Les Idées et les Hommes*—Deuxième série. Plon-Nourrit et Cie, 1915.

Beigbeder, Marc. *André Gide.* Bruxelles: Editions Universitaires, 1954.

Benda, Julien. *La France Byzantine.* Gallimard, 1945.

Billotey, Pierre. *Les grands hommes en liberté.* Bibliothèque des Marges, 1922, pp. 97–107.

Blanche, J.-E. "De Barrès à Gide" (Souvenirs) in *Les Oeuvres Libres,* Nouvelle série No. 28 (254). Librairie Arthème Fayard, 1948.

Blanchet, André. "André Gide et les Chrétiens" and "Encore Gide" in *La Littérature et le Spirituel* (La Mêlée Littéraire), Vol. I. Aubier, Editions Montaigne, 1959, pp. 151–63, 167–74.

Blanchot, Maurice. "André Gide et Goethe" and "Au sujet des *Nourritures Terrestres*" in *Faux Pas.* Gallimard, 1943, pp. 322–28, 348–53.

Boisdeffre, Pierre de. "Le Christianisme d'André Gide" in *Métamorphose de la Littérature: de Barrès à Malraux.* Editions Alsatia, 1950.

Boyd, Ernest. "The Protestant Barrès: André Gide" in *Studies from Ten Literatures.* New York: Charles Scribner's Sons, 1925, pp. 32–40.

Braak, Sybrandi. *André Gide et l'âme moderne.* Amsterdam: H. J. Paris V/H Firma A. H. Kruyt, 1921.

Brachfeld, George Israel. *André Gide and the Communist Temptation.* Geneva: Librairie E. Droz, 1959.

Brée, Germaine. *André Gide: L'Insaisissable Protée.* "Les Belles Lettres," 1953.

Brennan, Joseph G. *Three Philosophical Novelists.* New York: Macmillan, 1964.

Brodin, Pierre. "André Gide" in *Les Ecrivains Français de l'entre-deux-guerres.* Montréal: Valiquette, 1943, pp. 31–47.

Combelle, Lucien. *Je dois à André Gide.* Frédéric Chambriand, 1951.

Davet, Yvonne. *Autour des Nourritures Terrestres.* Gallimard, 1948.

Delay, Jean. *La Jeunesse d'André Gide.* Gallimard, 1956.

Derais, François and Henri Rambaud. *L'Envers du Journal de Gide.* Le nouveau portique, 1951.

Drain, Henri. *Nietzsche et Gide* (Essai). Editions de la Madeleine, 1932.

Du Bos, Charles. *Le Dialogue avec André Gide.* Editions Corrêa, 1947.

Fay, Bernard. "André Gide ou le triomphe du désir" in *Panorama de la littérature contemporaine.* Editions du Sagittaire, 1926, pp. 181–90.

Fayer, Mischa Harry. *Gide, Freedom and Dostoevsky.* Burlington, Vt.: Lane Press, 1946.

Fernandez, Ramon. *André Gide.* R. A. Corrêa, 1931.

Fowlie, Wallace. *André Gide: His Life and Art.* New York: Macmillan, 1965.

————. *Clowns and Angels: Studies in Modern French Literature.* New York: Sheed and Ward, 1943.

Gabory, Georges. *André Gide: Son Oeuvre* (Portrait et autographe). Editions de la Nouvelle Revue Critique, 1924.

Gagnebin, Laurent. *André Gide nous intérroge: Essai critique sur sa pensée religieuse et morale.* Lausanne: Cahiers de la Renaissance Vaudoise, 1961.

Ghéon, Henri. "Le Roi Candaule d'André Gide" in *Nos Directions.* Nouvelle Revue Française, Marcel Rivière & Cie, 1911, pp. 67-79.

Gide vivant, ed. Colin-Simard. Amiot-Dumont, 1952.

Gillouin, René. "André Gide" (à propos de *La Symphonie Pastorale*) in *Esquisses Littéraires et Morales.* Bernard Grasset, Editeur, 1926, pp. 1–5.

Gouiran, Emile. *André Gide: Essai de psychologie littéraire.* Ed. Jean Crès, 1934.

Guérard, Albert J. *André Gide.* Cambridge, Mass.: Harvard University Press, 1951.

Herbart, Pierre. *A la recherche d'André Gide.* Gallimard, 1952.

Hommage à André Gide. NRF, 1951.

Hytier, Jean. *André Gide,* trans. Richard Howard. Garden City, N.Y.: Doubleday Anchor, 1962.

Jammes, Francis. *L'Antigyde ou Elie de Nacre* (a novel). Mercure de France, 1932.

Klossowski, Pierre. *Un si funeste désir.* Gallimard, 1963.

Lacretelle, Jacques de. "Gide et le communisme" in *L'Heure qui change.* Geneva: Editions du Milieu du Monde, 1941.

Lafille, Pierre. *André Gide Romancier.* Hachette, 1954.

Laidlaw, G. Norman. *Elysian Encounter.* Syracuse, N.Y.: Syracuse University Press, 1963.

Lambert, Jean. *Gide Familier.* René Julliard, 1958.

Lang, Renée. *André Gide.* Egloff, 1949.

Lepoutre, Raymond. *André Gide.* Collection triptyque, Richard-Masse, Editeurs, 1946.

Lévy, Jacques. *Journal et Correspondance.* Grenoble: Editions des Cahiers de l'Alpe, 1954.

Lièvre, Pierre. "André Gide" in *Esquisses Critiques.* Le Divan, 1929, pp. 143–79.

Lime, Maurice. *Gide, tel que je l'ai connu* (avec 20 lettres inédites). Julliard, 1952.

Mahias, Claude. *La vie d'André Gide.* Avant-propos et commentaires par Pierre Herbart. NRF, 1955.

Mallet, Robert. *Une Mort Ambiguë.* Gallimard, 1955.

March, Harold. *Gide and the Hound of Heaven.* Philadelphia, Pa.: University of Pennsylvania Press, 1952.

Marchand, Max. *Le Complexe pédagogique et didactique d'André Gide.* Oran: Fouque, 1954.

———. *Du Marquis de Sade à André Gide: Essai de critique psychopathologique et psychosexuelle.* Oran: Fouque, 1956.

Marsalet, Maurice. *André Gide l'enchaîné.* Raymond Picquot, 1945.

Martin, Claude. *André Gide par lui-même.* Editions du Seuil, 1963.

Martin du Gard, Roger. *Notes sur André Gide, 1913–1951.* Gallimard, 1951.

Martinet, Edouard. *André Gide, l'Amour et la Divinité.* Editions Victor Attinger, 1931.

Martin-Mamy, Eugène. *Les Nouveaux Païens.* Bibliothèque Internationale d'Edition E. Sansot & Cie, c. 1914.

Massis, Henri. *D'André Gide à Marcel Proust.* Lyon: Lardanchet, 1948.

Mauriac, Claude. *Conversations avec André Gide* (Extraits d'un journal). Editions Albin Michel, 1951.

Mauriac, François. "Bref plaidoyer pour André Gide" in *Mes Grands Hommes.* Monaco: Editions du Rocher, 1949, pp. 231–36.

———. *La Mort d'André Gide.* Editions Estienne, 1952.

Mauriac, Pierre. "André Gide" in *L'Ecrivain et l'évènement.* Editions Siloë, 1947.

Maurras, Charles. *Réponse à André Gide.* Editions de "La seule France," 1948.

McLaren, James C. *The Theatre of André Gide: Evolution of a Moral Philosopher.* Baltimore, Md.: Johns Hopkins Press, 1953.

Michaud, Gabriel. *Gide et l'Afrique.* Les Editions du Scorpion, 1961.

Mondor, Henri. *Les Premiers Temps d'une Amitié: André Gide et Paul Valéry.* Monaco: Editions du Rocher, 1947.

Monglond, André. "Naissance d'un roman" in *Eventail de l'Histoire Vivante,* Vol. I. Armand Colin, 1953.

Naville, Arnold. *Bibliographie des écrits d'André Gide.* Guy le Prat, 1949.

O'Brien, Justin. *Les Nourritures Terrestres d'André Gide et les Bucoliques de Virgile.* Boulogne-sur-Seine: Les Editions de la Revue Prétexte, 1953.

———. *The Novel of Adolescence in France: The Study of a Literary Theme.* New York: Columbia University Press, 1937.

———. *Portrait of André Gide.* New York: Alfred A. Knopf, 1953.

Painter, George D. *André Gide: A Critical and Biographical Study.* London: Arthur Barker Ltd., 1951.

Pell, Elsie. *André Gide: L'Evolution de sa pensée religieuse.* Librairie H. Didier, 1936.

Peyre, Henri. "André Gide: Martyr and Hero of Sincerity" in *Literature and Sincerity*. New Haven, Conn.: Yale University Press, 1963.

Pierre-Quint, Léon. *André Gide*. Librairie Stock, 1952.

Planche, Henri. *Le Problème de Gide*. Editions Téqui, 1952.

Poucel, Victor. *L'Esprit d'André Gide*. L'Art Catholique, 1929.

Proust, Marcel. *Lettres à André Gide*. Ides et Calendes, 1949.

Reynaud, Louis. *La Crise de notre littérature: Des Romantiques à Proust, Gide et Valéry*. Librairie Hachette, 1929.

Rivière, Jacques. "André Gide" in *Etudes*. NRF, 1924, pp. 175–258.

Romains, Jules. "Consécration de Gide" in *Saints de Notre Calendrier*. Flammarion, 1952, pp. 197–202.

Rousseaux, André. "André Gide ou l'ange manqué" in *Le Paradis Perdu*. Bernard Grasset, 1936, pp. 187–283.

Rouveyre, André. *Le reclus et le retors: Gourmont et Gide*. Ed. G. Crès & Cie, 1927.

Sachs, Maurice. *André Gide*. Denoël et Steele, 1936.

Savage, Catharine H. *André Gide: L'Evolution de sa pensée religieuse*. A. G. Nizet, 1962.

Schildt, Göran. *Gide et l'Homme,* trans. Marguerite Gay and Gerd de Mautort. Mercure de France, 1949.

Schlumberger, Jean. *Eveils*. Gallimard, 1950.

———. *Madeleine et André Gide*. Gallimard, 1956.

Schreiber, Dr. Lotte. *Leben und Denken im Werk von André Gide*. Berlin: Verlag Dr. Emil Ebering, 1933.

Schwob, Marcel. *Le Vrai drame d'André Gide*. Grasset, 1932.

Simon, Emile. "L'Esthétique d'André Gide: La morale de *l'Immoraliste*" in *Patrie de l'humain*. Gallimard, 1948, pp. 75–112.

Slochower, Harry. "Absolute Doubt: André Gide, Ignazio Silone, John Dos Passos" in *No voice is wholly lost . . . : Writers and Thinkers in War and Peace*. New York: Creative Age Press, 1945, pp. 56–74.

Souday, Paul. *André Gide*. Simon Kra, 1927.

Starkie, Enid. *André Gide*. New Haven, Conn.: Yale University Press, 1954.

Stocker, Dr. A. *L'Amour interdit: Trois anges sur la route de Sodome* (Etude psychologique). Geneva: Ed. du Mont-Blanc, 1945.

———. *Désarroi de l'homme moderne*. Geneva: Ed. du Mont-Blanc, 1946.

Teuler, Gabriel. *Après Gide*. Nouvelles Editions Debresse, 1959.

Thérive, André. *Moralistes de ce temps*. Amiot-Dumont, 1948.

Thierry, J.-J. *Gide*. Gallimard, 1962.

Thomas, Lawrence. *André Gide: The Ethic of the Artist*. London: Secker & Warburg, 1950.

Turnell, Martin in *Nobel Prize Winners,* ed. E. J. Ludovici. London: Arco Publishers, 1956.

Uhlig, Helmut. *André Gide oder die Abenteuer des Geistes*. Berlin: Chronos Verlag, 1948.

Periodicals

Baldensperger, Fernand. "André Gide antigoethéen," *Revue de Littérature Comparée*, Treizième Année, No. 4 (octobre–décembre 1933), 651–75.

Bastide, Roger. "L'acte gratuit d'André Gide et le problème de la liberté," *La Grande Revue*, 38ᵉ Année, No. 4 (avril 1934), 302–14.

———. "Thèmes gidiens," *Cahiers du Sud*. Tom. XI, No. 328, 41ᵉ Année (avril 1955), 435–48.

Bataille, Georges. "André Gide: Journal 1939–1942," *Critique*, T. 1, Nos. 3–4 (août–septembre 1946), 367–68.

———. "André Gide: *Thésée*," *ibid.*, No. 5 (octobre 1946), 463.

———. "Le Journal jusqu'à la mort," *ibid.*, T. 7, No. 46, Sixième Année (15 mars 1951), 212–18.

———. "Nietzsche et Jésus selon Gide et Jaspers," *ibid.*, T. 6, No. 42, Cinquième Année (novembre 1950), 99–114.

Benda, Julien. "*Scholies*: de Gide, de Mauriac et de Barrès," *La Nouvelle Revue Française*, 21ᵉ Année, No. 229 (1 octobre 1932), 617–22.

Blanchot, Maurice. "Gide et la littérature d'expérience," *L'Arche*, Vol. 4, No. 23 (janvier 1947), 87–98.

Bodart, Roger. "André Gide en quête de la paix," *Revue Générale Belge*, No. 66 (avril 1951), 890–901.

Bouret, Jean. "Gide et la vérité," *Arts*, No. 301 (9 mars 1951), 1, 2.

Les Carnets Viatoriens: "André Gide, ou la synthèse du bien et du mal," 16ᵉ Année (juillet 1951), 220–21.

Carrier, Warren. "The Demoniacal in Gide," *Renascence*, Vol. 4, No. 1 (Autumn 1951), 59–65.

———. "The Devil and Monsieur Gide," *The Tiger's Eye*, Vol. 1, No. 4 (15 June 1948), 14–28.

Carrouges, Michel. "Les replis de la sincérité: Paul Claudel et André Gide," *La Vie Intellectuelle* (octobre 1950), 369–74.

Chadourne, Marc. "André Gide et l'humanisme," *The French Review*, Vol. 22, No. 3 (January 1949), 207–19.

Chaffiol-Debillemont, F. "Dans le sillage de *l'Immoraliste*," *Mercure de France*, No. 1082 (octobre 1953), 281–93.

Chazel, Pierre. "Gide et les cinq tentations du protestantisme," *Foi et Vie*, 48ᵉ Année, No. 3 (mai–juin 1950), 259–78.

———. "Le Procès d'André Gide," *Foi et Vie*, 28ᵉ Année, No. 4, Cahier A (16 février 1925), 189–96.

Cruickshank, John. "Gide's Treatment of Time in *La Symphonie Pastorale*," *Essays in Criticism*, Vol. 7, No. 2 (April 1957), 134–43.

Dieckman, Herbert. "André Gide and the Conversion of Charles Du Bos," *Yale French Studies*, No. 12 (Fall–Winter 1953), 62–72.

Doncoeur, Paul. De la ferveur: I. "La ferveur démoniaque d'André Gide," II.

"L'âme non-habituée de Péguy," III. "La ferveur du chrétien d'après St. Thomas," *Etudes*, 70 et 71 Années, Tomes 218, 219 (5 mars 1934), 595–606; (20 mars 1934), 751–61; (5 avril 1934), 35–48.

Ellis, Lowell B. "Some Existentialist Concepts in Gide, Malraux, and Saint-Exupéry," *Bucknell Review*, Vol. 10, No. 2 (December 1961), 164–73.

Estève, Louis. "Le 'Moi' selon Proust, Valéry et Gide," *Cahiers du Sud*, 26ᵉ Année, T. 18, No. 213 (février 1939), 118–25.

Etudes, 64th year, Vol. 193 (oct.–nov.–dec. 1927); (5 March 1934).

Le Figaro Littéraire: "Témoignages sur André Gide," 6ᵉ Année, No. 253 (24 février 1951), 5, 7.

Fowlie, Wallace. "Gide's Earliest Quest: *Les Nourritures Terrestres*," *Essays in Criticism*, Vol. 2, No. 3 (July 1952), 285–94.

———. "Who Was André Gide?" *The Sewanee Review*, Vol. 60, No. 4 (Autumn 1952), 605–23.

———. Review of *So Be It* or *The Chips Are Down* in *Saturday Review* (13 June 1959).

Frohock, W. M. "Gide and His Eagle," *The Catholic World*, Vol. CLXXV, No. 1,046 (May 1952), 97–103.

Gonzagne, Truc. "André Gide et la pureté," *La Revue Hebdomadaire*, T. 9 (1937), 135–41.

Green, Julian. "An Interview with André Gide," *Renascence*, Vol. 4, No. 1–2 (Autumn 1951), 58.

Grossrieder, Hans. "Der Dämon André Gides oder Konversion und leere Freiheit," *Wort und Wahrheit*, Vol. 4 (April 1951), 259–68.

Guitton, Jean. "André Gide et l'éternel présent," *La Table Ronde*, No. 83 (novembre 1954), 175–77.

Guyon, Bernard. "Le testament d'André Gide: *Thésée*," *La Vie Intellectuelle*, 19ᵉ Année, No. 6 (juin 1951), 51–67.

Herbart, Pierre. "A Key to André Gide," trans. Donald Windham, Noonday 2. New York: Noonday Press (1959).

Hoog, Armand. "André Gide et l'acte gratuit," *La Nef*, 3ᵉ Année, No. 18 (mai 1946), 130–32.

Hooker, Kenneth Ward. "Dostoyevsky and Gide," *Bucknell University Studies*, Vol. 3, No. 4 (November 1952), 168–81.

Kanes, Martin. "Whitman, Gide, and Bazalgette: An International Encounter," *Comparative Literature*, Vol. 14, No. 4 (Fall 1962), 341–55.

Kanters, Robert. "Nos grands hommes devant Dieu," *L'Age Nouveau*, XIᵉ Année, No. 94 (novembre 1955), 87–90.

———. "Le Siècle d'André Gide," *La Revue de Paris*, 70ᵉ Année (mars 1963), 107–18.

Kemp, Robert, Philippe Soupault, Armand Hoog, H. Bouillier, "Gide et nos vingts ans," *Revue de Paris*, 54ᵉ Année, No. 12 (décembre 1947), 140–45.

Lacoste, Henri de. "Quelques réflexions sur André Gide," *Foi et Vie*, 50ᵉ Année, No. 1 (janvier–février 1952), 32–37.

Lamarche, Gustave. "André Gide et l'anti-christianisme," *Les Carnets Viatoriens,* XIIIe Année (juillet 1948), 182–97.

Lang, Renée. "André Gide et Nietzsche: étude chronologique," *The Romanic Review,* Vol. 34, No. 2 (April 1943).

Lesdain, Pierre. "Un héros selon Carlyle: André Gide," *Synthéses,* 3e Année, No. 1 (1948), 82–95.

Magny, Claude-Edmonde. "A propos du *Thésée*: L'Ethique Secrète d'André Gide," *Poésie 47,* No. 36 (décembre 1946), 82–94.

Marcel, Gabriel. "André Gide," *Les Nouvelles Littéraires,* No. 1225 (22 février 1951), 1, 5.

Massis, Henri. "André Gide et Dostoievsky," I, *La Revue universelle,* Tom. XV, No. 15 (1 novembre 1923), 329–41; II, Tom. XV, No. 16 (15 novembre 1923), 476–93.

———. "L'Influence de M. André Gide," *La Revue Universelle,* Tom. VII, No. 16 (15 novembre 1921), 500–509.

Mauger-Clement, E. C. F., "The God of André Gide," *Journal of Arts and Letters,* Vol. III, No. 1 (Spring 1951), 62–67.

Mauriac, François. "Une âme sur les confins," *Le Figaro Littéraire* (11 août 1956), 1, 7.

Mehl, Roger. "L'attitude religieuse d'André Gide pendent ses dernières années," *Foi et Vie,* 49e Année, No. 6 (septembre–octobre 1951), 530–31.

Merchant, Norris. "The Spiritual Dilemma of André Gide," *The Colorado Quarterly,* Vol. VII, No. 4 (Spring 1959), 406–23.

Meyer, John. "Gide Today," *Renascence,* Vol. V, No. 2 (Spring 1953), 135–43.

Mitchell, John D. "André Gide, Rebel and Conformist," *The American Imago* (A Psychoanalytic Journal for the Arts & Sciences), Vol. XVI, No. 2 (Summer 1959), 147–53.

Nesmy, Dom Claude Jean. "Prestiges et Dangers du Désir chez André Gide et R. Rolland," *La Pensée Catholique,* No. 5 (1948), 112–20.

O'Brien, Justin. "Lafcadio and Barnabooth, A Supposition," *Symposium,* Vol. VIII, No. 1 (Summer 1954), 33–41.

Pell, Elsie E. "Gide and the Present Crisis," *The French Review,* Vol. XVIII, No. 4 (February 1945), 213–18.

Pierre-Quint, Léon. "Notes sur les idées de Défense Nationale et de Patrie—A propos de l'attitude d'André Gide à ce sujet," *Cahiers du Sud,* Tom. X, No. 149, 20e Année (mars 1933), 161–70.

Popkin, Henry. "Theories of an Artist," a review of *Pretexts* in *The New York Times Book Review* (4 October 1959).

Rhodes, S. A. "André Gide and his Catholic Critics" (review of Charles Du Bos' *Le Dialogue avec André Gide,* Victor Poucel's *L'Esprit d'André Gide,* and André Gide's *Un Esprit Non Prévenu*), *Sewanee Review,* Vol. XXXVIII, No. 4 (October–December 1930), 484–90.

———. "The Influence of Walt Whitman on André Gide," *The Romanic Review,* Vol. XXXI, No. 2 (April 1940), 156–71.

Ross, Flora Emma. "Goethe in Modern France, with special reference to Maurice Barrès, Paul Bourget and André Gide," *University of Illinois Studies in Language and Literature,* Vol. XXI, Nos. 3–4 (1937), 135–225.

Rousseaux, A. "Le drame d'André Gide," *Le Figaro Littéraire* (22 septembre 1951), 2.

——. "Sur la sincérité d'André Gide," *ibid.* (1 septembre 1951), 2.

Salz, Lily. "André Gide and the Problem of *Engagement,*" *The French Review,* Vol. XXX, No. 2 (December 1956), 131–37.

Sartre, Jean-Paul. "Gide Vivant," *Les Temps Modernes* (mars 1951).

Savage, Catharine H. "The Ideology of André Walter," *L'Esprit Créateur,* Vol. 1, No. 1 (Spring 1961).

Schmidt, Albert. "Sur la méthode morale de M. André Gide," *Foi et Vie,* XXXVIIᵉ Année, No. 6, Cahier A (16 mars 1924), 310–13.

Sender, Ramón J. "Freedom and Constraint in André Gide," *New Mexico Quarterly,* Vol. XX, No. 4 (Winter 1950–51), 405–19.

Simon, Pierre-Henri. "Le Christianisme d'André Gide," *Revue Générale Belge,* No. 71 (septembre 1951), 744–51.

"Souvenirs d'André Gide," *La Table Ronde,* No. 40 (avril 1951), 9, 14, 20, 33, 48.

Stock, Irwin, "André Gide: Apostle of Progress," *Accent,* Vol. IX, No. 4 (Summer 1949), 202–14.

Thibaudet, Albert. "André Gide," *Revue de Paris,* 34 Année, No. 16 (15 août 1927).

Trinh-Huy-Tien. "Gide en Annam," *France-Asie* (15 novembre 1947).

Vial, Fernand. "André Gide and the Problem of Sincerity," *The American Legion of Honor Society Magazine,* Vol. 23, No. 3 (Autumn 1952), 249–67.

Vicari, George. "André Gide et l'Italie," *Annales de la Faculté des Lettres d'Aix,* Tom. XXVIII (1954).

Vikner, Carl. "Gide et Dostoievsky. Esquisse de la psychologie d'André Gide," *Orbis Litterarum,* Tom. XV, Fasc. 3–4 (1960), 143–73.

Wilkins, Burleigh Taylor. "*L'Immoraliste* Revisited," *The Romanic Review,* Vol. LXXX, No. 2 (April 1962), 112–27.

Yale French Studies, No. 7.

Yanitelli, Victor R. "Gide versus Anti-Gide," *Thought,* Vol. XXVI, No. 103 (Winter 1951–52), 540–50.

Index